DEMOCRACY IN THE KITCHEN

Regulating Mothers and Socialising Daughters

VALERIE WALKERDINE
and
HELEN LUCEY

This book is dedicated to
Mary-Kate and
the memory of Rosemary,
two courageous working-class women, our mothers

Published by VIRAGO PRESS Limited 1989
20–23 Mandela Street, Camden Town, London NW1 0HQ

British Library Cataloguing in Publication Data

Walkerdine, Valerie, 1947–
Democracy in the kitchen: the regulation of
mothers and the socialisation of daughters.
1. Women. Education. Sex discrimination
I. Title II. Lucey, Helen
370.19'345

ISBN 1-85381-034-7

Typeset in Bembo by Goodfellow & Egan Limited, Cambridge
Printed in Great Britain by Cox & Wyman Ltd.,
Reading, Berkshire

CONTENTS

This is an old fiction of reliability
is a weather presence, is a righteousness
is arms in cotton

This is what stands up in kitchens
is a true storm shelter
and is taken straight out of colonial history,
                                        master and slave

arms that I will not love folded
                    nor admire for their 'strength'

linen that I will not love folded but will
                                        see flop open
tables that will rise heavily in the new wind
                                        and lift away
                    bearing their precious burdens

Of mothers who never were, nor white nor black
mothers who were always a set of equipment and a fragile
                                                            balance
Mothers who looked over a gulf through the
                                        cloud of an act and
                              at times speechlessly saw it.

From 'Affections Must Not' by Denise Riley

ACKNOWLEDGEMENTS

Many of the ideas contained in this book owe much to the work and insights of Diana Watson, who, with us, spent many hours slaving over hot transcripts. We would also like to thank Cathy Urwin, Diana Adlam, Nikolas Rose and Gillian Arnold who spent some considerable time reading drafts and discussing the ideas with us, and Ruthie Petrie, our Virago editor, who helped us clarify our ideas and gave magnificent editorial support.

Valerie would also like to thank the women students in the Summer School thesis workshop and critical psychology courses at the Ontario Institute for Studies in Education, Toronto, in the summer of 1987. They pushed me to extend my ideas and gave me an impetus and courage to develop and teach this work as I have never felt elsewhere. It was a privilege to teach them, to share my work with them and theirs with me. By their loving and supportive learning they helped make finishing this book possible.

This work was supported by grants from the Economic and Social Research Council, the Leverhulme Trust and the Nuffield Foundation. We would like to thank Professor Babara Tizard of the Thomas Coram Research Unit for generously allowing us access to the transcripts from her study 'Language at Home and at School' and for her consent to follow up the children from the sample.

INTRODUCTION

When John Osborne looked back in anger in the 1950s, what he saw was the kitchen sink. The focus of his anger was a working-class kitchen, with a mother leading a stultifying life.[1] The working-class grammar-school boys who at that time inaugurated the genre of realist kitchen-sink drama deeply despised their class. They especially hated their mothers with their piles of ironing and lack of conversation. By contrast, other men who grew up in those times eulogised their mothers, as Carolyn Steedman[2] has so clearly remarked about the writing of, for example, Richard Hoggart and Jeremy Seabrook.[3] And again, J. W. B. Douglas holds the working-class mother responsible for the success and failure of the new post-war equal opportunities.[4] By their teaching, argued Douglas, working-class mothers were the greatest and most important determiners of the educational success or failure of working-class children.

Mothers – heroines or victims? These stories have formed an important part of the present and its attempts to guarantee the success of a liberal democracy through the labour of women. In the 1970s, too, the equal-opportunities rhetoric extended its concern to all mothers, who may well be responsible for the so-called failure of girls within the education system, through their rigid róle models and gender stereotypes. All women then, as mothers, were failing. For they were failing to defend the certainty of progress by opening up the tiny gateways to the chosen among the oppressed.

We think that there is a story to be told about 'the kitchen', of how it came to be a place in which liberal democracy was to be guaranteed through the management of mothering, and how it came to be an oppressive space, where women's labour is so transformed as to make it appear to be the natural, normal and inevitable prop to free life as we know it. For it is our argument that women's labour, in the form of mothering, is an essential part of a story about class and social democracy in Britain, in which the regulation of women became seen as central, so great was the threat posed by the possibility that women would not properly mother. For this reason we are questioning the idea of the home as a place where mothers and children produce an easy democracy that will be that stepping stone to equality.

We write this story within another: our own histories as working-class girls. And we write out of anger, an anger in which working-class child-rearing practices have been either systematically pathologised or patronised, and in which the historical importance of mothering as the democratic fantasy has not been properly told. It is, in our view, a story of the complexities of gender, class and race as they are lived, but it is also a desperate bid on our part to speak about differences, so often seen as divisive within the women's movement. It is politically vital that we confront, rather than suppress, differences between us.

And what of the issues that led us to write this account? In our presentation, we want to dwell on our oppression, but not as a kind of additive sense: as in the idea that we are oppressed, doubly as women and working class, but not trebly, since we are white rather than black. It is too easy to draw up a list of oppressions so that middle-class white women come fairly near the top on privilege and low on oppression, or to argue that it is patriarchy and not class that matters so that all women are sent back up to the top of the oppression league again, asserting that differences and divisions between us can only harm the cause of women's liberation. It is black women[5] who have taught us that such arguments will not do and that we urgently have to confront the issue of difference and division, to understand how we might move forward together. In our view, ignoring or playing down those differences will do nothing but harm to a political movement, but we have also to learn to listen to each other, in order to think how it might allow us to move forward in our struggle. It is difficult to know where to begin, but let us try. A context comes to mind: a conference about migration, where a black writer asks the predominantly white audience to speak about the position of the coloniser, since, so far, all that has been said is about the pain of the colonial subject, the immigrant. The audience refuses the question. Many members of the audience speak, but all of them talk about their own alienation from their past, their own migration, their own pain. No one can even begin to address the pain and meanings of the coloniser.

When Valerie was a child she once asked about the dark skin of a friend of the family. She learned early and with pain that it was rude to ask such things. She learned, too, that watching the Black and White Minstrels on the television was a time of intense family togetherness and happiness. In addition, routine and unproblematic meanings were attached to the word 'nigger': it was the name of a fashionable colour for clothes. We are oppressed. They, the blacks, are dirty, taking our jobs; they are also the happy entertainers, singing and dancing on television. Since held in all that suppressed pain is the history, the cultural and psychic development of the racist discourse of the coloniser, it is so much easier, then, to deny that colonisation, to speak only of our own victimisation, our own oppression, and not to speak of racism. Black women have said this forcibly to white women, and yet we have defensively told them that to raise such issues as the racism of our universalising categories, like 'woman', divided us and diverted us from the liberation of all women. By the same token we too want to speak to white, middle-class women. We want them to listen to what we have to say. When they tell us they too felt oppressed, that it is divisive of us to point the finger at them, they are acting like the white audience in the conference. They want, we want, to hang on to our pain, our oppression, because it is so much easier to articulate it than to find a voice for the deep contradictions of power and powerlessness. We were brought up as white working-class women who have engaged in the history of a colonial imperialist power. Not because we are evil but, because, like the Black and White Minstrels, it is deeply imbued in the meanings and categories of our socialisation.

In his brave autobiography, *In Search of a Past* (1984), the British writer Ronald Fraser tells us of the pain of growing up upper class which he has explored in his psychoanalysis. The book has been widely celebrated, particularly by middle- and upper-class Left male intellectuals,[6] because it admits that such a privileged childhood, the site of intense political guilt, was also full of pain. How then to link this with the privilege of the childhood? Is it simply that we all feel pain, that we are all victims, all oppressed? In his analysis Fraser remembers an episode in which, as a child, he let a beggar into the manor house where he lived. There were no servants around and he felt pleased and important to be performing the butler's job. He thus treated the beggar as he would any guest arriving at the front door. His parents, however, did not react in the pleased way that he had expected. They were shocked and his mother returned white-faced from the front door to tell his father what he had done. Thus, instead of his parents expressing delight at his actions, he experienced intense guilt at having let them down, at his failure to understand that beggars are not ordinary guests, beggars are not to be treated like normal visitors. As the young Valerie learned that it was rude to ask about the colour of someone's skin, so the young Ronald Fraser learned that there are guests and there are beggars.

In Chapter Four we give the example of Samantha, a young middle-class girl who tries to understand and puzzle out why a window cleaner cleaning the windows of her house has to be paid for his labours. In her puzzlement she too learns certain lessons about who she is and about the status and roles of others, like the frightening working-class man with a dirty face and clothes that stares at her through the pane of glass which divides them. Like her, we all learnt meanings. In our childhoods, like Ronald Fraser, we all did things which shocked our parents and sent waves of guilt, deep traumas inside us, to remain there in our adult lives. Yes too, middle-class women felt pain, guilt, traumas as small children. But to remark that, is simply to agree that we are all, after all, oppressed and in pain. But in all the examples that we have given there were meanings attached to the traumas, the specific meanings which make up our experience of power and powerlessness. What Ronald Fraser remembered was a beggar, what Valerie remembered was the dark face of a woman. For Samantha, the window cleaner was both male and working class simultaneously. It will not do simply to assert one of the terms, male or working class, as though they explained anything by themselves. For it is the specificity that matters: in anti-sexist discourses it is precisely working-class men who are seen to be more fearful, more sexist, less understood, without ever exploring the deep oppressiveness in what is being said, the latent fears, circulating deep in middle-class psyches. Middle-class women may remember dirty working-class men and be afraid of them. They may remember that there are working-class women who will not let their children wander around and shout in public spaces, but keep a tight rein on them, a rein they do not understand and therefore feel must be oppressive. Despite themselves, such women join in the categories of the oppression of working-class women because they refuse to listen either to the stories that we are trying to tell or to their own constellation of pain and trauma, their own position in the bourgeoisie and what that means. We argue that in a struggle for the liberation of women we must listen to those voices, those painful voices which divide us, to understand the specificities of our own formation. In this book we seek to uncover and tell twin histories of oppression, of the regulation of mothers in the bourgeois order, which set woman against woman, rendering one normal and the other pathological, making one responsible for the regulation and oppression of the other. It is a history in which all women have been oppressed but not in the same way. It is a story which we wish to explicate with respect to the mothers and daughters whom we will meet on these pages, a story which demands to be told and which we have struggled to tell.

The data on which we will base our analysis come from a study of 'Language at Home and at School', written up in a volume entitled *Young Children Learning* (1984) by Barbara Tizard and Martin Hughes. Their aim was to explore the relation between home and school, by examining the roles of mothers and nursery school teachers in children's language and cognitive development. They came to the conclusion that many mothers were more 'sensitive' to the needs of young children than teachers and supported a position in accord with that taken by the sociolinguist William Labov in the 1970s, that working-class families were 'equal but different'. Fifteen white working-class and fifteen white middle-class mothers and their four-year-old daughters were audio-recorded at home and at nursery school. We re-analysed the transcripts of these recordings as part of a longitudinal study. Although this was not the aim of our research, we came to feel that we had to tell a different story about these mothers and daughters. To explain this we will say something about our childhoods and our response to the transcripts when we first read them. It began when we read the chapter in the account of an afternoon with a white working-class mother and daughter, produced by Barbara Tizard and Martin Hughes, entitled 'An Afternoon with Donna and her Mother'. Throughout the book, the authors are concerned to assert that working-class child-rearing practices are not deficient but *different*, the chapter on Donna and her mother being used to exemplify this notion of 'equal but different'. But there is an uneasiness in this assertion. Donna and her mother have rows, they get on each other's nerves, but all is not as distressing as you might think. For Donna's home and other working-class homes where mother and daughter constantly argue provide a rich 'educational environment' where 'the potential for learning, especially social learning . . . is considerable' (ibid.,

p. 92). This attempt to save the working-class mother and daughter from the ravages of deprivation theories made us just as angry as any of those theories themselves. This attempt to rescue, to make working-class families 'equal but different', still denies oppression in a liberal endeavour to produce equality out of a misplaced pluralism. It was felt necessary to single out Donna and her mother for scrutiny in order to convince the reader that something good is going on. Implicitly, then, the reader is led to assume that there is really something quite problematic that has to be accounted for. For it is only this afternoon which is singled out for special scrutiny, not the other 'ordinary' middle-class afternoons.

Next we went to the transcript itself. Neither of us could quite believe our eyes when we read it. Why was *this* afternoon chosen for discussion, this terrifyingly *ordinary* afternoon, which seemed to both of us so very like many afternoons we had spent with our mothers, completely recognisable and unremarkable? We felt that we were in deep trouble. For the hidden fear and contempt in the need to explain what was a perfectly ordinary afternoon like the ones of our childhoods was both deeply disturbing to us and made us feel an overwhelming fury. But the worst was still to come. We systematically read the working-class transcripts. These mothers and daughters might have been separated by ten or twenty years from our own childhoods but they were remarkably familiar. A feeling of confident recognition came over us. We knew where we were.

We then set about reading the transcripts of the middle-class mothers and daughters. What we felt is almost unspeakable. Helen felt contempt and Valerie hate. And both with a deep intensity. All the class hatred of our childhood, mixed with anger and disdain, hurt and humiliation, envy and longing, welled out in those moments. We felt such things about perfectly ordinary afternoons in perfectly ordinary middle-class homes, afternoons that women with middle-class backgrounds would doubtless identify in the same unproblematic way that we recognised the working-class ones, with a kind of 'yes, that's how it is'. But something inside us smouldered, a pain that we would rather not remember and could not easily articulate.

And in the background a question remained. Were we really that awful? We also learned as children that there was supposed to be something terribly wrong with the way we were. We were not wealthy, we didn't talk properly, we didn't know anything, on and on and on. So, by contrast, reading the middle-class transcripts was like stepping into a world of routine and unproblematic privilege. All the afternoons began with lunch. It may seem trivial but the food in the middle-class homes was one source of anger. The children were routinely asked what they wanted to eat, got a choice of menu, and there was more often than not a bowl of fruit on the table. The working-class homes did not have fruit or a choice of meals. It made them seem rigid by comparison, but they were also poor. But more than this, middle-class homes had more space and a different organisation of it, like the availability of playrooms. Their privilege and their prissy ways filled us with envy and we found it, at that time, almost impossible to see them as oppressed. But then, it was not they that were the problem so much as the hurt, pain and anger inside ourselves. As we gradually gained some distance, we gave the middle-class transcripts to Diana Watson, our co-worker, herself a middle-class mother, to look at. Of course, she began to show us the oppression that our anger had hidden from us. She began to make us see the awfulness of the way in which the middle-class mothers had to make every minute of the day into a pedagogy, so that they actually salvaged less time for themselves than the working-class women were able to do.

We want to insist that middle- and working-class families are not 'equal but different'. They are grossly unequal. The women oppressed by their labours in the middle-class households act out of a set of scientific ideas which tell them that they are right, that this is the proper thing to do. This deeply oppressive truth holds them responsible and full of unspoken guilt. But it also renders them powerful in their morality, and prepares them to be the very members of the caring professions who will come to regulate the working-class mothers, who may come to be seen as frightening, rigid and pathological.

We feel that leaves us with such a tangled web of powers and oppressions that it is important to attempt to untangle it. For part of that task lies in the unravelling of women's place in the making of democracy and the questioning of some assumptions about the governing of our modern order that are so easily taken for granted and which we want to begin to take apart. Our book is about those issues. It is not intended to be a critique of Tizard and Hughes. We are using their explanations of these data to demonstrate how certain ideas about child-rearing and its relation to class and gender have not only become common currency, but also been seen as liberal and progressive. It is this which we want to call into question.

Living in a working-class family

Our work is of course deeply contradictory. We are neither of us living in working-class families, but have become alienated from our class and part of the educated bourgeoisie, so that we are really no longer recognisable as working class at all. We have explored the pain of the distancing elsewhere and will not rehearse it here.[7] But that raises important problems about our position in relation to the interpretation of the transcripts and the story that we are trying to tell.

We both grew up in working-class communities, though separated by geography and historical time: Valerie in the fifties and sixties, in the industrial Midlands, and Helen in Hounslow, on the edge of London, in the sixties and seventies. We were both the first children in our families (and Valerie in her extended family) to go on to higher education. Both Valerie's and Helen's fathers were semi-skilled manual workers.[8] Valerie's father, who worked in the machine shop in the aero-engine division of Rolls-Royce, had suffered for most of his life from a heart condition brought on by having rheumatic fever as a child, the result of poverty and poor conditions. After some heart trouble at work he was declared unfit for manual labour and the philanthropic 'Royce's', as the family called it, gave him a job in the drawing office. He studied for years by correspondence course to become a draughtsman, sitting for hours in the bedroom, at a small card table, meticulously drawing bits of engines. He died from a heart attack at the age of forty-six, before completing the course, though the correspondence school awarded the certificate posthumously and it hung, a horrible reminder of all that pain, in the hallway. Valerie's mother had no paid employment until after her husband's death, since it was considered a sign of respectability that she did not 'have' to go out to work. After he died, she worked first as a cleaner and later in the kitchen of a local school, in the most menial and poorly paid employment, because it fitted in with school hours, so that she could rush home from work in time to be a mother who was still waiting for the return of her children from school. They were times of considerable poverty, during which the welfare state came to the rescue with uniforms and meals, but they were not made to seem like a right, they were presented as charity.

She later remarried a skilled manual worker who was by then the chargehand in the boiler shop at British Railways' carriage and wagon works in Derby. Ron suffered from three industrial injuries, none of which ever received compensation but were simply considered part of the job. He had industrial deafness and a skin condition produced by the intense heat, and the ends of the fingers of one hand had been severed in a machine. He died of a heart attack at the age of fifty-eight, four years after Rosemary, who died at the age of fifty- five, of cancer. It is a story of painful, brutal and short lives, which themselves provoke intense anger.

Helen's mother and father, both Catholic, were brought up

on small, impoverished farms in Southern Ireland (Mayo and Cork), left home and then Ireland to seek work: her father to join the armed services in 1935 and her mother to come to London to work in a munitions factory in 1941. Shortly after the war they married and two years after the birth of their first son they were housed on a council estate in Middlesex. Here two daughters, four more sons, and a last daughter, Helen, were born and brought up, and it is still 'home' to all of them. Things had got easier by the time Helen (the last of eight children), came along, as it was 1959 and a time of high wages for manual workers. Her sisters and brothers have much clearer memories of how little they had, of never having 'two ha'pennies to rub together'. But there was a price to pay for this time of so-called working-class affluence. Her father worked long, back-breaking hours, a lot of the time on night shifts because they were the highest paid, in Firestone's tyre factory. Her mother began work as a canteen assistant in a local technical college: like Valerie's mother, she took the only job she could find which would fit in with school holidays. Later on, when the local education authority tendered the canteen facilities of the college out to a private firm, they were obliged to offer the council employees alternative employment. By default almost, she became occupationally mobile, as she was offered and took the post of assistant welfare officer in the same college. When she was coming up to retirement age, but was adamant in not giving up work, she took up a post as part-time classroom assistant in the newly opened Special Needs Unit of the college. Her father worked in Firestone's, in the same factory and the same job, for thirty years, but in 1979 was, with three weeks' warning, made redundant. Fortunately, he was to retire the next year, and unlike men in their forties and fifties, though 'flush' with redundancy payments, he did not have to face the prospect of rapidly diminishing chances of getting another job. But his sense of worthlessness, of bitterness at having been 'thrown on the scrap heap' after all those years of gruelling labour, were crushing for him, and for the rest of the family to witness. Since then, he has worked as a gardener in private homes.

Our memories of growing up in our families bear little relation to the accounts of working-class life current on the Left. There is a set of fantasies invested in and surrounding 'the working class', all of which place them in an impossible position. Now we are not claiming to 'know' that class, but we object strongly to others who from behind microphone and notebook *do* claim to know them, but whose 'knowledge' understands working-class people as a constant disappointment. For they are the revolutionary class which fails to recognise its true mission to liberate *all* of society: who has failed the Left by swallowing the crafty but (surely?) transparent rhetoric of the Right: who put Thatcher into her third term of office, and buy their council houses. On the other hand, they are seen as a rigid and authoritarian class who have to be taught how to be democratic.

When we were at school, especially when we moved to the 'posh' grammar school, we became aware that there was only one way out. Only through education could we avoid having to become like our parents, to carry in our bodies the pain of having to do that kind of work. But, for all the eulogies to equal opportunities, comparatively little is written on the trauma of leaving and isolation, the disdain with which one is supposed to view the place from which one has come and the terrible guilt that we and not they have got out, have made it, and will work in conditions which they can never know. Conversely, our own mobility has made acute the awareness that often, academic accounts of working-class people's lives speak from a position of not knowing, of viewing, with fascinated horror, the conditions of our mothers' and fathers' lives. Academics often ask, 'How can they endure these conditions?' But this question is asked in several ways. Not only 'How can working-class people survive?' but, 'How can they be as they are: so horrific?' as though somehow these questions were not connected. For the academic can record, can theorise, but will never have to live that life.

For both of us, issues of belonging to and distance from our families, of making the difficult transition to the middle class, has been a prominent aspect of our lives. We have become, through our education, part of a class which, by turns, has invested the likes of our families with hope for the future, or has seen them as the problem in the bid for liberation. They have either nothing to lose but their chains if only they could see them, or they have to be taught the error of their authoritarian ways. The popular Left has deemed the white working class as beyond the pale. That they are lost to socialism, and are therefore to be dumped in favour of other groups who more easily seem to recognise and rebel against their chains.[9] What the Left does not seem to see is its own anger and hurt that the white working class did not come up to expectations, did not do its revolutionary job. Post-1968 accounts had the working class as variously 'affluent', 'never having it so good', and as having ended.[10] Reworkings of theories of ideology also attempted to account for how it was that working-class people could have become so reactionary.[11]

But we are sick of these accounts and their fantasies and fears, their investment and hopes, which simultaneously refuse to examine the position of the bourgeoisie who have the theories, hopes and fears. Since the late 1960s, Left intellectuals, mainly men, and more recently feminist academics[12] have penetrated the factory gates to discover for themselves the horror of the assembly line. Such accounts then get written up, but not for the workers, who, of course, like our families, live this as an everyday reality. No, the accounts are written for the intellectuals, who are taught about the routine brutality but who can scurry thankfully from work which they will not have to spend the rest of their lives doing. The latter found themselves as always in something of a quandary. What could they do or say about the conditions of an order they helped to support? It was clearly articulated that they, as the bourgeoisie, could do relatively little. What was needed was a mass uprising of the most oppressed people themselves. But something strange was going on. For people who lived these conditions as their everyday reality appeared to accept them as normal and not wish to rise up against the oppressor. These people had no need of an account, because they lived it. They not only did not need to talk about it, they would rather *not* talk about it. It is with some anger then that we read such accounts which 'reveal' the kind of butchery that Rosemary, Stan, Ron, Mary-Kate and Denis recognised as 'the way things were in life'. They accepted these things for themselves and tried to cope with them. They learned to accept that you cannot have what you want and that life is full of disappointment. This produced inside them terrible hurt and rage and bitterness. But it did not make them fight in the way the intellectuals of the Left would have them fight. Why not? The answer is difficult and only half understood, and it demands an exploration.

Rosemary had a phrase which she used when her daughters seemed to her to want so much. She used to say, 'Much wants more.' When Valerie left home to go to teachers' training college in London, Rosemary was filled with envy at the opportunities her daughter had that had not been open to her. Pride and envy mixed together. But, in this new place, Valerie again began to articulate desires for more, for other things. 'Much wants more' became a kind of password for these desires, a password which stayed inside Valerie's psyche, so that, many years later, in year after year of psychoanalysis, that phrase would return to haunt her. Every time she wanted something, love, comfort, possessions, her mother would enter the analytic space repeating that 'much wants more'. There was inside that phrase all the hurt and hate of people who have had to find ways of coping with constant denial, of constant refusals and failure to be able to have those things open to other people, things both material and psychic. 'Much wants more' was a coping strategy. It was used by Rosemary in her envy that Valerie, who had already so much more than Rosemary could ever have dared to hope for, still wanted more.

Just as we wanted to escape working-class jobs, so too we wanted to escape from the back-breaking domesticity of our mothers. Working-class girls who 'make good' want many different and contradictory things. Some of us want escape, romance and wealth. Others want a voice so that we can speak of our difference and not be ashamed of it. We want, too, not to be bound by the chains that bind our mothers and fathers. And yet it is their labour which gave us the opportunity not to have to live like that. And what of our mothers? When we didn't want to return home and get married, some of our mothers felt pain and envy: hurt that we wouldn't go back and give them children and envy that we didn't have to, that we 'had our freedom'. Some of us felt that our mothers were stifling us with demands that we no longer wanted to meet. Other mothers were excited by our independence, encouraged and pushed us, warned us off getting 'tied down and having kids'. And yet they were at the same time confused and dismayed that we had changed so much, had so many ideas they didn't understand, and were frightened when they caught glimpses of the terrible alienation we felt, both at home and at work. A wall of misunderstanding grows up, fed by fear and ignorance of 'what you actually *do*', of intellectual work and brainy people.

There grew up within feminism a new myth to cope with the kinds of problems that we were having with our mothers. It was the myth of the perfect mother. It was the myth of the mother who understood and who bonded with us, who didn't prefer our brothers or our fathers, who would love us, who would cure our alienation, who would take away our oppression, who would make for us a safe place. This fantasy of liberated women loving together has continued and built upon the very biological theories of bonding and natural mothering that feminists have been at pains to criticise. But we do not believe that the liberation of women is served by this fantasy, enticing as it is. Nor is it served by a feminist therapy with attempts to be that mother. The mother became the guarantor not only of the liberal order, but of the new liberation. It is this account which we want to challenge, by showing not only that women's labour of natural love is profoundly oppressive but also that natural mothering is a historically constructed phenomenon. While the production of the normal family has been seen as vital to the maintenance of democracy, this has meant the different regulation of proletarian and bourgeois women, often pitting one against the other. In this book we will explore some of these debates, attempting to open them up for discussion and action.

CHAPTER ONE

IT'S ONLY NATURAL

Here are two ordinary girls, Dawn and Amanda. They are four years old and at home with their mothers. Their mothers are ordinary too, and yet they are quite different and apart from each other. Neither pair has met or knows of the other, nor are they likely to, but within these pages they have been brought together, and not for the first time, to have their lives and themselves compared.[1] Here are some extracts of their conversations:

Amanda and her mother are having lunch together.

> C: Is ours a sloping roof?
> M: Mmm, we've got two sloping roofs, and they sort of meet in the middle.
> C: Why have we?
> M: Oh, it's just the way our house is built. Most people have sloping roofs, so that the rain can run off them. Otherwise, if you have a flat roof, the rain would sit in the middle of the roof and make a big puddle, and then it would start coming through.
> C: Our school has a flat roof, you know.
> M: Yes, it does actually, doesn't it?
> C: And the rain sits there and goes through.
> M: Well, it doesn't go through. It's probably built with drains so that the water runs away. You have big blocks of flats with rather flat sort of roofs, but houses at the time this house was built usually had sloping roofs.
> C: Does Rosie [friend] have a sloping roof?
> M: Mmm. Rosie's house is very like ours. In countries where they have a lot of snow, they have even more sloping roofs. So that when they've got a lot of snow, the

snow can just fall off.
C: Whereas, if you had a flat roof, what would it do? Would it just have a drain?
M: No, then it would sit on the roof, and when it melted it would make a big puddle.

Dawn, her small sister and her mother are also having lunch. The two girls are drinking juice.

C: I got the wrong straw. (She has a white cup and yellow straw, while her sister has a yellow cup and white straw.)
M: Huh?
C: I got the wrong straw.
M: Why's that?
C: That side that colour, that. (Points to cups.)
M: What colour's that then? (Pointing to Dawn's cup.)
C: That one?
M: What colour is it then?
C: Red.
M: White.
C: White.
M: What colour's Sue's [sister] then?
C: Blue.
M: Your dress is blue.
(Dawn then takes Sue's white straw to match her white cup.)
M: Give her back her straw before she hits you. (M gives the white straw back to Sue.)
C: That must be mine. (Pointing to white straw.)
M: Well, go without then.
C: I want that one. (The argument continues.)

Two different families, you may say, but the difference is as devastating as the idea that one mother is imperfect because she does not get her wash as white as the next. In using the wrong detergent, she is neglecting her children, being a bad mother. As in advertising, the mothers in these two examples are compared and one of them wins the accolade: one of them washes whiter. The game is called 'Find the Sensitive Mother', and it is a game beloved of psychologists and educators alike. Which mother do you think is sensitive and why do you think that this question is being asked?

Tizard and Hughes view Amanda and her mother's discussion about sloping roofs as 'a remarkable attempt by a child not yet four to explore an abstract topic'. This she does successfully, though she cannot do it alone. The pivot of her success is her mother, for it is she who responds to the girl's curiosity, her thirst for knowledge, by guiding, being explicit in her explanations and gradually building the basis for understanding the complexity of the concept. Contrast this to the 'failure' of Dawn and her mother's exchange where neither achieves being understood or understanding. No sense here of direction, resolution, the meeting of needs.

> [Dawn] was unable to express the concept in terms which her mother would understand, such as 'I should have the white straw to go with my white cup'. This difficulty was compounded by her mother's insensitivity or lack of patience. Mutual understanding was never achieved, and the conflict continued to escalate. (p. 147)

The reason for seeking out the sensitive mother is a genuine concern for the educational prospects of young children. Tizard and Hughes's study attempts to understand and intervene in the educational opportunities and performance of working- and middle-class girls, but in order to address these issues, like many studies before it, it addresses the preparation made in the home for performance in school.[2] The mother is to precede the teacher: she is to prepare the child. Her effectiveness in performing this task is judged in terms of her sensitivity to the child's needs.

On one level this argument seems obvious. Children have needs, and therefore mothering turns out to be an essential function. What we want to demonstrate is that things are not that clear-cut. Indeed, these arguments are ones that feminists too have balked at, and often, shared parenting has been put forward as a way of attempting to take the burden of child care from women's shoulders.[3] And yet, implicitly the argument remains: children have needs and mothering is necessary as a *function* to meet them. The crucial importance of 'mothering' frees it from biology, from gender. For while it is not coincidental that the ideal mother embodies all the characteristics of nurturant femininity, and while the bonds between this universal, ungendered 'mother' just happen to be made virtually unbreakable by the 'love bond' (see Chapter Three) between the baby and the woman who gave birth to her, the notion nevertheless stands that, in principle, 'anyone can mother', but that 'mothering' *must* be done by someone. We want to demonstrate that current ideas about children as having needs to be met by a mother are not universal, timeless laws, but were developed in specific historical and political conditions, which make mothering a function that is central to the way our modern state educational and social welfare practices operate.[4]

What characteristics are taken to define a sensitive mother? Firstly, while the mother is being sensitive to the child's needs, she is not doing any housework. She has to be available and ready to meet demands, and those household tasks which she undertakes have to become pedagogic tasks. A feature of the sensitive mother then is that her domestic life is centred around her children and not around her housework. The boundaries between this work the children's play have to be blurred and so it comes as no surprise that any household task can transform itself into the basis of domestic pedagogy.

Why should we concern ourselves with these issues? In the course of this book we will argue that modern mothering has become one of the central aspects of the regulation of women. Yet, many debates about the socialisation and education of girls and women end up implicitly or explicitly blaming mothers for the fate of their daughters.[5] This leaves women in a guilty impasse. In pursuing their own 'needs', are they damaging their children by not meeting theirs? Should they or should they not have children? Where lies liberation? Most of this work, feminist or not, takes as a matter of incontrovertible fact that there is a certain account of child development, a certain account of mothering, which is natural and inevitable. We do not believe that there are any simple matters of fact in this case at all.

The incontrovertible proof of mothering

In the Introduction we stated some of our anger, our feeling of a desperate need to engage in the possibility of a feminist politics that can take on the specificity of class. The story which we wish to unravel and explore here is one in which scientific proof about mothering has been so bound up with an account of the raising of working- and middle-class children that it is impossible to separate one from the other.

Over many years, a body of work condemning working-class child-rearing practices had grown up,[6] but now Tizard and Hughes, through their study, were seeking an alternative explanation of what had previously been seen as 'alien' and 'unnatural' practices. A diversion from much of the literature, the book bravely put forward a thesis of language development drawing on the work and ideas of the sociolinguist, Labov, who tried to revalue working-class child-rearing practices as different rather than deficient.[7] Although this kind of work was very important in criticising the concept of deprivation, the concepts of 'difference' and 'deficiency' are not the only ways of understanding working-class child-rearing practices. The idea of 'difference' frees us from one trap only to ensnare us in another, and that trap is to remove any idea of exploitation and oppression, to end up with a liberal pluralism of difference. Tizard and Hughes offered an explanation of what they saw as 'equal but different', seeking to normalise working-class practices and to defend them as not deprived. Although they produced an account based on empirical observation and on the interpretation of evidence, there are no hard facts in this matter. They asked certain questions about mothering, they collected evidence and used it within an already existing framework. This linked the education of working-class children to mothering and child-rearing practices, leading on to the possibility of regulating mothering, so as to pave the way for educational success. These questions are neither neutral, nor are they the product of bad people or bad science. They are, however, caught up in a politics of liberal democracy which we question here.

Central to our argument is that the story of girls and mothers has tended to validate middle-class practices and pathologise working-class ones; others have tried to suggest that all women's lives are similar and that class should be subsumed under the category of gender.[8] We do not share this view. Working-class and middle-class women's and girls' lives are different, although not in the sense that one is normal and the other pathological, one oppressed and the other not. They are both the object of regulation and oppression, but differently. We want to bring back that difference. It often pits woman against woman, but ignoring those differences will get us ultimately nowhere.

What is a sensitive mother?

The kinds of tasks which are supposed to aid the intellectual development of young children, and on the basis of which well-known psychologists have constructed their accounts of that development, are almost all routine domestic tasks transformed into a pedagogy: a pedagogy that the mother can engage in when she is, for instance, making the family meal. Laying the table can teach one-to-one correspondence,[9] peeling vegetables can become an excercise in sorting. In the following examples from a pre-school mathematics scheme this becomes clear:

> In the summer, washday may happen out of doors, and can stimulate lots of talk and valuable experience as children add soap to the water, wash the clothes (taking care that the water doesn't flood over the sides of the bowl), wring the clothes and peg them out on a line.
> (Schools Council, *Early Mathematical Experiences, General Guide*, 1978, p. 15)

Charlotte's mother is a sensitive mother. She tirelessly answers Charlotte's unrelenting questions and makes her home, her everyday life, an assault course of developmental tasks. This she achieves by constantly engaging her daughter in essentially domestic work which she herself cannot escape from. Some are routine tasks, like helping Mum put the shopping away, while others involve making things. Each becomes an opportunity for learning, growth and the monitoring of that growth. Charlotte mixes up a pudding and then puts coloured, decorative balls on the top. Her mother, as teacher, 'tests' Charlotte on colour and number concepts:

> M: How many colours are there?
> C: That many.
> M: Come on, how many?
> C: One, two, three, four . . . four!

Even 'insensitive' (Tizard and Hughes, ibid.) mothers get it right sometimes. Dawn watches her mother decorate her birthday cake with candles:

> M: Four.
> C: One.
> M: Mmm.
> C: Two. That one's got nothing on. (The candle holder has sunk into the icing.)
> (———)
> C: One, two, three, four.

On one level you might say that finding the principles of intellectual development in the routine activities of women's domestic labour is demonstrating that such activities or experiences are everywhere. But we could ask a deeper question, that is, why is domestic labour transformed into the very basis of children's cognitive development and what is the relationship between this and the idea that the sensitive mother is necessary to meet the child's intellectual and emotional needs?

The second feature of the sensitive mother is the way she

regulates her children. Essentially there should be no overt regulation; regulation should go underground: no power battles, no insensitive sanctions as these would interfere with the child's illusion that she is the source of her wishes, that she has 'free will'. As the psychologists John and Elizabeth Newson remark:

> Some conflict between parent and child is inevitable: it arises because parents require children to do things, and this interferes with the child's autonomy as a person, with wishes and feelings of his own. In disciplinary conflicts, by definition, we have a situation where certain individuals exercise their rights as people of superior status (in age, power and presumed wisdom) to determine what younger and less experienced people, of inferior status, may or may not do. If the child complies willingly of course (even if his willingness has been engineered by offering him the illusion of choice) his self-esteem can be kept intact: but whenever he is forced into an unwilling compliance by threat of sanctions, whether these be pain inflicted or approval withdrawn, he will inevitably suffer in some degree feelings of powerlessness and humiliation. (1976, pp. 331–2)

The mother, like Sally's mother below, who makes her power visible must be understood as abnormal and pathological. Sally shuts the connecting door between the dining-room and the living-room, even though her mother had previously told her to leave it open:

> M: Sally, open that door! Sally, open that door now! (M gets up and opens the door.) Close that door again and I'll give you a smack.

The sensitive mother therefore hides the fear, the spectre of authoritarianism, or rebellion which ensue if the child realizes herself to be powerless. This powerlessness must be hidden from her at all costs. At risk is not only what is counted in terms of the development of the child, but also the smooth-running society peopled by those who do not believe they are powerless, who believe they have some control. The sensitive mother therefore avoids conflict. She turns resistance and even violence from her children into 'feelings' that make themselves and others unhappy and she rationalises it so that it has no force. This is exactly what Julie's mother below does. Julie, jealous of her baby sister, shouts at the baby, who then cries.

> M: Oh, don't, love, don't be horrible to her.
> C: I'm not. Aaaahhhh!
> M: C'mon, you wouldn't like someone shouting at you if you were sad, now stop it!

Why do the Newsons, quoted above, think that disciplinary conflict is so harmful? They put together the possibility of autonomy, wishes and feelings which belong to the child. The adult has rights to discipline children, yet disciplining is considered potentially harmful, because feelings of powerlessness and humiliation will result, if the disciplining is not achieved by creating an illusion of choice where the child thinks that it is the agent of its own free will. The discourse of rights suggests a liberal analysis, but we are taken powerfully into libertarianism, where what is at stake is the production of a mode of disciplining free from overt authoritarianism. Newson and Newson do not go as far as to state that children must not be disciplined at all, but they suggest the creation of an illusion of the child as the originator of its actions. The autonomous child is the empowered child, the child potentially ready to take its place in a democracy. But wait, something is wrong here. The choice is an illusion, an elaborate charade.

There is a very common analysis, one that gained ascendancy in the late 1960s, which held authoritarianism to be the very basis of oppression, particularly of totalitarianism.[10] Libertarian theories depended upon an analysis of personal oppression as the stifling norms of coercion. Democracy was seen to be a sham, because hidden chains bound people together in oppressive personal and social relations. Equality was to be achieved through a politics of personal liberation, which stressed the removal of the 'bourgeois family' and personal growth. Utilising theories especially drawn from the Frankfurt school, such as the work of Herbert Marcuse,[11] other work began to be developed which documented the stifling nature of 'the family' as a bourgeois institution.[12] Therapy and consciousness change became political weapons and the sons and daughters of the bourgeoisie tried to find new ways of relating to each other. Traditional working-class struggles were no longer placed centre-stage because now a politics of liberation included a personal politics which criticised middle-class lifestyles. A pleasurable and free sexuality was emphasised. This was, as many women have documented, to free men from the confines of the commitment and trap of bourgeois marriage; women were exhorted to be free and gain pleasure in their bodies, but male sexuality was celebrated more than anything else.[13] Women began to feel that this liberation gave little to them as they were left at home while male members of collective households expressed their own liberation by not attending to any domestic or child-care tasks. The children of the bourgeoisie also began to 'drop out', they systematically disdained the careers mapped out for them and went off to the country in an attempt to escape the power and coercion of the System to make them take their place in society.

These were important attempts at revolt and a critique. They opened up a space for the possibility of middle-class women's liberation, and the exploration of sexuality and of the domain of the private, the domestic, as political issues, outside the scope of traditional working-class politics. In this context also a new Left politics began to be developed, one which was influenced by the sixties generation of middle-class children and their new questions. It stressed the politics of feminism, of anti-racist struggles, of cultural issues. All these have been very important. However, the concept of 'bourgeois' came to be rather over-generalised, as in the idea of 'the family' as 'bourgeois'. This meant that the working class were seen as a worse version of what the middle classes were struggling against. But, along with them something else happened. The white working class got dumped by the Left. They came to be seen, utilising the new theories, as failing to support the demands for liberation because they were reactionary, conservative and authoritarian, not because these demands simply seemed quite extraordinary to working-class people.

It is for this reason, among many, that we want to talk about the dual and different regulation of the proletariat and the bourgeoisie. We are arguing that the issues and conditions of the lives of the two groups are different, and therefore subject them to different modes of regulation in the bourgeois – of manners, stiff upper lips, stifling correctness and continuation of privilege and tradition – order. Thus it was the position of the regulative bourgeoisie that the students rebelled against in 1968. They demanded a politics of personal liberation because the chains that bound them were not ones which chained them to the factory floor, but to bourgeois morality. They felt stifled and oppressed, but what could be the basis of their oppression? Unfortunately the theories that they chose to support their claims were theories of liberation from authority and a kind of power which presented a threat to democracy. This led to the idea that liberation depended upon the removal of authority, and personal equality on people being free from demands. It became an extreme form of liberalism, which stressed the path to individual liberation in the politics of the personal and tended to ignore the possibility of collective action. If it was the System which oppressed then one had to find a way of living outside that system.[14] Such a view could only be held by people who had the wealth and position to make this possible. It was thus quite out of step and sympathy with working-class demands.[15] It must have seemed like a bourgeoisie demanding its personal liberation at the expense of the workers.

One of the main preoccupations of the work of what became known as the Frankfurt school was to document and explain the rise of fascism as a mass phenomenon. Extensive use was made of aspects of psychoanalytic theory, especially the idea of repression . Following the psychoanalyst Wilhelm Reich,[16] others argued that fascism depended upon an authoritarianism which related to the patriarchal authority of the father in the nuclear family and a set of family relations stressing power through position and hierarchy. Liberation thus depended on the removal of repression and the authoritarian family form which produced it. To save democracy and promote equality children had to be brought up and educated free from repression. This led to the view that the children of the working class were in even more danger than those of the bourgeoisie. There was a spirit of missionary zeal to save children from their authoritarian families, which stripped from them the few coping strategies they had to deal with and protect themselves against the brutal routines of their daily lives. Liberal capitalism and liberalism joined forces in campaigns to liberalise the workplace. In education children were to be set free, in factories workers, like managers, were sent on the heady path towards self-actualisation.[17] Not surprisingly, manual workers roundly rejected such humanism, pointing out that theirs was not the kind of work which led easily to the delights of self-actualisation.

Liberalism and libertarianism got hopelessly mixed up, and in the process working-class families were watched and monitored as never before. Bourgeois liberal culture, the culture of being laid back, opting out, became the new road to liberation. Working-class people were to be saved from themselves. None of this did anything for women or for their labour, except cement the strong distinction between the normal and the pathological family. The answer which was sought came time and again to centre on the regulation of practices of the mothering of small children. There followed the idea that there was a kind of human nature or essence which lay underneath the trappings of the social world. If we could know what human needs were then the sensitive mother could meet these needs, and children would not be brought up in the stranglehold of authoritarianism.

Although there seem to be very good reasons to assume that mothering is indeed an important function to ensure democracy, an analysis is possible that sees it as upholding a fiction of autonomy. For the Newsons, successful parenting rests on creating an illusion of autonomy so convincing that the child actually believes itself to be free. We believe that this fiction, the illusion of autonomy, is central to the travesty of the word 'freedom' embodied in a political system that has to have everyone imagining they are free the better to regulate them. In locating the problem of democracy in the home it is the mother who has to come to the rescue and the working-class mother who has to be watched above all others.

In the rest of the book we take apart several interlinking fictions. Science claims to tell the truth about natural mothering, but it is founded upon a set of fantasies and fears of what is to be found in the working class. Psychology has been centre-stage in providing the props to the production of these 'truths'. They leave mothers feeling that they have to 'meet needs', leave them feeling guilty for their inadequacy. We suggest that this guilt is bought at a high price. The mother has to underpin the fragile illusion of democracy, for this fiction of equality is propped up by her oppression. We want to question the very idea of 'meeting needs' and argue that it is not the best way to understand the relation of mothers to children.

A libertarian analysis of mother–child relations stresses 'freedom' for the child. Freedom from repression so that the child can be free to discover individuality and autonomy, free to learn self-regulation – the only luggage needed on the conflict-free path to democracy. But the picture of harmony is a fantasy, one which ignores and denies the possibility of resistance and power. The child may learn to live with and exercise her autonomy, but to do this she must first regulate the mother. An examination of conflict and resistance might tell us much more about mother–daughter relations than any analysis of 'harmony' can. Is there democracy in the kitchen? Is the kitchen the place where play and freedom and mother-love produce autonomous children, empowered and rational? The concepts of autonomy and empowerment are central to many analyses but we want to question their basis, suggesting that they may help to oppress rather than liberate women as mothers. Those mothers, almost exclusively working class, who separate work and play, who insist their daughters play by themselves and who insist also on getting the housework done, those mothers are insensitive, pathological. Their practices must be open to correction and scrutiny because they are abnormal. Some of these working-class families are poor, they live in cramped and unsatisfactory conditions, while some of the middle-class families seem wealthy in comparison. A few can employ cleaners and au pairs, the very jobs which some of the working-class women must do to keep the extra money coming in. But what do these differences mean? Are working-class mothers indeed pathological? How are class and cultural differences turned into perverse and unnatural practices?

Ours is not an argument which suggests that what is wrong with the working class is that we simply do not have the right conditions to allow us to behave properly. Rather, we are suggesting that the working class is constantly produced and reproduced as necessary, different, disgusting. Other – constantly told they are different in an order which ultimately depends upon their acceptance of oppression, exploitation and inequality as normal.

But it might be argued that mothering is a very pleasurable activity and we are making it sound totally oppressive. We certainly agree that such pleasure is crucial and yet we would also argue, following others,[18] that such pleasure is also produced and regulated – correct and incorrect, normal and abnormal – and cannot be seen as given. However, our purpose here is rather different. It is to point out the great investment in the 'naturalisation' of 'mother-love' and its place as a mode of regulation, examining the 'serious burdens of love',[19] because certain assumptions about mothering and specifically about the mothering of daughters have serious implications for the lives of all women and for feminism. For so long accounts seem to have concentrated on motherhood either as a state of love, a meeting of, or failing to meet, needs, or as a myth.[20] We examine the effects in practice of ideas about female sexuality and mothering as they affect the day-to-day lives of two groups of mothers and daughters.

When we think about the idea of mothering, we are immediately drawn to the incontrovertible fact of biology: of women bearing children. Only in science fiction, in novels like those by Ursula Le Guin or Marge Piercy, is that biology altered to produce equality.[21] In that case, are we at the mercy of our wombs, is anatomy our destiny? We are not going to challenge that, but we will be attempting to show that the line between scientific accounts and science-fictional narratives may be a lot finer than is usually thought. For many years now women have challenged the definition of ourselves presented through institutions, practices and theories dominated by men. We have argued that science was male 'control over nature'. We have offered theories of female power, matriarchy, nurturance, sensitivity. We have challenged scientific proof which claimed we were not as good as men. In many ways, over many years then, women have sought to challenge and resist those definitions. But biology returns to haunt us. Women mother because we give birth. We want to show how science has produced accounts of mothering which not only claim it to be natural, but state it as true. We are not out to 'disprove' these accounts so much as to show how and why they were produced and what effects they have on women and girls now, and therefore to challenge their validity. The purpose of this is to demonstrate a way beyond a certain set of problems in the existing accounts – ideas about women's work, the role of the family, the needs of children. The story we want to construct is a narrative about power and regulation, fact and fiction. To tell it we will need to explain some theoretical concepts and examine how they differ from ones that have been used before. Our aim is not to be exhaustive, to back up and substantiate all our points, but to suggest how we might go about examining the issues we are raising. In other words, we want to explore what it might mean to tell a different story.

Why do we use the term 'story'? We are arguing that scientific accounts are not true in any simple sense. Not that we are saying they are false, but rather, that scientists do not work in academic ivory towers, constructing unbiased, objective accounts, but work in and respond to particular historical and social conditions and concerns. The concerns we will spend most time exploring in this book are those of the creation and maintenance of what we will call bourgeois liberal democracy. This is the democracy of rights, of individualism, related to the rise of science, of capitalism, of the bourgeoisie. In this we want to oppose a simple idea of science as truth, and ideology as distortion, by claiming that scientific accounts are narratives in their own way and that the distinction between science and ideology is unhelpful, but also that they have particular effects in practice when it comes to regulating the lives of women.

Although the scientist in this regulation is presented in the position of the unproblematic purveyor of truth, we want also to ask what lurks behind the apparatus of regulation. Behind the assurance of rationality of the scientist lurks a set of fears of the observed, fears of the dark uprisings that threaten the safety of the bourgeois order. Experiment and observation attempt to predict and control through the modern magic of numbers, of data, timed seconds, moments. The rise of the bourgeois order was premised on the possibility of scientific government, with its own particular forms of control and regulation through science.

CHAPTER TWO

TAMING NATURE

Since the truths and stories constructed about mothering become tied in with ideas about how to produce democratic citizens, they are hard to disentangle. Yet, if we dig deeply into the empirical evidence produced by developmental psychology and sociology, we find that not only is women's labour transformed into the most routine and unchallenged aspects of intellectual development, but that this development is taken to be crucial to the production of the democratic citizen. In this way, by examining the most boring details of domestic and child-rearing practices, we are not simply engaging in a debate about education and development, but uncovering the most fundamental political questions about the production of democracy, about freedom and about women's oppression. Modern government works through the routine administration of our lives – in schools, social-work offices, law courts, tax offices, hospitals – and depends upon a set of facts gained from scientific research, facts about 'children', 'learning', 'clients', 'needs', and so on.

A historical narrative about the regulation of women and its place in the production of a liberal democracy would be a lengthy book in itself. The point we would like to emphasise here is how certain scientific ideas codified fears and fantasies about a proletariat who had to be tamed, so that a form of government became dependent on practices which were based on scientific knowledge about the population, producing covert forms of regulation, dependent on notions of 'free will', hiding exploitation and oppression.

The French philosopher of science, Michel Foucault (1979)

argues that central to modern forms of government is a shift from a kind of government invested in a sovereign, in which power is overt, visible and located in the monarchy, to a 'suspicious' and 'invisible' form of government, which is dependent upon a set of calculations about the population to be governed. The rise of science from the seventeenth century gave the tools through which the populations were to be known. This gives the human and social sciences a special place in terms of strategies of government. Although it is common, following Marx, to contrast science with ideology, Foucault (1979) sees also in this scientific project the construction of 'truths' which can hardly be described as objective. It is not that these are bad or false sciences, but that science itself is incorporated into strategies of government. The sciences claim to describe a population in order that they can better be governed. The rise of sciences therefore is not simply about academic disciplines, but, as we shall see, it is about the development of specific practices through which families, mothers, children, might be 'known' in order better to regulate them. Now, of course one could say that this is an entirely admirable project and the best thing to do is to calibrate the individual as accurately as possible. However, as in all struggles for power, this knowledge is constructed out of an uneasy compromise. Other things are suppressed. Regulation is not neutral, but is about a knowledge which suppresses and silences other knowledges in producing its own vision. What always has to be regulated is the threat of uprising, the bid for freedom of the oppressed. It is our contention that modern democracies operate upon a fiction of freedom – the fiction of autonomous individuals, who believe themselves to be free. To speak another story, a story of oppression and repression, is therefore somehow to be undemocratic.

It may seem at first sight that this project has little to do with what generated our anger in the Introduction, that is, the engagement of feminism with class. Let us return to the vision that Tizard and Hughes constructed of the working-class kitchen. Their attempt was indeed to defend working-class mothering, to render it equal but different. And yet, we argued, that did not save working-class practices from pathologisation or patronisation. Something, we said, was going on, some fear, some delight, some fantasy of gazing at the working class. So too we found our own fantasies – of wealth, plenty, happiness – in our vision of being middle class, as well as our hate.

What we are trying to link here is scientific accounts, democratic government and our own position and fantasies. This will inevitably take us into some methodological arguments. Where do the 'truths' produced through a scientific government place us? There have been many debates within the Left over the past ten or fifteen years which have argued that one of the problems of post-structuralist accounts is that they only tell us about power, not how that power is lived – a gap between regulative strategies and people's experience.[1] Although this book is not the place to go into a detailed discussion,[2] nevertheless, what we require is an analysis of how regulation is 'lived' and this demands an engagement with how we become subjects, a politics of subjectivity.

In this chapter, we will explore how these issues relate to methodological arguments, both in relation to how we conducted our own work and how the original Tizard and Hughes study was carried out. How do we justify and set about our own examination of these data given our anger at the previous workings of it? We want to set our analysis within an examination of precisely how studies such as these create a 'truth' about class, read it back as fact and intervene in practices on the basis of this knowledge. Are we not therefore falling into a trap by producing our own reading, our own 'truth' about it? Firstly, we want to record the gaps and silences, what is not spoken as well as what is articulated. And we want to examine how other arguments might be made. This is not an easy or unproblematic task. First of all, let us set out how Tizard and Hughes constructed their sample.

Quite specific criteria were used to select the girls and their families. Mothers who worked full time were not included as it was felt that this would have made it too difficult to observe the girls at home (Tizard and Hughes, p. 24). Families which were felt to be 'atypical', such as non-English-speaking, single-parent, black and families with more than three children, were also excluded (p. 25). The girls were 'paired' in nursery school so that working-class and middle-class girls could be compared at school.

The fifteen working-class and fifteen middle-class families were selected using the conventional indicator of social class, husband's occupation. Using the Registrar General's five main classifications, the middle-class fathers came from RG class I and II, the working-class fathers from RG III manual, IV and V. The mother's level of education was taken into account in the choosing of the families, so that only middle-class women who had at least qualified to enter college or university were included, and only working-class women who had left school at the minimum leaving age with no qualifications (pp. 137–8).

The Registrar General's classification is a method which uses five categories of employment as an indicator of class. In this way class becomes an occupational category, which, as many have said, ignores the problematic nature of women's status.[3] But, more than this, it sets up two groups, middle and working class, which are then contrasted with each other. The origin of this lies in 1950s mobility sociology, in which the main aim was to monitor the effectiveness of the post-war social democracy in promoting upward mobility.[4] In other words, the political strategy itself, a strategy which we are seeking to take apart in this book, already defined the working class as a group to be compared to the middle class and found wanting. The relationship of calculation, calibration and statistical facts of population to the rise of the bourgeois order is well documented.[5] But it is necessary here to point out that there is a very important link between the specific way in which the sample was constructed and the generalisations made from it about class difference.

These common-sense notions of 'working' and 'middle'

class as unproblematic, generic categories were taken up and have been used in education, psychology and sociology since the 1950s. These so-called universal categories are quite specific, referring to *white* families and based on the occupation of the male 'head of household'. The class structure of Britain has changed considerably, however. At the time this sample was drawn up, the numbers of black Britons and immigrants from various parts of the old Commonwealth made it ludicrous to talk of a British working class as a unitary body. And yet, all the families in this study were white and only their daughters were studied. The continuing prevalence of psychological and social disciplines to treat 'race' and 'gender' as 'additive' concepts is testimony to the reluctance to engage with the complexities of subjectivity and social life and the desire to hang on to the fantasies of unified and yet separate populations of working class, blacks and women. The logic of the Tizard and Hughes study was that if the sample was constructed only of white girls, stratified by social class, then the 'nuisance variables' of race and gender could be discounted, since only class was being varied. It was thus felt that no discussion of race and gender was necessary. The absurdity of such a methodology would be laughable if it were not also profoundly insulting and pernicious.

Some social theorists have recently argued that 'the working class' is a fiction, a group which once existed but no longer exists in 1980s Britain. While we would accept that class is a far more complex and contradictory concept that it was felt to be under Victorian capitalism, we suspect that '*the* working class' was always the object of fantasies and fears. Either we were going to save the world for socialism or we were a reactionary class, pathological and upsetting social democracy. It is hard, with those fantasies running riot, to understand the complexity of our exploitation and oppression. Yet that does not mean that we think the term 'working class' has no currency. Fictions and fantasies have real effects when they are inscribed in the practices and modes of government through which we are regulated, subjected, oppressed.

Although there has been little work about modes of government and fantasies in relation to class, the connection has been made in discussions about race and colonisation. In his examination of colonial government and the formation of colonised subjects, Bhabha (1983) makes reference both to post-structuralism and to the work of the revolutionary black psychiatrist Frantz Fanon[7]. He suggests that colonial government works by creating a knowledge about the colonised subject to be governed. Bhabha suggests that the stereotype of the colonised subject is not a false picture, clouding a true reality which could be known, but an elaborate set of knowledges absolutely central to forms of colonial government. Bhabha quotes Said's (1979) analysis of Orientalism, in which 'the Orient' is taken to be a repository of Western exotic fantasies, with both delight and fear inscribed in them – 'the yellow peril', 'the mysterious East'. The colonial discourse seeks to produce a knowledge of the 'colonised', to describe colonised peoples as Other to, different from, the coloniser, both to legitimise colonisation and to provide a knowledge of the colonised as a mode of government. But these knowledges which govern are also based on fantasies – they are fantasies of the coloniser about the colonised people – savages which have to be civilised, violent and closer to nature, who are both delighted in, exoticised in their difference and feared in their capacity to rise against the coloniser. Thus such discourses constitute colonised peoples as subjects. Bhabha suggests this is replete with ambivalence – delight and fear – and that the 'return of the oppressed' is always imminent. He speaks of 'those terrifying stereotypes of savagery, cannibalism, lust and anarchy which are the signal points of identification and alienation, scenes of fear and desire as phobia and fetish' (1983, p. 25). Using Fanon, Bhabha then suggests that the 'colonial unconscious' plays a central part in the forms of government; the power/knowledges are articulated through these fantasies, through the fear and desire. Thus the colonised subject has to be created through those fantasies. Fanon talks of being a black man who is the object of fear. He quotes a white girl saying to her mother about him "Look, a Negro . . . Mamma see the Negro! I'm frightened. Frightened. Frightened." (Bhabha, p. 28) In a related example, the black feminist, Audre Lorde in *Sister Outsider*, tells us of the horror of a white woman when, as a little girl, she sits next to her on the subway:

> Her mouth twitches as she stares and then her gaze drops down, pulling mine with it. Her leather-gloved hand plucks at the line where my new blue snowpants and her sleek fur coat meet. She jerks her coat closer to her. I look. I do not see whatever terrible thing she is seeing on the seat between us – probably a roach . . . . When I look up the woman is still staring at me, her nose holes and eyes huge. And suddenly I realize there is nothing crawling up the seat between us; it is me she doesn't want her coat to touch. The fur brushes past my face as she stands with a shudder and holds on to a strap in the speeding train. Born and bred a New York City child, I quickly slide over to make room for my mother to sit down. No word has been spoken. I'm afraid to say anything to my mother because I don't know what I've done. I look at the side of my snowpants, secretly. Is there something on them? Something's going on here I don't understand, but I will forget it. Her eyes. The flared nostrils. The hate.
> (Lorde, 1984, pp. 147–8)

What is it like to be the object of so much fear? And where do the fears come from? To live as a colonised subject is to live and see oneself through the fears and desires of the coloniser. While we are not saying that the fictions and fantasies about the colonised are the same as those about the working class, we are saying that there are similar processes going on. What fantasies therefore exist of working-class women? Simultaneously as threat and desire? As promiscuous, exciting, harmful, diseased, poor mothers, yet salt of the earth, hard workers with grizzled faces and home cooking, with community spirit, warm, washerwomen with big arms, big breasts, big hearts.

We find both fear and desire inside those very apparatuses

and practices of regulation which seek to produce the normal, healthy citizen and stave off the ever-present threat of revolt. This knowledge about 'the working class' therefore is central to the formation of ways of governing it. Strategies of government are replete with such views.

Bhabha suggests that the stories about the colonised have to be constantly and repeatedly told to make them sink in. In the same way the scientific stories about how to produce a kind of mothering to ensure democracy are repeated again and again. If the 'proof' is scientific and science claims to tell us about 'nature', about what is true, then the regulation based on science is legitimate, it is also true. Again and again, mothering is literally 'produced' as natural, that is, it becomes the object of a science which proclaims it as natural. Science tells stories about 'human nature' in an attempt to control nature. The rise of science from the seventeenth century sought to map and control a nature which was indeed delighted in and feared (noble savages, peasants versus lords, noble men). Nature had to be tamed. Civilisation meant taming the animal, the instincts, rationalising that outside reason. Those who were supposed to be living nearer their instincts – the masses – posed a constant threat. With colonisation, the so-called primitive peoples also threatened to rise up against the oppression of the coloniser. Democracy was to be assured through a process of knowing and taming. This process was never simple. It always involved horrendous suppression and oppression, like the suppression of witchcraft, which was the Other to the rise of science.[8]

The 'democratic kitchen' then, the mother as the guardian of the cradle of democracy, had to be watched, monitored, produced. Middle-class women were recruited into the 'caring professions' in this service. They too were positioned as normal, natural guardians of democracy. Theirs is no route free of oppression, but in being so positioned they came to monitor, regulate, oppress those who were the target of their 'caring'. They claimed to understand the working class, to know what it was like, to plumb the depths of human 'needs' through the daily regulation of lives – in school, clinic, hospital, social-work office, produced a knowledge which claimed to know working-class people. If working-class children were quiet in the waiting-room of a doctor's surgery they were repressed. If they were noisy they were hooligans. If middle-class children were noisy and ran around they were 'independent and autonomous'.

Working-class families have always presented a threat to the modern, bourgeois order. This order, founded upon Reason, supplanted magic, the supernatural, religion, with the guarantees of science. All the tools of magic were invested in scientific enquiry. Above all science was concerned with prediction. No longer was religion or the supernatural seen as the guiding force, but nature could be regulated, controlled, seen to operate according to laws. The subject of the new order was the unitary subject who could in turn be described, controlled, predicted, regulated. There was always that, however, which stood outside reason. As Michel Foucault describes in *Madness and Civilisation* (1967), this came gradually under the control of medicine and moralised unreason, that is, everything which could not be regulated as pathological. Irrationality became illness.[9] Yet irrationality threatened the new order. The masses, as we shall see, constantly presented ways of being which threatened the safe assurance of reason. Increasingly, they came to be pathologised.

The idea of democracy, with rights and responsibilities, became government by reason, in which individuals, at first men with property,[10] would have channels to power, a power previously accorded only to the aristocracy. While universal suffrage increased those channels, the concern with the threat to the bourgeois order grew. The masses had to be bought off, to prevent their rebellion and their disruption of liberal capitalism. In his analysis, Marx gave the proletariat a historic role. He assumed that they would see their oppression and rise up, defeating capitalism. When the threat had been kept at bay in Britain at a time when Russia rebelled, a new threat emerged to the liberal order. It was the threat of the defeat of the Left by the forces of fascism. The working-class family began to be blamed for the production of a regimented authoritarianism. Before and after the war, natural democracy was asserted with a new vigour. We argue that the Frankfurt school's position on fascism builds upon precisely what we are opposing: that the masses really are mad and irrational and that what has to be asserted is the rule of the rational. In particular, the guarantees of democracy were to be assured by a science of mothering which held women responsible for the future of the next generation. This task not only demands that women want to do this, a desire which first has to be produced, but that the task is different for the proletariat and the bourgeoisie. Working-class mothers have to be watched and prevented from being authoritarian, while bourgeois mothers have to nurture and promote rationality at all costs, especially since they and their children are to be the normal individuals who uphold the order and the professionals who do the surveillance.

How do we justify and set about our own examination of the data, given our anger at the previous working of it? There are several points that we want to hold up for future explanation, a set of 'working hypotheses' about how to understand the phenomena we are working with. The first thing to note is that the construction of the sample creates the fiction of the possibility of a working class–middle class comparison by occupational group, for the purposes of predicting what will lead to educational success. Secondly, a simple cause-and-effect model then maps middle-class practices and concludes that every difference in the working class is a pathology to be corrected, and that if this were corrected, the system of 'equal opportunities' would work.

One of the sciences of 'population management' was statistics, which defined the characteristics of the population by finding the average or norm. The idea of the norm, which was an artifact of a technique, then became widely incorporated as the 'normal'; such that patterns of development found across children were seen and told as 'normal'. This meant that any difference was a deviation from the norm and thus became abnormal, or pathological. Thus the 'fact' of sampling in this way helps to locate the problem and find the solution while naturalising the specific conditions of its production. Now, we are therefore placed in a dilemma. We want to take these categories apart and start again. We could construct a different sample, ask different questions, with a different analysis of class. However, we think it is important to work with the sample defined in this way precisely because that is the most commonly used definition of class at the present time. It is both a fiction and a fact which is acted upon. Educational, social, medical and legal workers *do* intervene in terms of the truth constructed by such sampling techniques and theories. They do so, often based on training which is filled with empirical material demonstrating the 'facts' of child-rearing, from studies such as these.

How then can we avoid falling into any number of traps in producing our account? In the end, we cannot, for it is so much easier to take apart than to build again, but at least we can try to outline the steps, the foundations of that work. We want to understand how we are positioned, how and why we live our lives in a particular way and therefore the basis on which we might work. We were working-class girls and are now middle-class women academics. How then are we to live that contradiction? We criticised Tizard and Hughes for the fantasies of Otherness inscribed in their account and the way it played right into oppressive truths.[11] Most social scientific research on the working-class claims to tell a truth – wants to 'know' – but we think that beneath the easy objectivity lurk more difficult emotions. What is it like to 'be' like that, 'how can they'? These and other questions are present in the way that the social scientist becomes a paid voyeur, who claims to tell the truth about working class families. Left and feminist researchers often assume that we can give a 'proper' account by 'siding with the oppressed', or being 'woman-centred'.[12] Yet we are not simply 'women', we are not the same as those we interview or observe. We (HL and VW) are not mothers, and we are indeed now part of the very class which monitors the working class. We therefore think it is crucial to monitor and understand *our* formation and its effectivity in our research, interactions and the story we produce.

If we do not engage with the psychic dimension and its inscription in the truths of regulative apparatuses themselves, then our political engagement is a sham. It is *so* easy for us to believe we are telling the truth, producing an objective account, without looking to our own place, our own positionings. We also object to the idea that 'we' have access to a higher truth while the subjects of our research are trapped in ideology. Indeed, we may well in producing 'proof' be engaging in the 'constant retelling of stories' through which things *must* be true (and always have been true) if you use enough methodological guarantees.[13] In Tizard and Hughes's study, an observer was present but refused to speak as though she would then not affect the interaction. It seems somewhat naive to assume that silence, especially from a middle-class academic, cannot be read as watching, evaluative surveillance in which you have to 'mind what you say'.[14]

Having said all this, of course, what we are looking at here is a set of transcripts. We have already said how much easier we felt it to work with the working class ones and how many difficult emotions we felt when trying to work with the middle class ones. We do not know what some of this means for our account and we would welcome an engagement with what it means to grow up a 'middle-class woman'. Yet to phrase it in this way demonstrates how difficult it is to pose the question. Middle-class white women often simply see themselves as 'women'. They do not have to try to set out and detail the specificity of their lives. Where then is the pain of growing up middle class? Where is the problematic struggle to be on the Left in feminism – are you positioned as a 'voyeur', a vanguard, on the margins? How do you live with the push, the careerism, the privilege as well as the pain?

The psychic dimensions to our work – the problems of what people remember[15] and how they interpret situations, mixing fact and fantasy, the defences against pain, the push of wishing, hoping, desiring – are rarely discussed in social analysis. A politics of subjectivity needs this engagement if it is not to succumb to a too simplistic determinism, for it shows the complexity of how we are struggling.

The set of transcripts which we look at in this book were collected by making audio recordings, of approximately two and a half hours' duration, when the girls were at home with their mothers. The recording sessions usually began when the families were having lunch. Another set of recordings of the same length were made of the girls at nursery school. These school transcripts do not form part of our analysis in this book. All the girls were within three months of their fourth birthday at the time of recording. In each case the girl wore a radio microphone inside a 'special' dress. During the home recordings, an observer sat with the families, making notes on what was happening but refusing to interact. The notes were then transcribed alongside the speech, so that the transcripts are divided into two columns.

Six years after the first study was conducted we contacted the girls. We wanted to find out what had happened in their educational careers. We interviewed the girls, talking to them about school, their families, classmates and teachers. We asked them how they judged their own school performance and that of their classmates. We also gave a standardised maths test to everyone in their class, and interviewed their teachers.

Of the working-class families, nine lived in council accommodation: six in flats and three in houses. The rest lived in privately owned or rented terraced housing. All the middle-class families lived in houses with private gardens while only six of the working-class families had access to a garden. We have not counted 'back yards', the sort found tacked on to pre-war terraced houses, as gardens. They were not designed as leisure areas, nor is there evidence that they were used as such by the mothers and daughters of this book, and thus we felt that they did not warrant the title 'garden'.

Just under two thirds of the women worked part time (none were in full-time paid employment) at the time of this study – five middle class and nine working class. The kind of work they did was as different as the kind of houses they lived in. All the middle-class women had formal qualifications, at least up to A level, and most had trained in a profession before having children. These were mostly the 'caring professions' – teaching, social work, nursing – and it was to this sort of post that the women returned to work part time. Contrastively, only one working-class mother had any educational qualifications. Most had worked in the service sector as waitresses, shop assistants or in factories as semi- and unskilled workers. At the time of the study, four of the working-class women had early-morning or evening cleaning jobs. Others worked from their own or other people's homes, one as a childminder, another as an agent for a popular brand of household ware.[16]

All the middle-class fathers were professionals, with occupations such as journalist, editor, teacher, social worker, which would locate their families as part of the 'new middle class'[17]. The working-class fathers were mostly semi- or unskilled manual workers, with a few exceptions, for example a carpenter and a hairdresser.

In the rest of the book we will go on to talk about the families in this sample in relation to debates about the production of mothering and the government of reason. The next chapter concentrates on the developmental psychology of the 1950s onwards which produced the idea of the sensitive and insensitive mothers that we met in Chapter One. We should begin to see how 'sensitivity', although produced as a fiction, was soon to become a powerful fact, incorporated in the hunt for the 'sensitive mother'.

CHAPTER THREE

CAGED ANIMALS

Wild and savage animals to be tamed, lions and tigers in jungles, children brought up by wolves, 'man' descended from apes. But, what have we here? Far from the steaming jungle, we find ourselves in a laboratory lined with row upon row of caged monkeys. It is 1958 in the psychological laboratories at the University of Wisconsin, Madison, USA. The president of the American Psychological Association, Professor Harry Harlow, has conducted a set of experiments on infant rhesus monkeys which will be the most quoted research to demonstrate the biological basis of maternal bonding for many years to come. For, the story goes, if we are descended from apes, then perhaps studies of apes, monkeys, laboratory rats and other animals can tell us something about human reactions too. But what has happened to the state of nature? It has been caged. Along the walls of the lab are cages of infant monkeys, not in troupes swinging across the jungles, but, for many, in solitary cofinement in cages. Nature has become the individual, one infant monkey alone with a mother or mother-substitute. The results of his experiments are first presented to the world in his 1958 presidential address to the American Psychological Association. The paper, entitled 'The Nature of Love', begins as follows:

> Love is a wondrous state, deep, tender, and revealing. Because of its intimate and personal nature it is regarded by some as an improper subject for experimental research. But, whatever our personal feelings may be, our assigned mission as psychologists is to analyse all facets of human

> and animal behaviour into their component variables. So far as love or affection is concerned, psychologists have failed in this mission. (Harlow, 1961, p. 673)

Harlow goes on to add that the 'authors and authorities have stolen love from the child and infant and made it the exclusive property of the adolescent and the adult'. In this way Harlow and others initiated a very important shift: they introduced the scientific validation of 'the new couple'.[1] No longer is love sexual and adult, it is based on the relation not of woman and man but of mother and infant. Harry Harlow set himself the mission of scientifically proving that mothering is natural, normal and inevitable.

We have already seen that there was reputed to be a 'biological bond' between the mother and her children, which was to ensure the smooth running of the state through the care of children. This biological bond postulated the mother–infant attachment process and the long period of dependency in humans as the climax of evolution. Mothers reared children in this scenario, not because of the history that we have recounted, but because it was evolutionarily inevitable for them to do so. What we are presented with then is a desire, a desire to secure the stable future of the state, a desire to prevent crime, a desire for a constant and stabilising presence. The fantasy created to fulfil this desire is the mother. The fantasy is lived out as fact in experiments such as Harlow's which translate it into scientific findings which are then incorporated into public policy. The myth becomes reality.

For there is no test of nature at all. Monkeys in cages with or without their mothers can hardly be described as ecologically valid. The appeal to biology fails the moment it begins. Indeed, the interest in monkeys is only a foil. The central concern is how to scientifically regulate mothering. The mother not only gives milk (the primary drive), she gives warmth and comfort. We will see that the 'sensitive mother' finds her forerunner here. For, ultimately, it has to be demonstrated that a supply of food is not enough. The mother has to care for her children because she is biologically equipped to tune into their need (secondary drives) for understanding, for comfort, for meaning. She and no one else will do. And moreover, if she is abnormal her mothering has to be corrected. So, first you put women at home with their children and then you demonstrate that they have special biological reasons for being best at the job, and those who do not do it correctly are described as abnormal and corrected or may have to give their children up to some other and better substitute. Here love has become the watchword. Remember earlier that the idea of wild and savage animals tapped into a fear of the inevitability of war, of inbuilt aggression, of death drives. These have disappeared in this story and we are left only with nice emotions, which will be there as long as there is correct mothering. No anger, no aggression, no fantasy, just attachment. Let us examine what this entails.

Harry Harlow's celebrated test of nature required that infant rhesus monkeys be placed in cages in one of three experimental conditions. They were placed in a cage with their biological mothers (but no other monkeys), or with a wire construction which was heated and had a supply of milk through a nipple. In the third condition, the 'wire mother', as the contraption was called, became a 'cloth mother', the wire being covered with terry cloth. Here, the laboratory cage provides our test of nature, the wire box the experimental version of the civilised home. Well, suprise, surprise, it turns out that what works best is a real monkey mother, the one that responds to the infant's need for comfort, a reactive mother, not a stiff and unresponsive cloth or wire mother. Presence is not enough, nor is food and warmth. In other words the satisfaction of the basic drives does not ensure civilised life. Ladies and gentlemen, in clinical trials, eight out of ten monkeys prefer their mothers to a piece of cloth or wire. The case rests. The necessity of the mother is proven; theories of mothering based on attachment begin with this proof.

> A charming lady once heard me describe these experiments, and when I subsequently talked to her, her face brightened with sudden insight: 'Now I know what's wrong with me,'

> she said, 'I'm just a wire mother.' Perhaps she was lucky. She might have been a wire wife. (Harlow, 1961, p. 677)

Here we have it, the point of the exercise. Some mothers, it is feared, neglect their children. They leave them alone, they deprive them of their presence, they go out to work or, worse, they go out for pleasure.[2] The point is not to tell us anything about monkeys in a laboratory, it is to calibrate and quantify human mothers caged inside their homes with their children. Here, like the psychologist in the laboratory, health visitors, social workers and others can monitor their performance. Is the mother at home reactive, or is she a cloth or, worse, a wire mother? Is she hard, rigid, unbending and depriving her children? It is here that we have the beginnings of attachment. It is not just the possession of breasts that is important to mothering. No, it is the bonding of skin to skin that attaches mothers to babies like superglue. Attachment theory takes off in its application to the psychopathology of mothering that was its purpose in the first place. In Harlow's work, the production of neurosis was the goal of this profoundly cruel exercise. In the interests of analysing neurosis Harlow kept infant monkeys in cages for periods of from two to five years. This produced 100 per cent neurotics. As we know only too well, mothers and children can be confined for a much longer period. Harlow states:

> One of our goals has been the production of neurotic monkeys raised on inconsistent and rejecting mothers. To achieve this, we have produced a mother whose ventral surface is lined with tubes through which jets of compressed air may be forced, for air blast is a strong aversive stimulus for monkeys. A buzzer serves as a conditioned stimulus warning the infant of approaching air blast. Our single subject to date has learned this conditioned response, and when the buzzer is presented, it clasps the mother's body with increased vigor, insuring that maximal blast intensity will strike its face and body. (1961, p. 83)

In 1959 John Bowlby, then head of the department of children and parents at the Tavistock Clinic, organised a conference, which was to be written up as a book edited by the psychologist Brian Foss and entitled *The Determinants of Infant Behaviour*. At this conference Harlow presented the paper cited above. Although Bowlby's name is often singled out for abuse because of his theories of maternal deprivation, a far wider movement took up attachment theory. Experiments such as Harlow's paved the way for a kind of scientific study of mother–infant interaction which has become the common-sense bedrock of developmental psychology. It is this path which will lead us straight to the 'sensitive mother'.

Bowlby stated in his book *Attachment and Loss*:

> In the countryside in springtime there is no more familiar sight than the mother animals with young. In the fields, cows and calves, mares and foals, ewes and lambs; in the ponds and rivers, ducks and ducklings, swans and cygnets. So familiar are these sights and so much do we take it for granted that lamb and ewe will remain together and that a flotilla of ducklings will remain with the mother duck that the questions are rarely asked: What causes these animals to remain in each other's company? What function is fulfilled by their doing so? (1971, p. 225)

The basis of Bowlby's presentation of this pastoral idyll for us is his reference, like Harlow's, to the 'nature' of love, a nature which has the animal and bird population bonded in mother-love. Scientific attachment work tied into the attempt to provide an experimental verification of psychoanalysis, but this verification transformed psychoanalysis almost beyond recognition. Bowlby turned to ethology to extend Freud's reference to evolution, needs, drives, instincts. But what he did was to take out any sense of an opposition of positive and negative, life and death drives, to give us a picture of realism, an adjustment which has harmony produced out of the reality of early environment, maternal bonding.

Around the time of the first and second world wars there had been tremendous concern about evolutionary theory. It was stated and feared by many that war was inevitable because it was evolutionarily necessary to the survival of the fittest. Further than this, others had found in it a biological basis to capitalism, a capitalism which stressed the necessity of competition. In other words, social Darwinism held on to a theory of drives which the more liberal thinkers were very concerned to overturn. Freud's use of drives smacked of the very negative aspects that liberal social reformers were keen to do away with. Thus, an ethology which stressed the evolutionary necessity of mother–infant interaction, not drives based within the infant (remember that in Harlow's work it was contact and not the satisfaction of needs or drives for food and warmth which was said to prevent neurosis), seemed a much more positive step. That this 'positive step' entailed the confinement of half the human race in the interests of liberal democracy seems not to have troubled the members of the scientific community that gathered in the Tavistock Clinic in 1959, just as it had not bothered the Victorian physiologists and psychologists before them.

Bowlby makes this move away from drive theories quite clear:

> The hypothesis advanced here . . . is built upon the theory of instinctive behaviour already outlined. It postulates that the child's tie to his mother is a product of the activity of a number of behavioural systems which have proximity to mother as a predictable outcome. Since in the human child ontogeny of these systems is slow and complex, and their rate of development varies greatly from child to child, no simple statement about progress during the first year of life can be made. Once a child has entered his second year, however, and is mobile, fairly typical attachment behaviour is almost always seen. By that age in most children the integrate of behavioural systems concerned is readily activated, especially by the mother's departure or by anything frightening, and the stimuli that most effectively terminate the systems are sound, sight, or touch of mother. Until about the time a child reaches his third birthday the systems continue to be readily activated. Thenceforward in

> most children they become less easily activated and they also undergo other changes that make proximity to mother less urgent. During adolescent and adult life yet further changes occur, including change of figures towards whom the behaviour is indicated. (1971, p. 223)

In the same chapter, Bowlby makes clear his difference from need and drive approaches:

> In this formulation, it will be noticed, there is no reference to 'needs' or 'drives'. Instead, attachment behaviour is regarded as what occurs when certain behavioural systems are activated. The behavioural systems themselves are believed to develop within the infant as a result of his interaction with his environment of evolutionary adaptedness, and especially of his interaction with the principal figure in that environment, namely his mother. Food and eating are held to play no more than a minor part in their development. (p. 224)

Here, Bowlby was also building upon the object–relations schools of psychoanalysis, which followed the work of Melanie Klein. Stressing the mother as an 'object' is a concept which feminists have long attacked in terms of the objectification of women. But here, the use of the term was intended to convey something 'relational', rather than Freud's stress on the drives. Bowlby sought to move beyond what was referred to as a 'cupboard love' theory of the infant's desire for the mother. In other words, there was taken to be 'something else'. It is to find this something else that Bowlby and others turned to ethology, to animal behaviour and to behavioural systems in general.

Although the importance of the biological mother has been disputed after ferocious attacks on the concept of maternal deprivation, what has never been seriously challenged is the fundamental concepts which underlie attachment theory. Most of the progressive changes suggest that the father or other female or male adults may 'mother', but mothering is still taken to be attachment and therefore necessary to mental health. We are not arguing empirically that children do not need attachments. Rather we are criticising the theoretical basis of attachment theory. We will see later that feminist approaches sometimes get rather stuck in the idea of attachment because it deals with what actually happens rather than reducing it to drives. However, in Chapter Eight, we will examine some problems with this approach.

Mother-infant interaction

Through this brief review we want to demonstrate how laboratory studies came to view what Denise Riley (1983a) has called the mother and infant in a bell-jar as a given and unproblematic approach to infancy and to the raising of children. Literally thousands of studies have mapped the so-called interaction of mothers and infants in laboratories in an attempt to calibrate 'natural mothering'. Others have intruded in their homes to observe this interaction *in situ* and map language development, for example.

The experimental study of mother–infant interaction builds not only upon the idea of an experimental test of psychoanalysis, but also on the foundation laid down for the possibility of a scientific psychology. A scientific psychology was, from its very inception, to be an *experimental* psychology. Hence, it was considered quite acceptable to take animals out of their natural habitat and put them in cages in laboratories. Only this, it was proposed, would give the conditions necessary for the *controlled* study of their behaviour. The fact that the controlled conditions might fundamentally change that behaviour was not a point at issue. It has, however, become a focus of debate in modern developmental psychology, around the concept of 'ecological validity'.[3] However, there has been little, if any, use of this term to criticise work which takes women as the object for granted.

When scientific psychology took off at the end of the nineteenth century, there were of course references to the debates of the day. In particular what should concern us here is the relation of work on evolution and on environmental conditions. We have already seen that work on the environment stressed the possibility of the management of change in the population. While there was no necessary opposition between work on heredity and that on environment, what is important for the development of the experimental tradition is that it concentrated on what was described as 'observable behaviour'. By this it was meant that what was avoided was any sense of 'mind' as a 'black box' which could not be observed. Thus, for example, one of the first behavioural studies, Pavlov's experiments on salivating dogs, attempted to produce changes in behaviour. Whether these were changes in thought was not under consideration. Pavlov produced what he described as 'experimental neurosis' in the dogs, that is, a state of anxiety resulting from confusing signals. Thus, states of mental distress and anxiety and confusion could be seen to be produced behaviourally. This kind of work was linked with experimental studies of mother–infant interaction to stress both the natural and evolutionary basis of what mothers did with their babies and introduced the concept of normality by demonstrating that some maternal behaviours could result in neurotic infants. It is this work which provided the basis for the intervention into maternal care and the regulation of mothering by the various state agencies.

There have been many critiques of 'Bowlbyism', which have examined his claims that attachment requires that mothers and infants bond at birth and stress the importance of the continual presence of the biological mother. Denis Riley (1983) suggests that while Bowlby did not claim that neurosis was produced in children if the mother was not at home all the time, the ideological climate at the time popularised his work to fit a set of post-war conditions and assumptions about women's labour. Cathy Urwin (1985b) has suggested that rather than popularisation we can look to the incorporation of these ideas in social welfare practices which regulate mothers and mothering. The concept of maternal deprivation became very widespread and was extended to linguistic deprivation in the 1960s. Several accounts have challenged the empirical claims of the deprivation literature and the claims made for maternal bonding.[4] However, because these approaches remain within a positivist framework they do not question the theoretical assumptions upon which the work was founded. Thus, while challenging the evidence, they do little to challenge the whole framework within which the problem has been formulated. This requires the taking apart of the conditions and assumptions of the work in the first place. It is this which we feel is so important to any feminist engagement with this debate.

Basically, what has been stressed in later work is that there is no evidence to support a biological basis to attachment in non-primate mammals.[5] In addition, it has been argued by psychologists Sluckin, Herbert and Sluckin (1983) among others that there is no evidence to support the view that the newborn infant must bond with its mother within hours of birth to produce psychic health. In addition, they suggest that attachments may be formed with several adults and that it is not the time spent with the adult which matters but the quality of the interactions. They utilise this to point out that social workers may now with good conscience make 'place of safety' orders on unborn or newborn babies if they consider that their biological mothers are unsuitable. They do not state by what criteria mothers are to be judged unsuitable. However, such work has also been used by feminists and others to suggest that 'men can mother too'. The concept of shared parenting as a solution to the problem of women's oppression as mothers is one which has many attractions. While we agree that it is important to stress the responsibility of others for parenting and child care, we do not accept that this concept is adequate to the task at hand.[6] Basically, such accounts adhere to the 'multiple attachment' approach. Thus, they do nothing to engage with the fundamental theoretical issues involved in the account of mothering as behaviour and the production of correct environments. If what is important in order to produce neurosis-free children is the quality of attachments, then what can be experimentally studied is the production of 'normal' mother–infant interactions. Mothering becomes a set of functions which can be experimentally mapped and articulated.

The making of the sensitive mother

We want here briefly to outline the development of the experimental study of 'attachment behaviour'. While the liberal scientific community might have rejected 'Bowlbyism', the study of mother–infant interaction continued unabated. Attachments formed the basis of all future empirical work, treated in such a way as to fundamentally ignore the theoretical and political questions that were at stake. The interactions of mothers and their offspring were calibrated and calculated in minute detail, so that, once again, the 'natural' could be determined and built into a model of how to ensure normal development.

Early laboratory and field studies such as those of Ainsworth (1964) and Ainsworth et al. (1972) and the developmental psychologist H.R. Schaffer and his team (1964) studied infants' reactions to various kinds of separation from the mother. They studied what happened when she left or was replaced by others and what resulted when she returned. By calibrating the infants' responses in minute detail, they mapped bahavioural responses, vocalisation, gesture and so forth, so that a whole battery of behaviours was produced.

Then they attempted to search for causes. At first the development of memory systems in the infants was thought important, but this did not provide enough explanatory data. Then, attachment to other figures was studied and cultural norms for separation from the mother explored, coming up with different ages for separation and distress in different cultures. Thus, it was suggested that different amounts and patterns of interaction between mother and child was then felt necessary because if it was not simply the presence or absence of the mother that did or did not lead to pathology, to neurosis, then what must matter, the argument went, was what happens in the relationship between the child and the attachment figure. In other words, there must be healthy and unhealthy ways of relating. Psychologists were concerned with what kinds of responses the mother made to her infant early on and how this related to later attachment behaviour, that is, signs of clinging, distress and so on. One such study, by Blehar, Lieberman and Ainsworth (1977), is worth quoting from because it demonstrates what kind of thing the researchers were looking at and for. They studied interactions in the homes of twenty-six American middle-class mother–child pairs at the ages of six, nine, twelve and fifteen weeks. What they concentrated on most was face-to-face interactions:

> A face-to-face encounter is defined as a full-face presentation of adult and infant to each other, occuring at a distance judged to range from 8 to 18 inches. Face-to-face episodes were coded when initiated by one member of a dyad (mother–child pair) even though the partner did not respond. They thus included instances in which (a) the baby initiated the episode by looking at a nearby person and smiling or vocalising but received no response; (b) the adult initiated the episode by presenting his [sic] face, but the baby failed to respond; and (c) one of the dyad initiated the episode, and the other responded by at least looking . . . (p. 185)

In this way they produced a coding of maternal behaviour and of infant behaviour. These related to the minutiae of the interaction. At twelve months the pairs were tested in a laboratory and the infants were left by their mothers for a few minutes. They then categorised the children's reactions on the mother's return. They divided the children into three groups according to their responses:

Group A actively avoided contact.

Group B sought contact, closeness or interaction.

Group C were ambivalent in their reactions. They both sought and resisted contact.

They further divided Group B into three sub-groups:

B1, called the 'normative' group, sought and maintained close physical contact.

B2 interacted over a distance with their mother, but did not seek proximity.

B3 were like B1 but their behaviours were less marked.

It will come as no surprise that the accolade 'normative', meaning normal, was accorded only to one group and that when the researchers checked what the mothers of these children had done in their early observations they had responded positively to their infants. By that they meant that the children in B1 who they thought showed the most normal attachment behaviour had mothers who paced their behaviour to that of the child, encouraged more interaction and were playful. It is only through setting up mothers with their infants in this way, by defining 'healthy attachment' that we come to find, unsurprisingly, that certain mothers do things which keep their babies 'attached' to them.

Here we have the studies which paved the way for the emergence of the fully fledged sensitive mother. Next came the idea that what mattered more than anything else was not whether the mother was with the child all the time, but how sensitive she was in the minute detail of her interactions. It is here that the work on emotional attachments was welded onto concerns not only for mental health but also for the educational success of working-class children.

Arguments about the daycare of infants and small children hinged upon the claims for the importance of the kind and intensity of the interaction. While some did not frown on daycare in principle, the child's mother just did a much better and more sensitive job. So, the debate got itself rather in knots. Some studies claimed that some mothers did a good job but that others, notably working-class ones, were not so sensitive; they were the latterday wire mothers. Thus, there were grounds for preferring day and nursery care and education to the harm done by abnormal mothers. H. R. Schaffer, like Harlow before him, waxed lyrical about the importance of mother-love. Like Harlow too he wanted to replace the romance of the heterosexual adult couple with the romance of the new couple, the mother and child. He leaves us in no doubt that the normal mother should be head over heels in love with her baby:

> Love also means a heightened sensitivity to its object. Anyone who has ever been in love knows of the increased awareness it brings to the other person, of the absorption in him that makes it so much easier to sense his moods, feelings, needs and wishes. To be attuned to the child is thus part of mother-love – so much so, according to the popular though quite unverified example, that the child's whimper will wake his mother when a thunderstorm fails to do so. (Schaffer, 1977, p. 87)

Rudolf Schaffer appears almost to speak from the position of the baby, the grown-up baby who wants a mother who is sensitive to his every whim, his every mood, who understands and panders to it. What an enticing vision! No wonder he believes that his universe will collapse if women do not readily and in love surrender themselves to this servitude. The sensitive mother is the one who is prepared to undergo this act of surrender to total love, to see things from her baby's point of view and to understand them.

However, Schaffer makes it clear that there are in the world women who do not love their children in the way we civilised peoples do. In a passage headed 'Some loveless people' he tells us of the Ik people of Uganda who have no place for love and reminds us that Margaret Mead's study of the Mundugamor people of New Guinea found that 'Here there is no such thing as mother love' (1977, p. 91). The absence of sensitive mothering will rain down the modern equivalent of pestilences upon the civilised world. Hate, aggression, violence and crime are all attributed to bad, insensitive mothers, who are not besotted by their babies. Softening a little he tells that even some emotionally disturbed women can mother adequately, but what matters most are those women who are egocentric: that is, they have wishes and desires of their own!

In a curious passage in which the mother is called by the 'generic masculine', (is he really talking about himself?) he leaves us in no doubt:

> We have repeatedly stressed the central role of sensitivity; let us now also stress that the insensitive parent is perhaps the greatest obstacle to the child's developmental progress, for he is likely to be more attuned to his own wishes and desires than those of his child. Being egocentric, he will have a distorted view of the child's capacities and may well attempt, in a rigid and authoritarian manner, to force the child into a mould that he just will not fit. (1977, p. 93)

Of course, we return to the woman who puts her own pleasure first, who wants to go out, enjoy herself, who has other interests than being besotted by her baby. Such women are *egocentric*. By defining them in this way Schaffer makes it clear that such women are pathological, for he uses a category from developmental and social psychology that is usually used to describe children who have not yet acquired the capacity to take another's point of view. The egocentric mother is the selfish woman, but here selfishness is a pathology that she could be cured of.

Because early sensitivity to the child was calculated by responses and interactions in the mother, it was argued that some mothers were insensitive. Some mothers did a great job, better than any nursery. Indeed some studies suggested that mothers were so sensitive to their children that they also became the best spontaneous teachers. So the message was: if you want your child to succeed in the educational system, become a sensitive mother. Nursery provision was threatened by the idea that if mothers could best teach their children, then they would, by implication, be better off at home. Tizard and Hughes, in the study which we quoted at the beginning of the book and whose transcripts form the basis of our data, got themselves into just such a tangle.

They wanted to demonstrate that the debates about social class which had used the deprivation literature to argue that, basically, working-class mothers were inadequate and insensitive, was incorrect. Tizard and Hughes tell us that there *are* sensitive working-class mothers. They do more than this. They imply that those mothers are more sensitive to their daughters' needs than their nursery-school teachers. Thus they leave open the implication that these children are better off taught by their mothers. They get themselves in knots because their adherence to the sensitivity discourse leaves them no other place to go. Nowhere do they really investigate the conditions for the production of mothering in working and middle-class women.

Their position seems to suggest that the only kind of response to class inequality understood as deprivation is that working-class mothers can be sensitive too. They are somewhat at a loss, however, to know how to deal with those working-class women who do not fit the description. They are left only with the alternative that they elect, that is that the daughters of such women get useful lessons in 'social learning'.

Many studies by psychologists began to map maternal behaviour in terms of intellectual as well as emotional sensitivity. Scales of sensitivity were developed and more and more behaviours mapped. Then sensitivity became linguistic. Normal mothers not only responded to their babies' emotional needs, they engaged in 'fine-tuning' to their meanings, they 'scaffolded' their responses, they expanded their children's utterances and made sense of their gestures.[7] The mother became the prime vehicle through which the child was to communicate with the outside world. Sensitivity to and development of the child's first steps to communicate was the mother's job par excellence. Mothers, many studies concluded, were so good at all this that they were inimitable and irreplaceable. It is they who would ensure their children's mental health and would prepare them for educational success both by teaching them and by developing their language.

Later commentators make it very clear indeed that this preparation is what is taken to be the forerunner of educational success and therefore the erosion of inequality and particularly of social class differences.[8]

With such burdens as these, women today struggle in their relations with their children. The fact that the future of civilisation is laid at the door of women, that science selects as its mission the minute mapping of the civilising process, gives us more than enough reasons both to take apart the arguments upon which these claims are founded and to explore in detail the lives of the women and girls who provide for the scientific voyeur all the elaborate detail of animals in cages. It is to the daily lives of these mothers and daughters, so clearly and closely described for us, that we will now turn.

CHAPTER FOUR

WOMEN'S WORK IS *ALWAYS* DONE

Women's work

What then do we have so far? We have a web of bonds between women and children, a tangle of needs met by undeniable mother-instincts. Women are bonded to their babies by their biology, as numerous rhesus monkeys under the grand ring-master of the laboratory circus, Harry Harlow, and countless ducklings and goslings pulled into the ring by Harlow's successors have proven.[1] Women's biology makes them the best suited to the job of child care, but this is not always enough, for, as we have seen, some abnormal women become wire, not warm, mothers. Nor is it good enough for the mother merely to 'be there'; her presence must be in mind, emotion, as well as body. This is easily achieved by the normal mother, for she and her baby are bonded by *love*, and she, like 'anyone who has ever been in love knows' (Schaffer, 1977), has neither eyes nor ears for anyone else, not even herself. But is it *really* that easy? The account of mother–infant love traced so far presents it as a 'state' (Harlow), a condition which descends upon the mother to overwhelm her. Love-induced inspiration attunes the mother acutely to her child's needs; a 'fine-tuning' never achieved by others outside this love-bond – the nursery school teacher, the daycare assistant. This uniquely satisfying relationship then equips the mother to be the best teacher. The fact that the mother has a life at all, outside the helpless gaze of the loved one, is never considered. Not surprising, since Schaffer's account is about an emotion so intense, so overwhelming that the person who is in love could not possibly want to *do* anything else, so great is her absorption in him, his majesty, the baby.

It seems ridiculously obvious to point out that becoming a mother does not instantly terminate all other aspects of women's lives. But we have shown how a tradition of work on mothering which emerged from evolutionary biology, ethology and the laboratory has constructed this very view: this isolated, romantic snapshot of motherhood. We want to take the mother-child pair out of that laboratory, to put them back into their real lives where the mother often has more than one child, a husband, a job and housework. We want (and this is sometimes much more painful) to reveal that the work of mothering – for it has not disappeared or been chased away by love – has been transformed and concealed.

We will also, in this chapter, be looking at how 'women's work' as a specific category has been understood in feminist literature, and how there are attempts made here also to transform women's domestic labour, this time from 'drudgery' into a commodity which produces a value within a capitalist system of production. But for now, let us return to psychology, for to understand how the work involved in achieving sensitivity in mothering has been metamorphosed, we must examine some crucial aspects of standard developmental theory.

If we examine closely the kinds of tasks which are supposed to aid the intellectual development of young children, and on the basis of which well-known psychologists constructed their accounts of that development, we will find that they are almost all routine domestic tasks transformed into a pedagogy; a pedagogy that the mother can engage in while she is, for instance, making the family meal. The following example, taken from a suggested school handout to parents on early mathematics, makes this clear:

> You are probably helping your child to get ready for Mathematics in many ways, maybe without realising it! Here are some of the many activities that you can do *with your child* which will help.
>
> Laying the table – counting, getting the knives in the right place, etc.
>
> Going shopping – handling money, counting items in basket.
>
> Dressing and undressing – sorting clothes into piles.
>
> Helping with cooking – weighing, measuring.
>
> Playing with water – at bathtime, washing up.
>
> Tidying away toys.
>
> *Left* and *Right* games.
>
> Spotting shapes (circles, squares, etc.) colours, comparing sizes, etc., whether at home or on walks.
>
> No doubt you can think of many more. The important thing is that you help your child to get hold of the basic ideas of Maths, such as sorting, matching and comparing. By sharing an activity with your child and by talking to him, you can begin to introduce the correct 'Mathematical' words such as big and small, few and many, longest and shortest and so on. *But don't turn it into a lesson* [our emphasis]. All these things can be done incidentally as a part of day to day events. (*Early Mathematical Experiences General Guide*, 1978 p. 11).

Diana's family have sat down to their midday meal. Diana is going to have a 'picnic' in the garden with some friends later on. She and her mother talk about how many glasses of juice they will need.

> M: How many children are there?
> C: Three.
> M: There's Mary.
> C: David. (C counts on her fingers.)
> M: David.
> C: Annabelle.

M: Annabelle. Now, have you got the right number of fingers? Diana . . . put these down.

Diana has in fact got *all* her fingers up. Her mother pushes them all down except one, and they start again. The first finger is for Diana, and she puts another finger up for each person they name. They end up with five names.

M: How many is that?
C: Four.
M: No.
C: Seven.
M: No. Count.
C: (C tries to count her fingers.) One, two, three . . .
M: Four.
C: Five.
M: Mmm.
C: Five. You have to give me . . . five juice out, five biscuits out.

Katy and her mother are in the garden planting seedlings and watering them:

M: Now, one more [to be watered]. How many's that?
C: Three. Can I do it?
M: No, it's four.
C: It's four.

On one level you might say that finding the principles of intellectual development in the routine activities of women's domestic labour is demonstrating that such activities or experiences are everywhere.[2] But we could ask a deeper question, that is, why is domestic labour transformed into the very basis of children's cognitive development, and what is the relationship between this and the idea that the sensitive mother is necessary to meet the child's intellectual and emotional needs? In order to answer this, we need to examine how domestic work became mothering. We will begin by looking at the terms in which 'women's work' as a specific category has come to be understood in feminist literature, and then go on to discuss the relationship between housework and mothering.

In our analysis we do not talk about the 'value' of housework, indeed in many of the examples we use, no housework as such is being carried out at all. For here we make a split from those diverse strands of thought within what became known as the domestic-labour debate in feminist writings during the mid- and late seventies. Consistently emphasised within the different strands of feminist and Marxist writings within this debate was a concern with women's waged and unwaged labour.[3] While this debate may have been exhausted by the late 1970s, it remains a landmark in that it raised issues about female labour which, up until that point had not been commented on. It may be true that 'nobody talks about' the domestic-labour debate anymore, but many of its concepts still underpin and echo in feminist writings of women's *paid* labour especially.[4] It is crucial therefore for us to, in a sense, 'go back' to the domestic-labour debate if we are to propose a different understanding of 'women's work'.

In our analysis of housework we make no distinctions between what counts as housework and what counts as mothering, the 'work' of being a mother. By using extracts from conversations had while mother and daughter were sitting together, eating lunch or writing out a shopping list, we can show how the work of mothering goes on, even though the event may be the result of or the prelude to domestic labour in a crude sense (cooking the dinner, say, or doing the shopping).

No longer can we differentiate between the physical tasks which make up women's housework and the work of mothering. The two are the same. Housework can no longer simply be seen as physical 'valueless' drudgery, designed for the constant maintenance and reproduction of an exploited workforce. These tasks are not just keeping the house clean, the family healthy and fed, fit for another day's work. There is another function of this labour, a function ignored or missed by the domestic-labour debate. We have suggested in Chapter Two that housework and the regime of cleanliness, health and fitness were historically used to regulate women's sexuality. More recently, women's domestic labour has become the basis of modern ideas about how children learn, and housework, in its metamorphosis, has become integral to the function of sensitive mothering.

Writing in the late nineteenth century, Karl Marx talked of how the home became a point for the reproduction of the labour force, both on a day-to-day and generational level.[5] At this point, women's oppression was seen as inextricably bound up with the family. For here, within that self-contained unit, women became isolated, dependent on men.[6] But within this analysis the enormous significance of women's position as reproducer of the labour force was at one and the same time confirmed and completely undermined, made trivial. The unseen labour of the woman in every home then became one of the mainstays of the capitalist system. Capital needs women's housework, and yet, within this analysis, her labour has no 'value'.

According to Marxist logic, class position is dictated by one's relationship to the means of production; between those who own capital, who employ, exploit, and those who own nothing but their labour, who do not employ but must engage in an exploitative relationship with the capitalist owners to make a living.[7] Class membership depends upon whether or not the surplus value you produce through your labour is creamed off by your employers in return for a wage unequal to the value of that labour. Much discussion on class within feminism has relied heavily on this Marxist conception of class, although the refinements to it have been great.[8] Nevertheless, this position has consistently posed massive problems when considering the class position of women. For within this framework, the *work* of reproduction produces no obvious surplus and therefore no 'value'.

What then of women's class position? Can it simply be read from the position their husbands occupy in the outside world, or are they, by virtue of their valueless yet crucial drudgery, classless? Does capitalism exploit women through their domestic labour, or are they oppressed by their position in the family? Who benefits most from this labour, capitalism or men? And how can women develop a sense of class, of class consciousness, like their menfolk if they are not incorporated into capitalist production, if their labour is not waged, and if they are not subject to the severest exploitation as 'proper' workers?[9] How can they enter the struggle for liberation, without first experiencing this? These are some of the thorny questions which feminist writers on women, their work and their class have tried to answer, and tried to struggle free of in the last twenty years.

Feminist analyses of housework, after an initial descriptive period of the mid-1960s to early 1970s,[10] had two main concerns. Firstly to present a balance to the psychoanalytic and developmental view of motherhood as an intrinsically satisfying relationship between mother and child based on nature – on drives and instincts. Secondly to compare housework with waged work, at which point housework had to be connected with capitalist production. Taking up the traditional sociological perspective of labour has provided important insights into the examination of motherhood.[11] It has highlighted the fact that housework and child care are work and as such can be as tiring, oppressive and alienating as waged labour. However, as Boulton (1983) points out, this has lead to a number of accounts which separate the experience of motherhood into two elements, the *work* of child care, which is boring and frustrating, and the mother-child relationship which provides many emotional rewards, but which are hampered by the social context in which the relationship exists. These studies then imply that motherhood (the mother-child relationship) is basically satisfying, while only the structure and context of the mother role, the 'conditions of maternity' produce frustration and negative feelings.[12]

The conceptualisation of the housewife or mother role as involving work inevitably led to other questions being asked, mostly centring around the ever-present concern of 'value'. Is housework productive? Does it too produce surplus value? Many women felt that if only these questions could be answered then it would be possible to decide once and for all (a) whether or not working-class housewives were truly a part of the working class and (b) on the common experience of *all* women, a belief in the classless nature of women's oppression.

Some feminist writers tried to deal with these questions within a Marxist framework, but there are other, varied strands of thought on this nevertheless.[13] We do not want to engage here with all the various theoretical positions within this debate, but rather point to the basic inadequacy of the framework dominating all of them. For the domestic labour debate and other analyses within that debate around housework are essentially about comparisons. Despite the advances made by highlighting women's hidden and unpaid work, throughout the literature, we find that 'women's work' is compared with male manual workers' waged labour. It is this category of worker which is held up as the ideal working-class member and the yardstick by which membership of the working class is measured.[14] This theme runs through feminist studies of women's waged work also. Here the question is, 'Do women have a class consciousness?' Most of these studies represent women's consciousness as problematic. It is fragmentary and contradictory[15] and while women appear to reveal 'work consciousness', their main identification of themselves is as housewives and mothers. This self-definition distinguishes and separates them from 'workers'. Again we have comparisons, this time with an ideal type of consciousness, but one which overlooks the fragmentary nature of the consciousness of *all* workers.[16] With notable exceptions[17] women as both workers and housewives are represented as a conservative force, unable to recognise their oppression as women or exploitation as workers.

Although the domestic labour debate was vital in making possible the posing of certain questions about women's work, hitherto unasked, it completely elides the issue we are trying to raise in this book. That is, it is not simply a question of labour or value, but the way in which the mothering and child-rearing labour of bourgeois and proletarian women became a central guarantor of the possibility of a liberal democracy. Thus, it is not simply the 'fact' of the labour, nor its power in the 'reproduction' of labour, but the central place in the production of women as mothers and the facts of their regulation. Our argument is that middle- and working-class practices are differently regulated and in order to investigate this we need to examine the organisation of mothering, housework, child-rearing, and the meanings through which they are produced and understood.

One of the most striking features of most of the middle-class homes is the way in which housework is organised and actually carried out. Generally, domestic tasks are rendered invisible in the middle-class homes. They are spoken about far less and often the only indication that these women do indeed do any housework is in the field-notes made by the observer. Housework thus goes *underground*, with the effect that it is presented as far less pressing for most middle-class women than for their working-class counterparts. Ownership of or access to a car and enough available money to do a weekly shop or bulk buy at a supermarket makes shopping for a family less time consuming, less physically tiring and, in the long run, much cheaper.[18] A couple of the middle-class mothers employed cleaners and one an au pair. Nevertheless, to suggest that these factors account entirely for the massive differences observed in time spent engaged in visible house-work between the working- and middle-class mothers would, we feel strongly, be unfair. Some studies of house-work suggest that even though the possession of a dish-washer or other domestic appliances may ease the sheer physical work, they make very little difference to the actual time spent in household chores. They may be labour-saving devices, but they are certainly not time-saving.[19]

What we are concerned to explore here is why we *see* in some working-class households women whose day is one continual round of domestic chores, the constraints of which are painfully evident to both mother and daughter (not to mention the researcher), whereas in most middle-class homes there is no sense of drudgery, of not having enough hours in the day to get everything done. We *find* and *read* a relaxed mother creating a relaxed and unharried environment. And yet, of course, most of these women have cleaning, cooking, shopping and so on to get done.

Naomi's mother lectured in English one and a half days a week, had two pre-school children and was expecting twins in a few months at the time of these recordings, and yet her labour remains hidden, does not intrude on the day we witness in the transcript. Did she organise her day so radically differently from Jacky's mother? The latter has a young baby, and works at home as a childminder. Although she and Jacky have a friendly relationship, she makes her labour apparent. When did Naomi's mother fit in all her chores? In the evening, for example?

To demonstrate how this invisibility is achieved we will cite the example of Sarah, whose mother gets her to clean out the fish tank. When it comes to transferring the goldfish back into the now clean tank, her mother sets up the task as a problem of logic for the child.

> M: Now, how are we going to get the fish out of the big bowl and into the little one, d'you think?
> C: I know, well, we get a thing and then we put some water in it and then put it into there. Catch the fish.
> M: And catch the fish?
> C: Yes.
> M: How about something like that? (M holds up a plastic pot.)
> C: Yes, I think that would do. Wash it out!

Notice how the mother defines the task as pedagogic, as an educational task from which Sarah can learn about capacity, size and even more complex mathematical concepts such as the effect of refraction through glass and water on the size of objects.

> M: They look a bit bigger through their glass, don't they?

C: Yes.
M: Even the small one looks pretty big, doesn't it?
C: Through the glass.
M: Look over the top and see if it looks different.
C: No, that one's little now, when I look from the top. And it's bigger when I look from through the glass.

We have argued that women's domestic labour had become the basis of modern ideas about how children learn so that tasks taken to aid the accomplishment of intellectual development were nearly all domestic tasks, like sorting cutlery, making cakes, doing the shopping. But the interpretation that is used is that cognitive development is everywhere and therefore anything can form the basis of an intellectual task. It is a mode of analysis of tasks which sees them as embodiments of a particular structure of action and of thought. In this way the fact that they are domestic tasks, and that women must aid their children's development by transforming their domestic labour into a pedagogy, is completely hidden. Of course, not *all* housework is endlessly transformed in this way: there are obviously times when the children are not around. But from these examples we can begin to see how these women's housework can get hidden and transformed into something else. That something else is the very basis on which they are judged to be sensitive mothers, because in responding to what is described as children's needs, they are aiding their development.

Work, play and time

We can immediately see how something as pressing as domestic work could conflict with demands made by a small child, but the sensitive mother must be constantly ready to meet needs (though not *too* much as this would undermine her developing autonomy: D.W. Winnicott's account of healthy neglect). Theories of child development stress the need for a 'free atmosphere' in which the child can explore and discover. How sharply this notion contradicts the just as powerful idea of the 'ideal home' which is always clean and well ordered. We can see then that the mother must walk a tightrope of conflicting and impossible demands. For the sensitive mother her work becomes the basis of the child's play. This was much more common in the middle-class homes. In working-class homes, the distinction between the mother's housework and play with her daughter is much more marked in terms of time.

Let us take a closer look at what we mean by the mother transforming her labour so that it becomes the foundation of play. Sarah does not work at cleaning the fish tank: it has become a kind of game. This is just as it should be! Many developmental texts insist that play is the proper medium of expression for children. Many curriculum materials for young children are totally based on the idea that every task must be presented as play and not work.

> It was found that there were many different methods of presenting activities and learning situations to the children, but these could be grouped loosely into four main categories:
>
> 1. Children *playing* freely with as many activities and materials as possible, without adult intervention.
> 2. Children *playing* with materials which had been deliberately provided by teachers to encourage the acquisition of certain concepts, but still without adult intervention.
> 3. Children *playing* with materials of their own choice with the active participation of an adult.
> 4. Children *playing* with materials which had been selected by a teacher who was leading and guiding them towards the acquisition of certain facts.
>
> (*Early Mathematical Experiences, General Guide*, 1978 p. 6, emphasis added)

Housework appears to be a far less pressing demand in middle-class homes. It is something which can be and frequently is abandoned in favour of the daughter's demand for help, attention or for a playmate. While a few working-class mothers do no housework during the afternoons of the recordings, this is certainly not the norm. Most working-class mothers make their domestic labour apparent and a priority over the child's demands, especially to play. On the other hand, the middle-class mothers seem to find it even more difficult to refuse their daughters' requests to play, even when, on occasion, they make it clear that they do have housework which needs to be done.[20] Some of these women do attempt to resist such demands, expressing how busy they are. But the strategy which we wish to explore here, which more middle-class mothers use in relation to housework, is to incorporate it into play.

Penny and her mother have been playing a card game called 'jumble sales', but when it is finished, Penny insists that they play another game:

> C: I said, what are you going to play with? Mummy?
> M: Don't want to play with anything. I, I should do some cooking really.
> C: No.
> M: Get the dinner ready.
> C: No.

Her mother complies and Penny initiates a fantasy game, which her mother is drawn into. Eventually she decides that she must get on with preparing dinner and ends the fantasy episode by saying:

> M: Would you like me to make you some pastry?
> C: Oh yes! (Squeals.)
> M: Don't scream! You can make, you can play with the pastry while I do some cooking.

What is interesting here is that this task begins with Penny's nagging and the ineffectual resistance by her mother to the child's demands for play. Now, developmental accounts would point precisely to how much Penny learned from 'helping Mummy cook': the valuable mathematical concepts of shape, size and quantity in making and manipulating the pastry. There might indeed be such concepts involved in domestic work, but that structural description misses the point that we are trying to make. That is, that the mother is forced to make her domestic work the basis of her daughter's play and in this way becomes seen as sensitive to her needs and aiding in her development. Had she refused her demands, we could not possibly have understood her in the same light. She would have been seen as blocking the child's possibilities for development. It is interesting to note by looking back at the transcript how ineffectual Penny's mother is in her resistance to her demands.

Charlotte's mother is considered sensitive. Charlotte constantly asks questions which her mother answers patiently and explicitly. Throughout the afternoon, her mother engages Charlotte in essentially domestic tasks. Some are commonplace, like helping Mummy put the shopping away, while others involve making things. During the afternoon, Charlotte's mother gets Charlotte to help her make muesli and this becomes the basis of number work. Unlike Penny's mother, she does not have to resist her daughter's demands, because she immediately and consistently sets up what she must get done alongside strategies for amusing her daughter. This form of mixing domestic work and play forms a particular mode of regulation, a way of disciplining the child. Penny's mother gets her to play with the pastry because her attempted strategy for resisting the child's demands has failed. Like Charlotte's mother, she can get on with her own housework, regulate the child and pass on new knowledge. Either she must find some way of giving in, like incorporating the demand into her work, or she must reason with the child, explain to her, a strategy which may not work.

For example, Emily's mother tries to resist Emily's insistence that they play another game by explaining patiently how she must 'get on' and carefully suggesting they play the game after lunch:

> C: Shall we play – Mummy, I want you to play this with me.

> M: All right . . . No, shall we, shall we start our lunch and play it afterwards? Do you think?
> C: No . . . Orange, blue, yellow, green, red. (C has already got the game out and is pointing to different-coloured clowns on the box.)
> M: Shall we do our lunch and then do it afterwards?
> C: No.
> M: I think it's going to take us rather a long time, that game.
> C: No! (Screams.)

These working-class women have a tendency to regulate and discipline their daughters in a completely different way, one which makes strong distinctions between domestic work and play and which delineates clearly that domestic work has to be accomplished in a specific time, usually before father gets home or she has to go off to work. This means that work has to be done and what is important is that the child does not interfere, can learn to play by herself, to be self-reliant. If the child interferes, she can be told not to be demanding, be told off. In this way the mother makes her power explicit, especially her power to withhold her attention. This is what the Newsons consider so harmful (see Chapter One). This makes possible explicit power struggles. So, while the working-class mothers do use domestic settings to 'teach' their daughters, this does not occur as often and they are much more likely *successfully* to resist the child's demands. They do not use such instances as regulative devices. When her daughter wants her to interrupt her housework and play, or 'come and look', the working-class mother is far more likely to insist that her daughter must realise how busy she is and that her work cannot be abandoned. So the daughter is also learning a very important lesson and some new concepts, but they are different lessons, different concepts, in different circumstances than her middle-class counterpart.

> Nicky: I wanna do some painting.
> M: I've gotta do washing first, then we'll do painting.

This is a very different scene to the middle-class homes where helping Mum make muesli becomes a rich educational and social context in which the child can interact, talk to and learn from her mother.

Joanne wants her mother to come and look at what she's playing with. She calls for her to come.

> M: I said I'll come and see you in a minute when I've done this. Won't be a minute, I must do some washing first or else I'll get shot.

A very different picture to the one where helping Mum put old Christmas cards away becomes a counting exercise, while the mother, as an incidental bonus, can at the same time complete her chores. But, much more importantly, the pair can 'discover' mutuality.

> Sally: Are you going to sit down with me?
> M: Not yet, I'm going to peel, finish peeling the potatoes.

There is no sense in the middle-class transcripts, unlike the extracts above from some working-class mothers, of the harassed housewife, the 'drudge'. No, the middle-class women can be read as discovering the mutual enjoyment of time spent with their daughters as well as discovering that housework *can* be fun. We gain a different sense of what time means in such homes. There is *more* time, to talk, to play, explain, explore and enjoy. Or is there? Later we will see just how much hard work goes into this apparently effortless scene.

It is important to note here that there were a few working-class mothers who did little or no housework during the recordings and spent almost the entire afternoon playing with their daughters. Conversely, a small minority of middle-class mothers spent little time playing compared to the rest of the sample. However, in the majority of working-class homes it was evident that housework was a quite separate activity from, and had priority over, play. This apparent contradiction between work and play in working-class households became the site for much resistance between mother and daughter. The working-class girls did make more demands than the middle-class girls, but crucially, these were successfully resisted by their mothers much more frequently. So, while it is true that middle-class girls appeared less demanding, this, we would argue, is a consequence of their mothers actually going in to them more frequently. The effect of the working-class mothers' successfiıl resistance to the girls' requests (in this discussion, to play) is contrastive. It opens up a site for conflict and struggle between mother and daughter.

Nicky's mother is working in the kitchen. Nicky hangs around the kitchen, constantly asking for biscuits, which her mother, after giving her one or two, thereafter denies her. Nicky then gets out a glass bottle that she intends to play with.

> M: No, it's glass, and you're not playing with a glass bottle.
> C: A, I did play with my glass bottle.
> M: Will you please get out of that cupboard and go upstairs and play before I get cross with you!
> C: I wanna get a biscuit, I'll put these upstairs. (C then sits on the stairs eating her biscuit.)
> C: I'll say I've finished and then I can have another one [biscuit], can I?
> M: No, you cannot have another one.
> (————)
> C: No, when I ate it.
> M: You're not having any more!
> (————)
> Go on, upstairs! Go and play.

Many things can be read into this short extract from their conversation. That Nicky's mother is impatient of Nicky's constant wanting. That she has much to do before she goes out to her evening cleaning job and Nicky is clearly under her feet, hindering her. All these things we can understand and have sympathy with. But can we see her as a sensitive mother? Nicky is making her 'needs' clear – she wants her mother's attention, and yet her mother is as clearly quite *in*sensitive to those needs. She refuses to stop what she's doing, *or* to shift her own tasks in order to incorporate the child into them. What is more, she overtly displays her own power and authority over the child. She adopts a 'positional' stance,[21] devoid (some might say) of reason, explanation. It is then only too easy to come to the conclusion that she is a *bad* mother who realises what the child needs but is more concerned with her own needs. She is 'egocentric'.[22]

Nicky's mother, like most of the working-class mothers, does not operate as though work can become play. Work and play are opposites and must be kept separate – the distinction between the two activities is often implicitly stated when the working-class girls ask their mothers to play.

> C: Mum, will you come upstairs and play.
> M: Nicky, I'm sorry, I cannot come up yet.
> C: Oh, you said when (————————)
> M: I'm just going to do this work first, love, I've got washing to do.
> C: Yeah?
> M: Got ironing to do.
> C: Yeah?
> M: I got altering to do.
> C: Yeah?
> M: Yeah, well, it all takes time, love.

Why is it that middle-class mothers make this shift in their labour, to blur the distinction between work and play so that they *can* be sensitive mothers as well as good housewives? Why can the working-class mothers not achieve the same? The idea that play is the 'educational context par excellence', especially in the pre-school years, became an educational doctrine in the 1930s and was popularised in the Plowden Report, 'Children and their Primary Schools', 1967. The fact that play was stressed can be related to several issues. Firstly, the emergence of compulsory schooling had meant that children should not *work*, therefore, childhood became defined as a distinct state, and the employment of children was considered to block the possibility of children 'being children'. Thus, play, the opposite to work, was defined as a childish activity, though the historian P. Aries (1960) points out that previously people of all ages played. Research from ethology was used to demonstrate that young animals 'played' (thus rendering it 'natural'[23]). Melanie Klein and others used play as a means of getting at fantasy for child analysis, and psychologists like Piaget saw it as a basis for the evolution in children of intellectual knowledge, produced by children's acting upon the objects in the physical world.[24]

By the 1930s, the First World War had added 'freedom' to the list. Children were to be free to play, and this was part of ensuring the free citizen.[25] The facilitation by mothers of young children's play thus became loaded with all the investments that we have been describing. Throughout the 1960s and 1970s such notions were popularised and special 'educational' toys and kinds of play were favoured, usually those which were supposed to aid language and cognitive development. Parents could aid their children's educational success by provision of the 'right kind' of play materials and by playing with them. The 'wrong' kind of (non-educational) toys were frowned upon, as was overt teaching.[26] More than anything, however, play was the opposite of work. It was not considered to be labour because it was pleasurable and intrinsically motivating to children, just as mothering was not seen as work either, but as 'love'. On this basis, it became impossible for mothers to extract themselves guiltlessly from so monumental a role.

Play and learning then become inseparable. The learning environment becomes the entire home, every possible permutation of events, actions and conversations becomes a 'not to be missed' opportunity for a valuable lesson. But the lesson cannot be discovered by the child alone. It must be directed carefully and sensitively taught, directed, by the mother, to ensure that the right lesson is learned. The good mother must always be there. And so, not only the 'formal' lesson or the 'educational game', but imaginative play, mealtimes, housework, conversations, questions, demands, resistance and arguments *all* become the site of learning. Given this, it is not so difficult to see why the middle-class mothers especially allow their time and space to be invaded much more than the working-class mothers. And how, also, mothers who readily give up their own work to talk, play and rationalise with their daughters are 'read' by the researcher as *sensitive* mothers, constantly attuned to their daughters' needs. We do not see a woman who is, in a very real sense, chained by an awareness of her child's cognitive and developmental 'needs' and how she fits into fulfilling those needs, but a relaxed and nurturant facilitator. In short, we see but one facet of the fantasy mother.

Housework, by its very transformation, has achieved a different value. It is no longer enough just to view it in terms of 'reproduction' of the labour force, for this analysis glosses over the differences too easily, between women's labour and what housework means to women of different classes. Housework oppresses, of that we are sure, but not in a universal way. For, while the middle-class women in this study are manacled to sensitivity, whereby even the way they peel the potatoes becomes a site for proving their worth as good mothers, as well as the worth of their labour, the working-class women, through the different economic circumstances they live by, are chained to time. In their jobs it is their time, not their skill which is bought. At home, similarly, it is their time that housework takes up. Both the working-class and the middle-class women must get their work *done*, but the middle-class women must also make it *fun*.

So the relationship between work and play and work and time relates to different circumstances of the women, their work, their wealth and poverty, but also to the way in which these things are cross-cut by their understanding and familiarity with modern accounts of child development. Consonant with developmental theory, housework becomes fun and learning is accomplished through play. Now you see it, now you don't. Is the sensitive mother really only a sleight of hand? Does a woman become a sensitive mother if she can become a conjurer, pulling play out of work, like rabbits out of a hat?

Both sets of women are 'managers' of a domestic economy, but under very different circumstances and with very different modes of regulation. Some have to say 'no' very often, while others can seem to offer an abundance of everything. How then one group must seem like saints, while the other are so obviously sinning against the great god of developmental psychology, of children's needs.

CHAPTER FIVE

A QUESTION OF MEANING

Maureen's mother and father both do paid work; he as a foreman in a confectionery factory, she as a part-time cleaner. Neither has any formal academic qualifications. Helen's parents work also. Her father is a journalist and her mother, a trained teacher, gives remedial tuition in her home three mornings a week. All are workers, but are all working class? Anne Phillips (1987) points out that 'When company executives jostle promiscuously alongside cleaners and cooks, such a definition evades a sense of ourselves' (p.22). For within such a framework, the gloss is too thick; thick enough to cover crucial differences in work and how it is experienced, how some of us come to be company executives, while others work machines or clean floors. Common sense tells us that the conditions of a cleaner's and a teacher's labour cannot possibly be the same or equal. Cleaners do not enjoy the same degree of autonomy, security, wages, expectations. The cleaner could be said to have a 'job', the teacher a 'career'.[1] And yet at the same time, this analysis elides the very real similarities between Maureen and Helen's mothers' work. We seem to be caught at all turns.

What does *work* mean for the women and girls living and growing up in different circumstances? Arguments which treat women's labour as a unitary category do not engage with the different circumstances and differential meanings of that labour within the contexts and practices in which the families exist.

The subjective and objective meaning of 'work' is not only constructed on the factory floor. Class consciousness is not only spawned within the factory walls, through the exchange of one value for another. Marilyn Porter (1983) acknowledges that 'in most work-based studies we never follow the wage out of the factory gates'. She is one of the few writers on women's and men's class consciousness who stresses the importance of considering not only the experience of the daily eight hours spent away from the home in waged labour, but also the sixteen hours spent at home. This is important given the way in which the categories of 'work' and 'worker' have come to refer to men in manual, male-dominated, waged labour. But none of the women whose lives are discussed in this book were working in manual jobs at the time of the study, although some had previously done that type of work. Significantly, too, many studies of the formation of working-class consciousness and how it relates to their experiences of work confine their investigation to men. Assumptions are made about working-class women which leads them to being either omitted altogether from such studies (but added on all the same, as if the forces which shape their husbands' consciousness can legitimately be said to be identical to their own) or referred to as a conservative force, as putting pressure on their menfolk to withdraw from issues about work (involvement in unions, striking etc.). We want to make the argument, through our examples, that their husbands' work (and this applies to the working- and middle-class women equally) did have an important effect on the meaning of work, especially with regard to the relationship between labour, money and goods, but that their own experience of their *own* work, waged and unwaged, housework and the work of mothering, were crucial.

In the extract below, of the conversation between Samantha and her mother, we will show how an everyday conversation became the place where meanings about women, about work and about class were explored and produced. We propose then, in this chapter, to look at 'women's work' in a different way – in a sense, to turn the way it has been traditionally studied on its head. We do not compare the conditions of the women's housework with manual or other jobs, we do not try to put a 'value' on that work. In the Introduction, we argued that we (VW and HL) did have a sense of being working class when we grew up, but that this was not the sense of class put forward in most Left analyses. What was important to us was what our lives meant to us, and the meanings ascribed to us, like being 'bright working-class girls' who went to grammar school. Those meanings come from the intersection of the conditions of our lives and the way in which those lives were regulated. Those meanings have psychic effects which can often be difficult to deal with.

We are now going to explore a piece of transcript in which Samantha and her mother talk about the work being done by a window cleaner. We will see how Samantha's mother tries to explain that work to her, but also how Tizard and Hughes ascribed particular meanings to the transcript which serve to regulate child-rearing practices by designating certain meanings as proper development and others not.

Samantha and her mother are sitting in the dining-room having their lunch when the window cleaner arrives in the garden to do their windows. Samantha's mother goes into the kitchen and talks to her neighbour, Marion.

> C: What did Marion say?
> M: She's having to pay everybody else's bills for the window cleaner, 'cos they're all out.
> C: Why they all out?
> M: 'Cos they're working or something.
> C: Aren't they silly!
> M: Well, you have to work to earn money, don't you?
> C: Yeah . . . if they know what day the window cleaner come they should stay here.
> M: They should stay at home? Well, I don't know . . . they can't always.

The event – the appearance of a workman – may seem like an everyday occurrence. Yet in the conversation that follows we see how this presence evoked not only curiosity, 'puzzlement', and the need to clarify the knowledge imparted to her, but possibly also darker elements: confusion, fear and disgust.

While the pair are eating their lunch, the man cleans the windows of the dining-room where they are sitting. Samantha whispers to her mother.

> C: The window cleaner got dirt on him.
> M: What?
> C: (Whispers.)
> M: Don't whisper.
> C: The window cleaner get dirt on him.
> M: Gets dirt on what? On his rag?
> C: On his face as well.
> M: Oh, does he? (Laughs.) Well, doesn't really matter, he can always wash it, can't he? –
> C: Yes.
> M: When he's finished work.

The conversation continues, Samantha's fear of the 'dirty' window cleaner allayed by her mother's lighthearted and amused replies. She is alarmed, as many four-year-olds would be, by the appearance of the strange man in the garden; that too is obvious and cannot be ignored. The window cleaner is both a man and working class, simultaneously, and this will have effects for her puzzlement and her fear. We wish to suggest that she is worried by and trying to understand something else; something about work. Who does what kind? Why are they paid and who works for whom? She clearly finds the discussion difficult. Why?

> C: Mummy.
> M: Mmm.
> C: Um, she can't pay everybody, er, the win, or all the bills to the window cleaner, can she?
> M: What?
> C: Marion can't give all the bill, all the bills . . .
> M: No, she can't pay all, everybody's bills.

C: To the window cleaner.
M: Well, she sometimes pays mine if I'm out. She sometimes pays Ruth's up the road if she's out. I always pay her back though.
C: 'Cos it's fair.
M: Mmm, it is.
(———)
C: Umm, but where does she leave the money?
(———)
M: She doesn't leave it anywhere, she gives it, she hands it to the window cleaner, after he's finished.
C: And then she gives it to us.
M: No, no, she doesn't have to pay us.
C: Then the window cleaner gives it to us?
M: No, we give the window cleaner money, he does work for us, and we have to give him money.
C: Why?
M: Well, because he's been working for us cleaning our windows. He doesn't do it for nothing.
C: Why do you have money if you have . . . if people clean your windows?
M: Well, the window cleaner needs money, doesn't he?
C: Why?
M: To buy clothes for his children and food for them to eat.
C: Well, sometimes window cleaners don't have children.
M: Quite often they do.
C: And something on his own to eat, and for curtains.
M: And for paying his gas bills and electricity bills. And for paying for petrol for his car. All sorts of things you have to pay for, you see. You have to earn money somehow, and he earns it by cleaning other people's windows, and big shop windows and things.
C: And then the person who got the money gives it to the people . . .

Why is it that she seems not to understand these issues? Is it simply that she is a small child or is there more to it than that? A window cleaner is being paid to clean the windows of Samantha's mother and those of other women in the street.

What Samantha does not understand is why the man has to be paid for his work. In the end she works out that the window cleaner needs money to buy food and support his family. But why had she not worked this out before? One possible reading is that a manual worker, for Samantha, appears to be somebody who is different from herself and who is dirty. In the view of work that she is formulating, work appears to be something which is done by some people, not very nice people, for other people, like her family. They are the kind of people who pay for the services of others. In other words, implicitly, she is learning something about the division of labour and her place in it.

The pane of glass which he washes clear of dirt, and which Samantha gazes through to observe him, will continue to divide them in many ways. The chances of her having to earn her living at such a job are slim. She will learn not to be afraid to look out, will not see the dirt that pays the workman's mortgage in the same way. This example has been interpreted (1) as demonstrating 'the power of a puzzling mind', the power of the four-year-old mind. Tizard and Hughes state that Samantha's search for meaning is indicative of a concept they describe as 'intellectual search', which they suggest gives an indication of 'the power of a puzzling mind' (p.123). They go on to assert that this presents new ideas about what four-year-olds are capable of and that this puzzlement and searching represents greater intellectual achievements than psychologists such as Piaget credited children of this age with. Now, all this seems very laudable. After all, the interpretation appears to give children more credit than has previously been accorded them. But wait a minute. What at first sight appears to be an argument about *all* children, about the 'abstract epistemic subject'[2], the universal four-year-old, the species-being that we mentioned in Chapter Two, belies the fact that there are some four-year-olds who do not need to puzzle over work and money. Tizard and Hughes point this out:

> Confusion about the relationship between work, money and goods seemed to be less common among working-class children. Perhaps because their fathers' work was more clearly related to money, rather than the interest in the job, or because with a more limited income the arrival of the weekly pay packet was a more important event, the relationship between money and work was more often discussed in working-class families. (p.123).

What then does this mean for the concept of a generic four-year-old with a puzzling mind? Tizard and Hughes seem to be struggling to deal with difference yet, by implication, because of the universalised model they are using, they treat difference, that is absence of puzzlement, implicitly as a problem for the theory. Because they have set up the puzzling mind of a four-year-old as their developmental model, then children who do not puzzle must themselves be a puzzle for psychologists to solve. After all, they do not come to the conclusion that such working-class children are more advanced than puzzling middle-class ones. How can we avoid this? How can we provide an account of meanings which engages with the specificity of their production, which does not pathologise difference or subsume it into a sociological universalism as 'work' with a 'value'?

We are arguing that this example quoted above tells us not something generic but something very specific about the meanings produced for and by a girl in a specific place in the gender and class division of labour. Yet we also have to account for the fact that the interpretation such as that placed on the example by Tizard and Hughes has real effects in the regulation of the life of this mother and daughter. For such universalisation links in with a particular view of the mother as creating meanings for the child that we came across in Chapter Two. That is, it is the *sensitive mother* who engages effectively with her daughter's puzzlement and extends and expands her meanings. This is 'scaffolding', 'fine-tuning'.

The idea of a generic four-year-old and a 'puzzling mind' are concepts which suggest that all minds possess the same qualities. In other words, they are universals, suggesting a natural sequence of development which renders all minds an exemplar of 'mind'. This is not unlike what we said about the concept of mothering. It creates the idea that if a mind is not 'puzzling' at four then there must be something wrong, something abnormal and unnatural. Lack of puzzlement is produced because the mother is insensitive to the child's needs and curiosity. That some four-year-old girls should have to puzzle over who works for whom and why then becomes implicitly the norm. What is worrying about this is its specificity. It is normal for four-year-olds not to understand certain things, but what things and why? We would argue that what Samantha fails to understand is not general. It is precisely related to the position of her family; a family in which there are no explicit worries about money appearing in these transcripts, a family in which the window cleaner is not the only person paid for his services; they also employ a cleaner. The father works in a well-paid job as a solicitor, and the mother works part-time as a publisher's editorial assistant.[3]

Some of the girls' mothers have the kind of worries about money which lead Margaret's mother to have to wait to buy food until her husband gets home from work with his pay packet.

> M: Haven't had Daddy's money yet.
> C: I've got no money.
> M: No, I haven't got enough to get my shopping. All of it.
> C: Not all of it?
> M: Mary [neighbour]'s just taken five pounds. If she's got some she'll bring some change back. It's not enough to get all that. (Points to shopping list.) So when Daddy gets paid I'll get some more money and then I'll go and get the rest.

In other cases, girls are very explicit in their understanding of a clear relationship between money earned through the labour of the mother and father and that this buys goods and that wages are low and money is scarce. For example, Nicky's mother says that if her father doesn't go to work:

> M: No, he won't get lots of money and then you won't get no new slippers.

Tizard and Hughes cannot adequately explain this difference. The generic concept used elides its specificity, namely, that the puzzlement is not general. What matters here is what is being puzzled over compared with what is common knowledge in some working-class homes. So, what is related to poverty and manual labour becomes abnormal, unnatural in a general view of development.

Our aim here in exploring these examples is not so much to criticise Tizard and Hughes as to understand why certain views of development, which are common to most modern developmental psychology, make the assumptions that they do and the effect this has when used as an interpretative framework on data to produce a truth about development and therefore also about mothering. We end up with a framework which is unable to link what a particular four-year-old does or does not know to any theory which takes into account the social, material and economic specificity of the lives of the children concerned. Instead a concept of development is invoked which only tacks these things on as effects.

Let us return to the window cleaner, the discussion of whose labour so puzzled Samantha. We argued that her idea about work was related to the social position of her family. Similarly, the working-class women's differentiation of their work from other activities relates both to their material circumstances and to what work means to them. Work for the middle-class women is not the same work. The category of domestic labour is the same for both groups of women, but it is not lived in the same way, it is not understood by them in the same way, nor by those agencies (teaching, social work, medical) and discourses which regulate and speak of them, and it is cross-cut by the exigencies of waged work, wealth and poverty.

The working-class women who work outside the home

often present a picture of having to *rush* to work, to clean an office or pub. In addition, their husbands' work is regulated in a way that is made explicit and in a way which is never spoken of by the middle-class women. That is, they have to be at work at particular times, they are subject to rules and regulations, they do back-breaking work for poor money. They may be giants in the home; they are not, as Carolyn Steedman (1986) has remarked forcibly, the gods of patriarchy outside the home, but pathetic and often powerless figures.

This is very clearly understood by the working-class girls. Fathers cannot come home for lunch because they are not allowed to, goods cannot be bought until there is money, demands cannot be met because scarce resources do not allow the illusion of power to the child. The exchange relation is learned firmly, painfully, not puzzled over as in Samantha's case. For instance, Nicky begins by asking her mother why her father is not at home for lunch that day:

> M: It's gone dinner time, doesn't come here for lunch, does he? Not now, works too far away.
> C: Why don't he come up here for lunch?
> M: 'Cos it takes too long for him to get home and get back to work again.
> C: And he's not allowed to?
> M: No.
> C: Or he get, or he won't get lots of money?
> M: No, he won't get lots of money and then you won't get no new slippers.
> C: No, or new pumps.
> M: Won't get them both this week, love.

Conversely, when we began our original analysis of the middle-class transcripts we convinced ourselves that none of the mothers worked outside the home, so hidden was any reference to their employment. Not one middle-class mother mentioned it during the recordings. There is also no sense of poverty, no going without. So, puzzling over a window cleaner can indeed afford to become an intellectual exercise because it does not contain elements of lack, absence or going without.

How then have current developmental accounts managed to universalise those meanings and in doing so pathologise those which do not fit? We have seen that Samantha and Nicky have different ideas about work, because the term, 'work' and the meanings surrounding it relate in different ways to their place in the division of labour. Samantha does not understand, and has to puzzle over, the idea of waged labour, which she associates with dirt and with something another kind of people do. Nicky, on the other hand, is only too familiar with waged labour, what it means that her parents go out to work, and what the money earned can and cannot buy. So, how do we understand how these different meanings are produced? One common way is to assume that the meanings children make are dependent on their 'stage of development'. The writers of a standard textbook on primary-school mathematics give the following advice to teachers:

> [money] is used only for buying and he pays in coins for what he asked for, two pence, four pence, etc. The idea of money as meaning the exchange value of goods will be beyond him for a long time to come. (Williams and Shuard, 1976, p.51)

What the authors are implying is that the idea of money as exchange value is an abstract concept and that young children can only reason with concrete materials, actual coins and so forth. This appears to tie in with Tizard and Hughes's idea that the 'puzzling mind' of the four-year-old cannot fathom certain complex ideas. But the idea that a concept such as exchange value is abstract is only a problem if it is considered as part of a concrete/abstract dichotomy. This is part of the taken-for-granted assumption of developmental psychology that children's minds develop towards abstraction and that complexity equals abstraction. But exchange value is only 'abstract' in its inclusion within economic theory. The exchange relation for girls such as Nicky quoted above is painfully concrete. She demonstrates forcefully that she knows as part of her everyday life that parents go out to work, that they earn money, that this buys food and other necessities and that often there is not enough money to go round. Such understanding is, in one sense, very 'concrete'. But for a child such as Samantha, who does not have to confront those realities (but confronts others such as people working *for* her family– it can indeed appear as a puzzling, abstract idea. The *meaning* of work or money therefore must be seen as intimately tied to the particularity of the lives of the different children. On one level it could be argued that the circumstances of some of the working-class girls teach them very early a complex lesson about exchange. Yet it is nowhere suggested that this might indeed be more advanced than the puzzling mind of Samantha.[4]

Another kind of theory would explain meaning as developing according to universal features of meaning. The Semantic Features Hypothesis has been very influential in work on the development of word meaning in children.[5] This suggests that meaning is derived from a universal system based on perception. Words contain 'semantic features' which are added together. Words said to contain fewer features are acquired first by children. In this analysis there is no sense of a social world in which meanings are made differentially as in the case of Samantha's and Nicky's understanding of 'work'. This idea of semantic universals has been seen as radical because it assumes that since these features are universal there is no sense of environmental deficit. However, one problem lies in the way this opposition is posed, as in the concrete/abstract dichotomy discussed above. The debate which surrounds the idea of universals grew up in opposition to the idea of linguistic deficit or deprivation, which often explicitly blamed the mother for failing to provide a rich enough linguistic environment to produce proper language development.

Thus, the idea of universals came to be seen as a better bet. But we want to show that the problem need not be posed in these terms at all. In later accounts, the 'social' seems to be equated with enough attention, sensitivity to needs, a rich enough environment. This means that certain questions about the production of meanings cannot be raised. The idea of work, of how to understand women's work and of children's understandings of this that we raised at the beginning of this chapter, simply cannot be posed within these frameworks. Yet these issues are as much about the meaning of words as any other. What we are asking, therefore, is how word meanings are produced and become part of the way in which the social regulation of women and the socialisation of girls operates. Work 'means something' to the participants, but it has different meanings and different effects.

There are already a number of discourses which claim to tell us what work means: the domestic-labour debate, Marxist analyses of value, ideas of sensitive mothering, the concept of the puzzling mind. All of these and more create meanings through which we are led to understand the phenomena that confront us. These meanings are regulative, that is, they are used in the ways these girls and women are led to understand themselves, inasmuch as they are public discourses, and they are used, as we have seen, to regulate the lives of women as mothers. This latter view of meanings then understands them as socially generated but in a complex interplay of conditions. Those conditions are material – differential wealth, kinds of labour – and discursive, that is, created historically in those public texts and practices which claim to tell us the truth about women and children. So, the meanings through which the women and girls will be led to understand themselves and each other, through which the mothers will regulate and socialise their daughters, will be a complex mixture of those. We will give further examples of what we mean in later chapters, but here let us begin with one small example.

Using the Semantic Features Hypothesis it is commonly asserted that word meanings are acquired by children in a particular sequence. This sequence is supposed to have nothing to do with ideology, discourse, or the materiality of which we have spoken. Rather the complexity of the terms within the linquistic system is the determinant.[6] So, why should some girls understand the meaning of work at four and others not? We have already been told by developmental psychology what a difficult and abstract concept money is, yet some four-year-olds seem to understand something about it. Why? Are they aberrant? A word pair, 'more/less', commonly discussed in the literature on early development and education, illustrates this problem. This is viewed as a contrastive opposition which is about the relation of quantities. 'More' is said to be semantically simpler than 'less' and therefore acquired first.[7] Here, there is no sense that terms like 'more' may have meanings which vary according to particular conditions or social practices. We analysed the occurrence of 'more' and 'less' in the conversations of these mothers and daughters. There were many instances of 'more' but not one of 'less'. It is tempting to conclude that this is because 'more' is linquistically simpler. But, when we examine the practices in which 'more' is used, we discover that they are very specific indeed. That is, for all families the main place that it occurs is in the regulation of the girls' consumption of scarce or expensive commodities, as in examples like this, where Gill, a working-class girl, is asking for more:

C: I want some more.
M: No, you can't have any more, Gill.
C: Yes! Only one biscuit.
M: No.
C: Half a biscuit?
M: No.
C: A whole biscuit?
M: No.

Here, Gill's mother has to regulate her consumption. It may well be that Gill had eaten enough biscuits, but the point we are making here is that the meaning of 'more' is inscribed in the regulative practices themselves. In these cases, 'more' is not being used to make a comparison of quantity. The appropriate opposite would be something like 'no more' rather than 'less'. There are plenty of occurrences of comparison of quantity, although these do not use the more/less pair, but other terms. We have discussed this analysis in detail elsewhere and cannot elaborate it here.[8] The main point is that there is a social production of the meanings which varies according to particular circumstances. Meanings are made in practices, involving regulation. This regulation within domestic practices is primarily the province of mothers. This presents the mother as the originator of meanings. But this is to elide their social formation. The mother carries the meanings, she is not the originator of them. It is because she has to regulate her children in a variety of conditions that she appears to generate meaning. Yet other common theories see her as the originator without any sense of her positioning in a wider social network. The idea of 'fine-tuning' and of 'scaffolding' that we mentioned in Chapter Three suggests that it is the sensitive mother who makes meaning for her child by interpreting the needs of her child. She is sensitive to these needs and to the child's primitive attempts to communicate, by cries, gestures and so forth. She interprets these and shapes them into language. Meaning is therefore said to be produced 'intersubjectively', that is, between the mother and the child. In this analysis, meaning comes out of need and the mother provides the social shaping of that need into language. There is no sense that she is positioned as the sensitive mother or that she too is regulated, that she is not the originator of meanings.

But we can see how the 'sensitive mother' account is further developed to demonstrate that the sensitive mother is necessary to develop meaning and language. This holds the sensitive mother responsible and pathologises once again the meanings produced by some of the working-class mothers. For example, Nicky's mother is berated because she appears to misunderstand the needs of her daughter (as we saw in Chapter One). On the contrary, meaning is a much more complex phenomenon than this. The meanings of work vary both according to the conditions that the families are in, the understanding and experience of labour, and the discourses through which the meanings are regulated by external agencies. This provides us with the basis of a view which sees the women and girls as positioned, as actively making meanings but not as the originators of those meanings.

CHAPTER SIX

DEMOCRACY IN THE KITCHEN?

There are many democratic kitchens, where harmony reigns, mothers smile and well-fed, happy children have their needs met. Such enticing visions are presented to us in colour in magazines sold at supermarket checkouts. How is this delightful dream, for dream it is, constructed? We have argued that the regulation of women as mothers and their regulation of their children is central to the production of the modern dream of bourgeois democracy. In this chapter we will examine just how conflict is transformed into discourse to present us with a fiction of harmony.

The path to democracy begins in the kitchen of the sensitive mother. Here, there is supposed to be a nurturant presence which facilitates the development of her child towards natural language and reason. These develop because the sensitive mother is finely tuned to her child's struggle for meaning, extends and elaborates her utterances, transforms her own domestic work into play for her child's cognitive development. All these and more are the ways in which so-called natural development is produced. This development, getting at the child through the relay point of the mother, aims to produce a reasonable citizen. This citizen imagines herself empowered, autonomous, free. Here, democracy is ensured by the removal from consciousness of any sense of oppression, powerlessness, division or exploitation.

It is difficult to understand an apparent freedom – to talk, to discover, to play – as regulation. But that is what we are claiming it is, because it is through the regulation of women that they too have become regulators, those who will ensure 'normal development', which is the central part of the warding off, the guarding against, antisocial activity (delinquency, crime and so forth). This has been particularly apparent in a discourse which has contrasted 'democratic' with 'authoritarian' child-rearing practices. Here, 'democratic' means without apparent coercion, but the term 'authoritarian' signals the danger of presenting children with their own powerlessness, which they can then kick against, becoming delinquents.

Women's sexuality has been regulated so that any passion or activity – danger signs – have been converted into safe nurturance. Passion is invested in reason. Woman becomes the mother who nurtures reasoners. Now, we are not saying that in any simple sense this is what actually happens, but discourse, policies and practices are produced to try to make it happen. But, as we will explore in the next two chapters, things that are not supposed to be there actually do erupt onto the surface. Socialisation, in our view, does not work, there are no guarantees.[1] The story goes, however, that if the mother is sensitive, social conflict need not arise, because it is produced out of aggression, itself the result of frustration, through insensitivity.

In this vision there is no excess of passion or conflict. It is a humanist dream in which all relations become interpersonal relations. Social conflict has traditionally been viewed in Marxist terms as the result of exploitation and oppression, in feminist terms as the result of patriarchal oppression. In the democratic vision, such social conflict can be potentially eliminated, not through political struggle, but through mothering. Conflict will disappear if children have their needs met. Power and powerlessness have become, in this analysis, personal tyranny – power over others, which can be removed by the meeting of needs. Libertarian analyses of power have played right into this by asserting that all adults and children are 'people' with equal rights.[2] So the mother is left guarding democracy, asserting a sense of herself outside the needs and development of her children at her peril. This has left many feminists in a double bind, full of guilt that 'women's needs' are in conflict with those of their children. Our aim is to demonstrate the problems with such an account. Power cannot be reduced to democratic mothering (or parenting); the removal of oppression and exploitation cannot be achieved through the policing of socialisation practices, leaving every other aspect of the social body intact.

Let us then state two central contentions about our data. Firstly, we claim that many working-class mothers do not regulate their daughters in the 'democratic' mode. They make power and conflict visible and painful. For this they are pathologised. We want to view it in a different way. Secondly, power and conflict are *not* dispersed or eliminated in the democratic kitchen, they are suppressed. Harmony is only on the surface – beneath reasonableness lie the passions.

This illusion of harmony depends upon the regulation of conflict in a particular way. That is, a way that appears above all else to be non-conflictual and reasonable. A utopian vision indeed, but sadly it remains that; illusions of harmony and democracy in the mother-child relationship run alongside the fortification of the child's illusion of power. There are fictions and fantasies everywhere. One of them states that working-class families are highly disputatious. They fight and quarrel: the mothers are not reasonable, and their dealings with their daughters are devoid of reason. Middle-class women, on the other hand, debate with their children, all opinions are given equal status, everyone has a voice and everyone will listen; more fantasies. The working-class women do not entertain debate (or, as they are supposed to see it, argument). 'I'm not going to argue with you,' says Nicky's mother to Nicky – making it clear who has the last word.

The democratic rule decrees that all citizens shall have a voice, that all shall have access to equal power. Only bad mothers deny their children the right to their voice, their power, by being authoritarian, saying no all the time. Only insensitive mothers will refuse to reason with their children. Many of the working-class mothers of this study, if judged by this criterion, must be said to refuse to meet their children's needs. The spectre of authoritarianism lurks around the council-estate stairways. But there is hope; this ghost can be chased away; mothers can be educated; even bad mothers can be converted to the democratic way. How then to achieve harmony where discord previously ruled, to replace temper with reason, bad power with equality? For this is exactly what many of the middle-class women especially strive to achieve but never can, precisely because the search for harmony is the search for a pot of gold – it does not, cannot exist in this way except as a fantasy.

We want to make it clear that we are not denying the possibility of an easy-going, pleasurable mother-daughter relationship. The illusion is not that there is no pleasure for the pair. The illusion lies in the harmony we see. It is the notion of mutuality, of constant equality, of a fantastic home where violence and tempers are never raised. Of course these mothers enjoy their daughters' company and can achieve an intimacy with their children perhaps never reached with adults. But not all the time, and not without pain, upset, quarrels and fights. The possibility of a mother-child relationship without these elements eludes us.

Nevertheless, in striving for this fantasy, many women do achieve an illusion of it – an illusion that may seem real, that presents us with a picture of the mother-and-child haven. We want to deconstruct this flimsy illusion to argue that, rather than mothers achieving a conflict-free mutuality with their daughters, in many cases, women become chained in their homes to suffer the tyrannical rule of their children.

There is no way that, for instance, power conflicts will not arise, that they will be absent. The secret of their apparent disappearance, however, lies in how that conflict is dealt with; how particular strategies for dealing with power and conflict make it seem as if they had simply gone away. One of these strategies we have called 'intellectualisation', a phenomenon we noted particularly in the middle-class transcripts. For example, all the girls in this study were at times very demanding of their mother's time, energy or attention. Overall the middle-class girls were as demanding and argumentative as the working-class girls. But there are important distinctions to be made when examining the girls' strategies for gaining attention, as well as differences in the mothers' strategies for coping with such demands. We are not suggesting that these demands always led to conflict in the sense of quarrelling or fighting, but often it lay in the conflict of interests between mother and daughter. That is, the girls often made demands which conflicted with the mother's own wishes, or other constraints on her attention. We have already noted in Chapter Four that the middle-class mothers were more likely to give in to their daughters' demands, either to stop what they were doing and attend to the child, or, importantly, to incorporate their work to accommodate the girl. Here we want to examine another strategy important to the conflict-free regulation of children and the maintenance of the fantasy of the democratic kitchen.

Within the idea of intellectualisation there are certain transformations which produce the illusion of democracy, which eliminates inequalities by transforming them into attributes, possessions of the participants. Passion becomes 'feelings', which one must be sensitive towards. They belong to people who are 'upset' or 'frustrated'. These feelings are distressing and the girls have to be taught to understand them. The irrational has to be transformed into the rational. Conflict can therefore become apparently dissipated through rational argument. Power relations become interpersonal relations. Conflict is no longer dynamic or relational (as in the idea of social conflict, for example), it is reduced to a possession of the individual psyche, put there because of faulty behaviours on the part of the mother. This is the normalized view of psychoanalysis as 'healthy adjustment'.[3]

Creating an 'illusion' is central to this process, as we

demonstrated in Chapter One. The quote from John and Elizabeth Newson (page 24) made it clear that the idea of personal autonomy, rights and choice for children is, in fact, an illusion, but one supported by the mother, who collaborates in allowing the child to believe that she is the orginator of her actions, that she is not regulated. Regulation has gone underground. But if it is an illusion, this democracy, what lurks beneath the fantasy?

Educators rave on and on about the rich learning environment of the home, where children can 'discover' and learn about a wide range of topics from practical skills, lessons in self-reliance, pedagogic skills, difficult concepts such as life, death and the outside world. This learning is said to be achieved by mutuality – the mother understands the child's needs and helps her to make sense of her complex world, mostly through everyday routine. 'The child's mother is thus very salient to her, constantly available to answer questions, provide information and act as a conversation companion' (Tizard and Hughes, p.250). *Nobody* within a discourse of meeting needs talks about the mother: what effect being 'constantly available' might have on her. No one talks about how she must constantly struggle to maintain the rich environment of which she is guardian or how much hidden effort is made; while the child is enjoying 'liberation' and autonomy, this to some extent depends upon the mother's oppression.

Samantha and her mother are redecorating the doll's house with a book of free wallpaper samples her mother has got from a decorating-supplies shop. There is constant emphasis on choice, and Sam is given a free hand to choose which wallpaper she wants for each room. Sam's choice also becomes an intellectual problem, for she must make sure that the sheet of wallpaper she wants is big enough to cover the room. At one point she suggests cutting up bits of paper so that they will fit.

> M: Why will we have to cut it off?
> C: Umm, because, you see this is why we have to cut it off, because this big piece here is rather big to fit on, isn't it?

This phenomenon of girls being pushed to intellectualise

practical problems was much more common in the middle-class families, where their mothers were much more insistent that they think the 'problem' through for themselves; where they have to justify a particular course of action; or, for instance, in the context of games (mainly educational games) where the girl has to get the right answer. One of the effects of this sort of intellectualisation is to maintain the idea that anything is possible within reason; that it is the art of rational debate which gives you power. The girls, however, know that there are other bases for power. They can challenge their mothers in particular ways that violate the democratic rule – e.g. cheating, blackmailing, refusing to intellectualise – all these things give the child power. More specifically than that, they give the middle-class girls power. The working-class women are less likely to stand their own power being challenged in such a way. They are far more open and overt about the use of their supreme authority over the child.

Samantha (like Sarah in the episode with the fish tank in Chapter Four) is given considerable power during the event both to negotiate and challenge her mother's knowledge and authority. At this point her mother is concerned that there won't be enough paper of the same colour for the room they are about to decorate:

> M: We want some that's the same as that, don't we, ummm?
> C: There are none the same.
> M: Really, I'm sure I saw another page of the blue somewhere.
> C: I'm sure you didn't.
> M: Never mind. This one page isn't going to be quite enough, I don't think.
> C: I think you didn't really, what . . .
> M: Never mind, well, let's start with that one.

It is important to note that while it is mostly the middle-class mothers who create this kind of space with their daughters, there were a few working-class mothers who did very much the same thing. Teresa helps her mother construct a wendy house. While her mother does most of the physical construction, presumably because the frame parts are too heavy for Teresa, there is constant consultation with Teresa, who is never shy to make suggestions about which piece should fit in where, nor is her mother impatient or dismissive of these suggestions. When Teresa asks a question, she explains patiently. Teresa's mother does not appear at all threatened by her daughter's challenges to her authority. Like Samantha's mother, Teresa's mother encourages 'equality'.[4]

What the illusion of choice creates is not harmony without power, but the creation of the possibility for the daughter to challenge the mother, to reason with her, to regulate her. The democratic fantasy holds that power gained through reason rather than coercion is good, reasonable power. In psycho-educational discourse this is the power gained from discovery and proper conceptualisation. It is the mastery of reasoning.[5] If conflict is regulated through reasoned argument, power is gained through challenging the basis on which the argument is posed. In schools this often means that the pupil is led to challenge, not the teacher's power to regulate the classroom, but the teacher's mastery of the discourse (her knowledge).[6] Much stress is laid upon knowledge as structure and process, that is, as reasoning and not as facts. So, making a challenge confidently is what the discourse of mastery is about. Considerable stress has been laid on this in debates (particularly in the USA) in relation to girls' education. Girls are said to lack 'mastery orientation'.[7] So it is once again sensitive mothers who will impart this to their daughters. (We will examine some of the problems with this argument in the last chapter.) This transformation of power into mastery understands it as a possession and therefore implicitly denies it as regulative at all. Right at the heart of it is another fantasy, of omnipotent mastery over a universe which acts according to the laws of reason. This mastery over time and space is guaranteed by play. But whose work makes play possible? The playful reasoner, whose violent conflict now only surfaces as argument, is supported by the work of others, the hidden servicing of manual work, domestic work and nurturance. Here then is the bourgeois subject who believes all are equal, not recognising that paying for services is not a million miles removed from the aristocratic status that the bourgeoisie so desired for itself. It is women's nurturance which is supposed to promote and prop up this fantasy of mastery. This 'healthy' model of challenge, of autonomy, of democracy depends upon the removal of any power dimension. At least, that's what is supposed to happen! We will demonstrate later on that what in fact we 'see' is the removal of power from the *overt* – power goes 'underground' as well as housework. But just as this concealment of women's labour does not make it vanish, so the removal of overt power from the mother–child relationship does not mean that power is absent.

What we want to show is how easy it can be to read the sensitive mother as the democratic guide of the actively discovering child in an unproblematic way, but also to show how this model falls apart if we shift our analytic framework so it may incorporate resistance, struggle and power. By using a number of examples, we hope to show how the idea of challenge being an indicator of autonomy in these girls can swiftly break down.

The child's power to reason, intellectualise and challenge is also a fantasy on one level. The mother works hard to construct and repair this fantasy, and in doing so, loses some of her own power. It is this loss of her power which is the building material of the 'false state'. Mutuality is not a state of equality, where mother and child have an equal, specified relationship. It is achieved by the mother actively suppressing her own authority.

Naomi plays a number game with her mother, which consists of picture cards that correspond with numbered cards. Sitting on the floor, they set the game out together. Naomi's mother stresses choice and negotiation:

> M: Which number are we going to start with?
> C: We got those and that.

M: What are you going to start with?
C: Ah, this one.

The game goes well. Naomi gets most of the answers correct, some with her mother's guidance, but she is allowed to take cards out of the game that she feels are 'too difficult'. This episode exemplifies both good mothering and good teaching practices – stressing the child's own pace, pushing but not too hard, negotiation, harmony and so forth.

When the game is finished, Naomi's mother suggests other games to play – they eventually decide on picture snap. From the moment this game begins, the negotiation, mutuality and sense of democratic harmony Naomi's mother has achieved fall apart and are quickly replaced by resistance and struggle. For Naomi not only wants to play the game, she wants to, *must*, win the game. Eventually she begins cheating. She wails when she loses. Throughout this episode her mother tries to maintain her own calm and cope with Naomi's cantankerousness. She continually attempts to point out the moral disadvantage of cheating; threatens to pack the game away, but never does; tells her it's 'silly' to play like that and, when all this fails, tries to reason with her:

M: Why do you cheat, Naomi?
C: I dunno.
M: You like to win?
C: Yeah.
M: Never used to bother about winning did you? Doesn't matter, you know, if you don't win. Does it? Not really? Hmmm? . . . Doesn't matter if you don't win.
C: (Unclear.)
M: Sometimes it's nice just to play, isn't it?
C: (No reply.)

In other words, the regulative system consists in making the girl see that certain demands are not sanctioned (in this case the child's desire to win), not because they cannot be met, or because the mother lacks resources, is tired, depressed, overworked or whatever, but because they are not reasonable. The system of regulation par excellence therefore is

Reason: reasonable demands can be met; everything is possible, within reason. It forms the bedrock of modern pedagogic practices, designed to produce reasonable citizens; reasoning is the key to morality and that is the key to a stable democracy.

The 'democracy' which we witnessed in the previous number game which Naomi and her mother played quickly disintegrates in the new game. Naomi's confident challenge, previously encouraged, even praised by her mother, turns into something else, something not 'nice'. This is partly because, in the snap game, the basis of Naomi's challenge is no longer intellectual, as it was in the number game. Naomi's investment in the game is transformed. She is not driven by a thirst for knowledge, the 'natural curiosity' of the child, but by a much rawer desire for power – the power gained in *winning*! But she cannot achieve this by reason, for this game is not an exercise of intellect. The only way she can win, short of good luck, is by cheating, and win she must. Thus Naomi's confidence and autonomy take on a very different slant.

This example shows how a model which views autonomy as divorced from any conception of power is bound to fall apart eventually. An essential element of libertarian self-regulation – one of its goals – is to achieve a sense of self-power. What such an analysis would like to do, however, is render this power 'nice' and 'safe' – ideally to make it go away altogether.

One strategy for 'making safe' this potential for 'bad' power is again to intellectualise. Most middle-class and a minority of working-class girls are given the impression that they share power and that they are equal in their sharing. As we have seen, they are given space, indeed are pushed to reason with and challenge their mother's authority to know. This 'space' can have important effects on the pair's struggle for power. In situations of potential conflict, where daughter or mother wishes to resist the other's demands, the mother takes the lead role in trying to diffuse the conflict by setting whatever is the particular bone of contention up as a 'problem' which must be reasoned out. Naomi's mother becomes increasingly perturbed by Naomi's incessant cheating. Although she does call upon her supreme authority several times, in threatening to pack the game away, she never carries out this threat. It is by appealing to Naomi's reason that her mother tries to take out, dissolve the power struggle. Reasoning becomes a way then to diffuse and at the same time deny that struggle.

This strategy is most often used as a regulative device, to thwart the child's resistance. However, if it does not work as a regulative strategy (and, after all, its effectiveness depends to a large extent on the child's acknowledgement of and cooperation with the strategy) then the basis of the mother's power is seriously threatened. Undermined also is the fantasy of the conflict-free democracy and the notion that the child's power is equal to her mother's.

The mother, by taking the 'conflict-free' stance, actually loses some of her power to the child. We can see this most clearly in relation to girls expressing violence towards their mothers. In a sense, intellectualisation is a game. If the child refuses to play this game, it gives her large amounts of power, while the mother has lost the ground from which she can be a covert authority.

Angela is playing with a box of Vim. Her mother is obviously worried that Angela might get some in her mouth. She explains the dangers to her daughter.

> M: No, you mustn't drink it, darling. You won't put it in your mouth, will you?
> C: No, it's only for Marcus [teddy bear].

Angela's mother does not take the Vim away from the child, but explains patiently that she must not eat it, and if she agrees to this, then her mother will allow her to play with it. Angela now knows that even though the Vim could be dangerous if she ate it, her mother, having explained that she shouldn't eat it, trusts her with the Vim and won't take it away. This, in effect, gives Angela the opportunity to blackmail her mother:

> M: It's not good for you, you can pretend . . . you'll have to pretend but you mustn't put it in your mouth . . . you won't, will you?
> C: No . . . but it, I will if you, if you don't get a, a, a saucer for my dolly.

Angela takes up the space created by her mother's explanation and intellectualisation of the problem to demand something which she was previously denied by her mother – a saucer for her doll. Angela intends giving the Vim to her dolls for a pretend lunch. Her mother eventually tries to subvert this by giving her a biscuit to give them instead. This Angela promptly mixes up with the Vim and gives it to the dolls. Her mother's reaction is to say what a 'silly' thing it was to do.

Caroline and her mother are playing a card game. They call the game 'trumps', and it is a version of knockout whist. The game moves very fast, fast enough to make it quite difficult to follow its progress. Caroline appears to have an excellent grasp of this complex game. She makes it clear that her object in playing is to win, which is not surprising, since, as in snap, winning is the goal of this game. This is not to underestimate, however, the obvious pleasure the pair get from playing the game. But the pleasure is different from that sought by Naomi and her mother in their game of snap. This game of trumps certainly does open up space for the negotiation of power positions, with both mother and daughter making confident challenges. It is intellectual also, the game has logical rules which require mathematical knowledge and reason. In this extract, Caroline has already won the first round so she must then decide on the 'trumps' for the next round – this means there is no need to 'cut' the pack for 'trumps'. However, Caroline thinks the pack still needs to be cut:

> C: Cut.
> M: No, you got four.

C: No, see [three].
M: Four.
C: See [three].
M: Four.
C: See [three].
M: There's only seven. Mummy had three and you had four.
C: And . . . I had four so we can, do have to cut.
M: You have to call.
(———)
(M: deals out cards.)

Even though Caroline was wrong, she was not at all shy to challenge her mother. Conversely, her mother does not seem to mind when she is challenged in this way. Caroline cheats and bends the rules constantly to suit herself, consenting on occasion to 'let' her mother win a 'trick':

C: I trump that.
M: Oh, ho ho, that wasn't a trump.
C: [unclear] . . . 'cos only got two of them so I trump it.
M: All right, go on then. (M lets C take the trick even though she did not really win.)
C: And you can . . . I'll let you have that one. (C lets M win the next trick.)
M: Cheat.

Caroline and her mother have now won two tricks each. Caroline cuts the pack to see which suit will be the trumps next.

M: Diamonds.
C: I wish I had cutted that ace. (C looks through the cards and has found an ace.) I want it.
M: We'll do it again then, go on.
(C cuts again and cheats so that she gets an ace.)
M: Ha ha, oh Caroline you are . . . Go on then.

So Caroline's mother doesn't exactly allow the cheating to go by unnoticed. She does protest at times, but her reaction is nothing like Naomi's mother's dismay that Naomi is being so unreasonable. In this game of trumps the 'rules' are quite different, as is the pleasure. While Naomi and her mother are at odds during their game of snap, and in the end get very little pleasure from the game, Caroline and her mother, despite Caroline's refusal to play by the rules, achieve an intimacy and pleasure never reached by the former pair. They both bend the rules of the game: Caroline cheats and her mother accommodates this, in order that the game may meet their needs. Caroline's mother accepts that she will want to win, and Caroline in turn 'allows' her mother to win occasionally. But the objects of the two games, although quite similar in content, are very different. It seems that the main aim of Naomi's mother in both games is to teach the child certain rules relating to morality, indeed to the concept of 'reasonable rule' itself. Thus her cheating is judged as 'unfair' in terms of these rules. In the trumps game, however, the logical rules become irrelevant because the space for the game is created out of a desire to gain intimacy between the pair. Thus Caroline's cheating is called 'cheeky'.

Winning, the desire to beat the opponent, is part of a very overt game of power. How much easier then to suppress this as not nice, not fair, not reasonable, and to pretend that it has really gone away. Many working-class mothers shatter the illusion of equality. This is why they have been the object of such heavy intervention in the 1960s and 1970s, for 'depriving' their children, for displays of overt power, for authoritarianism. But what such mothers do is fail to put up with the sham democracy of the bourgeoisie. They constantly tell their children that they cannot have what they want, when they want it. No fantasy of autonomy and control here.

In Chapter Four we pointed out that working-class children often live, painfully, as a practical necessity, the wage relation which middle-class girls like Samantha can only puzzle over. Power does not disappear by a sleight of hand. How much more painful, though, to be told that out of material necessity you cannot have what you want. How much more enticing is a fantasy of plenty, of freedom, even though it is an illusion. Intellectualisation is a strategy of puzzling, reasoning things out, things which, for the bourgeoisie, are not matters of survival.

Not all the working-class families were poor. But what we are talking about here is an overt mode of regulation which is explicit. Ironically, this mode, described as authoritarian, has been accused of being 'restricted' or 'implicit', because of failure to give reasons for control strategies.[8] We would argue quite the opposite. Here, power and powerlessness, regulation, are visible and explicit. Boundaries are clear, as we demonstrated in Chapter Four, between work and play, for example. Yet, not only do these shatter certain bourgeois illusions foisted upon working-class families, but they may also be practices which have grown out of a necessity of the conditions of working-class existence.

Manual waged labour is hard. It has fixed hours, with boundaries between work and non-work which are central and important in a way quite untrue for intellectual work. In the bourgeois scenario, boundaries are felt to be bad.[9] Is this so? Wendy Hollway (1989) has pointed out that when experiments in the 1960s sought to extend job fulfilment and 'self-actualisation' beyond management to manual workers, the latter stated forcefully that their kind of work did not have that kind of rewards. This discourse simply did not apply.

The larger democratic fantasy rests upon the oppression of women. Because they form the bedrock of the caring professions, it is women, as nurses, teachers, social workers, secretaries, who prop up the nurturant democracy which claims to meet all reasonable demands. Indeed, some of these women are trained to be the ones who regulate 'bad, authoritarian working-class mothers', attempting to render them 'sensitive mothers' or, if that is impossible, take their place in some other institution. Women, therefore, as mothers or quasi-mothers, hold up this humane democracy; they are the price paid for autonomy, its hidden and dispensable cost.

This kind of preparation of the young citizen is considered so central to the democratic order that educational and psychological texts are full to bursting with advice on the importance of the mother's preparation of the child's education at home. This preparation paves the way for the intellectual demands of the school. The mother should aid the child's development by helping her along the path to reason. The bad mother is the one who either does not prepare or prepares the wrong thing. She may teach her child facts instead of reason, or present an authoritarian instead of nurturant view of the school.[10]

One final fantasy, therefore, is that while harmony is said to reign in middle-class homes, discord is the feature of working-class life. Thus, frustration and aggression are said to come from the rigidity of boundaries. In the next chapter we will challenge that fiction too.

CHAPTER SEVEN

THE SUBURBAN TERRORIST

The suburban house, the sensitive mother, the clean, healthy and nurtured children – this scene is often presented to us as a snapshot on other people's mantelpieces. The desire to take up our place in that family portrait is fuelled by the many 'photographers' who construct the picture. There are many different 'angles' to be seen, but the theme which gives all images of the 'real' family their clarity, which makes us want to be that mother, that father, that child, remains constant. And yet we know that this family is not always happy. There are things which are not chosen to be photographed – the moments of conflict, of strain, of pain. Have these moments been repressed not only from the photograph – have they been suppressed too from the account? For the family has been seen as a place of safety, the only site where violence and conflict *can* be, *has* been, erased from the memory.[1] The dream of harmony is one shared by the builders of the New Democracy, where there would be no more war, and by those concerned to eradicate delinquency and crime. In the 1980s this dream is difficult to sustain, since violence inside families has blown apart that idyll. Not only has domestic violence become a burning issue for feminism, but so has child abuse. The 1960s and 1970s discourse of harmony looks, therefore, increasingly unable to be sustained. Earlier debates, such as those around maternal deprivation, concentrated on getting mothering right, without examining the position of the father. Unfortunately, such arguments get hopelessly tangled up when it comes to class. Although discourses of domestic violence and child abuse are not class specific, it is frequently the case that the targets of medical and social-work intervention are working-class families. Yet the feminist stress on masculinity and violence has searched for some curious solutions, which end up theoretically banishing the father as perpetrator of violence and almost substituting a feminist Bowlbyism which locks mothers and daughters in pre-Oedipal bonding, in a kind of harmony of 'a society without the father'[2].

That the above accounts seriously fail to engage with violence is, for us, a real problem. Some feminist accounts of violence consistently counterpose men's violence to the 'peacefulness' of women, as if women did not have violent emotions. We want to assert that violence is not simply located in men. The little girls on these pages express very violent emotions towards their mothers – emotions which shatter myths of harmony as well as a sense of middle-class propriety. We are left with no way of relating violence to power and to oppression.[3] We have no answer to these urgent issues. But we think that it is vital to talk about this violence in a new way.

We want to point to what has happened to conflict, to resistance, to violent emotions. In the last chapter we argued that conflict had not disappeared in the middle-class homes, but had effectively gone underground. That is, the mother had to deflect certain demands made by the child by designating them as unreasonable. In other homes, the power relations between mother and daughter were far more explicit and this led to the designation of those child-rearing practices as pathological. Here, we want to produce another account of conflict to demonstrate how the little girls resist their mother's attempts to regulate them and how the dream of harmony itself denies violence, erupting not far beneath the surface. But how are we to understand that violence?

The first thing to notice is that very little is written about violence in middle-class homes. While the finger points at the alleged disputatious nature of working-class families as one of the myriad explanations of working-class educational failure, bourgeois family life is commonly explained in terms of harmony and the resolution of disputes.[4] Only in working-class homes are we presented with the ever-imminent possibility of authoritarianism; of violence about to erupt, of rows and fights between mother and daughter. The picture of the middle-class home is a pretty one: everything in that garden looks lovely. But wait, there are other issues. Are these homes so different? Have the 'damaging effects' of emotionality, of envy, fear, love and violence really been eradicated? Has the power of reason really triumphed over the power of passion? We would argue not, for there is much to upset the harmony we so easily read in the homes of these fifteen middle-class girls. There is envy of siblings and hatred of the mother (or violence towards the mother). Conversely, in the working-class homes where mother and daughter seem constantly at each other's throats, there is sometimes resolution.

In addition, in two of the working-class homes that are designated harmonious, the two girls in question, Kerry and Patsy, are failing educationally and having emotional difficulties at the age of ten. By comparison, the most disputatious working-class homes have produced the two girls who are doing well at ten. There must be something wrong here, mustn't there?

Our arguments about conflict are necessarily about power. We take it as axiomatic that discipline is part of the regulatory role of parenting. This produces a power relation, but it is a different analysis of power from that in the Newsons' quote in Chapter One. Power is not the possession of the adult. Rather the mother is invested with power only because of her position as regulator of her children. The power does not belong to her by virtue of her adult status. It is contained within the discursive space. By this we mean that power is not her possession, but invested in her by positioning her as 'mother', with a responsibility for domestic regulation. Her power comes from this and is not unitary, since in other positions (most notably outside the home and in paid employment) she is relatively powerless. Also, her power is not all one-sided or good. This power invested in her as *mother* is one aspect of her oppression.[5]

The children's expression of violent emotions in these transcripts is most commonly displayed in attempts to control and regulate their mothers: they want to make their mothers do what they want them to do, to regulate the mother as they are regulated. In addition to this, they also express violent emotions about siblings. They are jealous of younger siblings and older siblings alike. They are attempting to negotiate their own position and this is difficult and dangerous. They try too to have power as helpless babies, to avoid having to do things for themselves. In this way they can be waited on by their mothers and it gives them enormous power. We will explore these aspects of helplessness further in Chapter Eight.

Violence – not seen, not heard

How is violence handled in the mother-daughter relationship?[6] As we discussed in Chapter Six, a libertarian analysis of mother-child relations argues that the child must not be repressed, she must learn and discover individuality and learn to exercise her 'right' to be a 'person'.[7] The mother must facilitate this liberation by ensuring the absence of any power struggle, never displaying her ability overtly to regulate the child. Power is bad, it is repressive and coercive. The child must learn to regulate herself, not be regulated by others, 'taking out' any form of power from mother-child relations. We must stress again that dealing with power by deflection, reasoning, intellectualisation, does not, and cannot, mean the absence of it.

By focusing on violence in the mother-daughter relationship, we will argue that this libertarian analysis simply does not work. Violence and violent emotions do exist, even in 'innocent four-year-olds'. How do working- and middle-class mothers cope with the very real presence of these emotions, whether they reside in themselves or in their daughters?

What we find are mostly middle-class girls whose violent emotions are consistently ignored or misrecognised, while the working-class girls (but not all of them) tend to be given space which allows for the venting of these negative emotions, as well as having, themselves, to recognise it in others, particularly their mothers. However, on no account do we want to fall into the trap of celebrating any notion of working-class violence. The painful material conditions which some working-class families live under, and which play a large part in producing situations where mothers are depressed, frustrated and on the edge of not coping, are no cause for celebration. Nor is the expression of this frustration in violence a positive or healthy resolution to their problems. But we do want to demonstrate how the denial and repression of negative emotions in the middle-class homes has extremely important effects on the mother as well as the child. By examining some of the middle-class girls in Chapter Ten when they are ten years old, we can see how much difficulty they have in dealing with the 'bad me', the 'me' who is *not* good, kind, generous and helpful; the 'me' who harbours many violent emotions. We will also examine the effect of 'the neglect of hatefulness' on mothers.[8]

It is important to note that twice as many middle-class girls expressed *direct* violence towards their mothers, or actually hit them. Of course, this is seen as 'better out than in',[9] and mothers, like teachers, have to put up with, even encourage it. Later on we will look at some of the ways in which violence was expressed obliquely, during games or fantasy play. But for now, the question to be asked is, how do the middle-class mothers cope with such flagrant violations of the democratic rule?

Liz, a middle-class girl, enjoys the benefits of having a 'sensitive' mother, who encourages Liz to intellectualise. She engages her in all sorts of 'good' and 'right' play during the afternoon, constantly pointing out things of interest, imparting information and complex concepts as she does so. For example, walking around the garden gives rise to a discussion about the growth of plants. Liz's mother tries at all costs to avoid conflict, but not so Liz. When Liz is resisting her mother's wishes, her mother will reason with her, intellectualise, try to get Liz to think about it. If Liz insists on having her own way, her mother either gives in or will entreat her not to be 'silly'. The term 'silly' was often used by the middle-class mothers as a regulative device. In this example, the pair are in the garden sitting on the swing. They are chatting about the plants, when Liz's mother absentmindedly whistles:

> C: Don't whistle, if I hear you whistle again I'll smack your bottom!
> M: No, you won't.
> C: Whistle again then. Whistle again!
> (M whistles and C hits her on the back.)
> M: Don't, Liz. I'm harder than you so I should be very careful.
> C: I'm going to be harder than you.
> M: Quite frankly, I'm not interested in that game at all. It's rather silly.
> C: I'm going to poke you in the eye one day.
> M: You'd better not. That's a very unpleasant thing to say, why d'you say that?
> C: 'Cos . . . you're being naughty.
> M: No I'm not. What have I done wrong?
> C: You . . . I don't want you to whistle.
> M: You're just being silly.

Her mother's first reaction to the comment 'I'll smack your bottom' is to treat it as a daring game that Liz is playing. Her 'No, you won't' is said in a jokey way, However, Liz continues to play her 'game', not reading or recognising the risky nature of it. Liz also in playing this game takes in fantasy the position of the mother who can discipline a daughter. It is thus a form of resistance and a bid for power. While her mother actually warns her not to do it again, still the boundaries to how far Liz can go are not firmly set, nor are they read by Liz, who continues to express violence towards her mother. Her mother, however, does not act in an authoritarian way when Liz announces, 'I'm going to poke you in the eye one day.' Instead she tries to reason with the child. When her attempts to render Liz and the game 'boring' and 'silly' fail, she intellectualises with her.

Sarah's mother responds similarly. Like Liz's mother, she chooses to ignore Sarah's disturbing comments, and quickly changes the subject, acting as if nothing particularly untoward or noteworthy had been said:

> C: So, er, er, I'll poke your head off! (C pokes at M's hair.)
> M: Oh, will you?
> C: I'll poke your eyes off, and then you won't be able to see, will you? Then you won't . . .
> M: That's not very nice.
> C: . . . able to look where you're going. You'll have to go the wrong way round. Then you'll have to think, and I'll cut your mouth up so you can't talk. Ug, ug, ug, ug, ug, ug, yeah!

Julie, another middle-class girl, was probably the most violent of all the girls towards her mother. On one occasion she actually slapped her mother and on three others she verbally expressed her wish to be violent towards her. Overall, Julie is not a particularly 'naughty' child, although she is quite demanding. And it is quite clear throughout the recordings that Julie is intensely jealous of her baby sister, resentful of the time and attention which her mother lavishes on the infant, who is only a few months old. Her mother must bear the brunt of Julie's resentment of the new baby. We will go into Julie's case in much greater detail in Chapter Nine. Suffice it to say here that Julie's mother, a trained teacher, has much difficulty in coping with Julie's frequently and forcefully expressed violent emotions. In the following example, Julie expresses hatred of the mother through a fairy story. Her mother is clearing up in the kitchen while this conversation is going on. Julie is singing and her mother asks her what the song is about.

M: What is it?
C: A nursery rhyme.
M: A nursery rhyme?
C: Mm.
M: About a princess? You know a nursery rhyme about a princess, don't you?
C: What?
M: (unclear)
C: Why did she?
M: You know why . . . (unclear)
C: Why?
M: Because a wicked fairy cast a spell.
C: What for? What for?
M: Because the princess's Mum and Daddy, the king and queen, didn't invite the wicked fairy to the christening party and she got so cross that she became ever so nasty. (Unclear) . . . fall asleep. And how did she wake up? Do you remember?
C: No.
M: How did she wake up?
C: Don't know.
M: How do you wake me up in the morning?
C: Don't know.
M: How do you wake me up, when I'm asleep? You come in and kiss me, don't you?
C: I have a kick . . . I kick you!
M: Oh, really.
C: . . . to wake you up, not really.
M: Well, the prince didn't kick the princess. He kissed her . . . and he woke her up.
C: He kicked her, kicked her in the face.
M: Yes, that's right.
C: Ah, ha ha ha. He didn't really, did he?
M: When I come in in the morning to wake you up, I'll just kick you in the face, all right?
C: Noooh!
M: Well then!
C: Yes, do that to me, all right.
M: You'd like to do that, would you?
C: No, I kick your face, all right?

M: I think that's really horrible.
C: Huh huh [laugh]. Do you think it's nice?
M: No, I don't.
C: I kick you in your face.
M: I really don't.
C: I kick you in your face.
M: If you carry on saying it I'm going to ignore you.
C: Kick you in your face. Are you 'gnoring me?
M: *Ig*noring you?
C: Yes.
M: Taking no notice, yes. It's not very interesting. It's very boring.
C: Please!
M: Please what?
C: Please don't 'gnoring me.
M: *Ig*nore.

Julie's reworking of this fairy tale is interesting in many ways. She certainly subverts the romance and harmony implied in the kiss, by substituting a phonologically close word, 'kick'. Here, she takes the active, masculine, position, (the prince) and substitutes hate for love. In the next chapter we will explore the way in which the phonological shifts have been used in psychoanalysis. Here, the shift helps to articulate the ambivalence of love and hate that Julie seems to express. But her mother appears to find it difficult to deal with being the subject of her daughter's hatred. Although Julie clearly articulates that she doesn't 'really' 'kick her mother awake', her mother calls it 'horrible,' not nice, threatens to ignore it and resorts to describing it as uninteresting and boring. This way, although she deflects Julie's violence, she does so by operating as though it were simply a not very nice and rather impolite emotion. She eventually attempts to convert the conflict into a lesson on pronunciation, by correcting Julie's ''gnoring'. What then is Julie to do with this emotion her mother so forcefully displaces? No matter how hard Julie tries, her mother will not reciprocate. This leaves only two options – escalation or suppression. Julie goes for escalation. It could also be argued that Julie's mother allows the violence to be expressed rather than suppressing it and therefore permits her to work through the difference between fantasy and reality. This seems to us to ignore the dimension of power and the oppression of the mother entailed.

Jenny, a working-class girl who has been persistently demanding and naughty, has been leaned on heavily on occasion, with threats and warnings from her mother. On one other occasion, when Jenny is splashing water all over the kitchen, she says she is going to pour it over her mother, after being admonished for making a mess. Her mother makes it quite clear that Jenny is stepping over the boundaries of acceptable behaviour; she threatens to, and eventually does take the water away from her. Note, however, in the following extract how her mother does use the term 'silly'.

Jenny is playing with water in the kitchen. Her mother sits drinking her coffee. Jenny splashes water on the floor.

> C: Well, that is it. No, we – water over you.
> M: Now that is enough! You're acting silly now, Jenny.
> (C splashes again.)
> (M takes bowl of water and pours it away.)
> C: (Screams.) Yes! I want to play with it! I want to play with it! Yes!
> M: No.
> C: Yes!
> M: No.
> C: Yes! (C spits at M.)
> M: No spitting.
> C: I want to play with that! (Screams.)
> (M sits looking at leaflet in the living room and drinks her coffee.)

Even though Jenny's mother carries out her threat of taking the water away, Jenny's aggression continues to escalate. It is interesting that it is at *the* most conflictual point in the argument, when Jenny spits at her, that her mother adopts a different strategy. Ignoring her daughter's spitting and screaming, and under a blanket of pretence of calm uninterest, she sits down with a cup of coffee and a leaflet. Thus we can see how some working-class mothers can only deal with violence from their daughters up to a certain point, and when faced with mounting violence they too stop confronting it and use similar ignoring tactics. So, actually, Jenny's mother's ignoring tactic is the finale to quite a long *overt* power struggle between the pair.

We have called these girls 'suburban terrorists' to point up the unspoken nature of their violence. But the object is the middle-class mother, who has to be the target of this, and accept or deflect it. Her position then is not unlike that of the nursery teacher who was the target of abuse for four-year-old boys, accepting it on the grounds that to stop it would be to repress the emergence of their childhood sexuality.[10] The discursive understanding of mothering equates aggression with frustration and therefore gives the idea that the mother is doing something wrong. This puts considerable pressure on her to accept violence. We are not suggesting that children are conscious manipulators of their mothers, though the effects of their struggles for power are manipulative. It can be very powerful to be helpless and waited on and turns the mother into a virtual servant.

These emotions become 'feelings' which are not nice or are unpleasant. Thus, they hark back to the issue we raised in the last chapter of a universal morality of feelings. Here then is no understanding of power or oppression, simply that there are feelings which have to be understood and dealt with. Sensitivity to those feelings is designated as women's work par excellence. It is a central component of modern accounts of a nurturant femininity and it is our contention that in the production of this femininity there is a transformation of violence into feelings, which is a denial of active and violent emotions to women,[11]. It is also a denial of power and oppression.

But, before going on to consider how this has arisen and how it might be understood, we need to look at some examples of working-class resolution of conflict. We mentioned in the last chapter that many of these mothers make power explicit, and that this was considered pathological. But they also do something else. That is, they permit the expression of violent emotions on the part of their daughters, but they do so in a way which renders them safe, as part of a game.

How some working-class women cope with violence from their daughters

When a child hits her mother and shouts 'I'll poke your eye out', the mother may choose to ignore this, to point out that 'it's not very nice' to say things like that, or call the child 'silly', but none of this means that there is not a real power struggle going on or that the girl does not indeed have 'hateful' emotions towards her mother. Or indeed, and just as importantly, that her mother does not experience resentful, hateful or violent emotions towards the child. For what of the mother's anger and humiliation at her daughter expressing such violence? The mother also, if she is to achieve that hallowed status of 'sensitive' must repress or somehow be able to deal with her own emotions as well as those of the child. The middle-class mother's strategies of diffusion and intellectualisation allow the child to openly express her power and resist that of the mother. Once she has done this she can then regulate the mother.

Some working-class girls in these transcripts seem to have a much clearer idea than the middle-class girls of where the boundaries of bad or naughty behaviour lie, though this certainly does not mean that they try to traverse them any less. In fact they were more overtly demanding than the middle-class girls. But their mothers were far more resistant to such transgressions of power boundaries and less likely to give up their position of authority. Only on two occasions did working-class girls express violence *overtly* towards their mothers. Sally is upstairs; her mother is cooking in the kitchen. Sally calls for her mother to come up because she wants her to do something for her.

> M: I will in a minute, I'll do the pastry first.
> C: Now!
> M: Sally! Don't tell me what to do.
> C: I want to beat you.
> M: You're getting too cheeky and you're going to get a smack.

Perhaps Sally's mother's reaction would not be praised, nor used to exemplify the notion of 'sensitivity', but the stance she takes certainly ends the argument. The boundaries have been set out and the consequence of crossing them made clear.

Dawn is sitting close to her mother, making noises into her ear. This is taken as 'playful' at first and her mother doesn't mind. Dawn then 'growls' into her mother's ear, obviously hurting her mother. The boundaries of what is acceptable quickly come down.

> M: Don't! You do it again I'll smack you.
> C: I won't!
> M: 'Cos it hurts!

A short while later Dawn screams into her mother's ear.

> M: Stop screeching! Don't screech in my ear like that! Don't! You do it again and I'll smack you!

This is very different to most of the middle-class mothers, who tend to appeal to 'feelings', who convert this sort of violence into emotion, bad emotions whose expression will make people 'sad' or hurt them.

On the few occasions where working-class girls expressed violence towards their mothers, or, much more commonly, when they openly defied their mothers' wishes, most of the mothers took up a stance of positional power. They did not intellectualise 'the problem', or turn their own or their daughters' negative emotions into 'feelings'. They warned or threatened much more, and made it quite clear that they were angry, that they too harboured such emotions.

Space for expressing violence

These working-class mothers created space where violence towards them could be expressed 'safely' in a way which seemed impossible in the middle-class homes, given the middle-class mothers' modes of regulation. More working-class than middle-class mothers engaged in physical play with their children. These were basically 'fun' games, like tickling, turning the child upside down or 'chase'. They were often exciting games which both mother and daughter seemed to enjoy. But often there were underlying themes to these games, themes of violence towards the mother, which were treated in quite a different way.

Jacky is in the bedroom with her mother who is sorting out old doll's clothes. Jacky pretends to hit her mother who then pretends to hit her back.

> C: You can't even touch me. You can't do it. (Laughs.)
> M: You didn't even touch me.
> C: I did. Did! (Laughing.)
> M: That doesn't hurt. Doesn't hurt.
> C: Look! (C really hits M.)
> M: Next time you do it I'll smack you.
> C: I 'macked you!
> M: No, *I'll* smack *you*.
> C: (Laughs.) You didn't know what to do, what to do.

It's interesting how often that kind of sing-song word-play features in this type of exchange. It seems to denote levity and yet at the same time the message is made quite clear – 'don't do it again'.

Patsy and her mother have been singing 'Dear Lisa' to each other earlier on in the afternoon. 'Dear Lisa' consequently becomes a catch-phrase throughout the recording in quite a specific way. It is used by the mother as a way of deflecting potentially conflictual situations, but it also allows the resolution of that conflict.

The pair are in the kitchen and Patsy's mother looks at the meat that is cooking. She shows the meat to Patsy.

> C: Can I see, dear Lisa, dear Lisa?
> M: Dear Lisa, dear Lisa. There's a hole in my bucket, dear Lisa. (M shows C the meat.)
> C: Dear Lisa, dear Lisa.
> M: I'll give you dear Lisa, I'll give you dear Lisa, you saucy thing. (M cuddles C.)
> C: Then I'll eat you, dear Lisa. (Pats M's bottom.)
> M: I'll eat you, dear Lisa.
> C: Can I eat this, dear Lisa? (C takes a sweet.)
> (———)
> (C smacks M's bottom and laughs.)
> M: Dear Lisa, that hurt.

A few minutes later Patsy smacks her mother's bottom again.

> M: Stop, stop, dear Lisa.

These word games are often noted as a source of pleasure for mother and child, as well as educationally important in that they are valuable ways of learning how to manipulate words. While we would not argue with this, we want to stress their importance as places in which the expression of resistance, and even violence, can be negotiated in a non-conflictual way, and always with the possibility of resolution. Nor must the mother intellectualise the resistance, reason it away, for it is not understood as a threat to her autonomy. At the same time, she is not afraid to *regulate* the child, for the phrase, in Patsy's case 'Dear Lisa', is also used as a form of regulation. Later on in the afternoon, Patsy's mother tells her not to run down the hallway. Patsy promptly denies that she was running, even though she was.

> M: Don't run.
> C: I wasn't.
> M: I heard you.
> C: I wasn't running.

M: Who was it running down the hall when Patsy brought the milk then, dear Lisa?

Boundaries for violence

Violence or the potential for violence may emerge and be contained in games which have some physical component. Anna is playing the game of 'running' her mother over. Her mother is sitting on the back steps with her legs stretched out in front of her. The object of the game is her pulling her feet away before Anna can run her toes over in her pedal car. This game is fun for a while, but her mother soon tires of it.

M: No, you're not running me over.
C: Why?
M: 'Cos you're not.
C: I'll run you over. I nearly ran you over.
M: I know you would.

Anna's wanting to run her mother over is actually an expression of violence, but in quite a different form. Her mother acknowledges that her daughter *would* like to run her over, but she doesn't get angry, is not hurt by this. The game somehow provides the context in which these emotions can be both expressed by the child and controlled by the mother.

Often, physical play provides such a context. This is not to say that the mother tolerates violence or physical abuse, but that space is created for their expression, within limits. For example, Kerry is lying on the sofa next to her mother and is putting her feet on her mother's head.

M: Do you like putting your feet all over my head?
(C stops.)

After a while, Kerry again rests her feet on her mother's head. At this point her mother is no longer prepared to tolerate the 'game', it has gone past being a game and is actually very invasive of the mother's space. A sharp 'Kerry!' lets her know that she is going 'too far' and Kerry takes her feet down.

In another instance, Patsy's mother tells her off for chewing an elastic band, Patsy clearly resents this and threatens her mother with:

> C: Watch out, otherwise I'll get my big horse out of his stable.

This could be viewed as creating a potentially conflictual situation if the mother were working on the premise that there should be an absence of 'bad' emotions – of power.

> M: Yes? And?
> C: It will give you a beating-up.
> M: Oh! That big horse in the stable will tell you not to eat elastic bands as well.
> C: Won't.
> M: Will too.
> C: Won't.

This is a 'sensitive' mother who nevertheless recognises her daughter's violent feelings towards her. She does deflect the conflict, not by intellectualising nor by ignoring or refusing to recognise the power-play, nor indeed by tolerating it. But she does create a space in which the emotion can be expressed without any threat to either herself or the child. This space also creates the possibility of resolution.

Nicky and her mother quarrelled for much of the afternoon. Her mother was clearly very tired and rushing to get everything done before she went to work, while Nicky was particularly demanding and could be very awkward. However, like all the mothers and daughters, the pair shared warm moments, occasions which were obviously very pleasurable for them. This is such a moment: they are sitting on the front step together. Nicky, despite her mother's warnings, keeps jumping from the steps onto the pavement.

> M: You've only got to fall and you'll hurt yourself . . . and you'll tell Daddy I've gone and beaten you up, won't you?
> C: I'm gonna tell him, later on, when he comes in tonight.
> M: Are you?
> C: 'Cos you been beating me up.

M: If you're gonna tell him, I'm *gonna* beat you up! (M tickles C.)
C: I'm gonna tell him! (Laughs.)
(———)
M: What you gonna tell him?
C: 'Cos Mummy's been beating me up.
M: Oh ho ho ho, fibber!
C: Beat me up and then I *will* tell him.
M: Beat you up and then you will tell him, no. (Laughs.)
C: Beat me up and then I won't tell him then.
M: Beat you up and you won't tell him? You want me to beat you up, do you?
C: Yeah.
M: What, like this? (M pretends to hit C and 'pull' her nose off.) Oh, get you in a lock, oh, that's a good lock, an arm lock and a nose lock, mmm? You're supposed to say, 'I suppose you think that's funny.'
C: I'm gonna tie you up.
M: You're gonna tie me up now, go on then. That's right, twist it round me.
(C pretends to tie M up. C and M tickle each other.)
M: Oh yeah, I can do that. And I got you here, right here.
C: Not there!
M: Here! I can!
(C tries to pinch M.)
M: No pinching. That's spiteful.
(C and M tickle each other.)

This turns into a fun game, with tickling and word-play, but there are also strong elements of violence, blackmail, power and authority of the father.

What is important about these examples for us is that they reverse a set of arguments about working-class mothers. We want to point up the positive aspects of these practices in a different way. They allow conflict, violence and anger to be expressed safely. When Anna wants to run her mother over, the mother allows her to display this within the safe confines of the game. She accepts her daughter's feelings towards her power and helps her daughter to render these frightening emotions sayable, handleable. Compare this with Julie's mother, who cannot confront her daughter's expressions of violence towards her baby sister. She tells her it's not 'nice', she rationalises it and makes Julie go to her room until she can express nice emotions.

It may seem odd that we appear to validate an expression of violence today, when there is so much talk about opposing violence, of working for peace. Perhaps it is because violence is so clearly pathologised, so difficult to articulate. In no way do we want to simply and unproblematically compare violence done towards men and the effect this might have on them and their actions, to women. But there is a connection. Fanon talks of the effects of violent oppression on colonised peoples. It produces anger and hatred, violent feelings. Are women not also the victims of oppression, of horrendous violence, both inside and outside the home? Is the effect of this experience to make them peaceful?

While there is little discussion of girls' violence towards their mothers, there are other discourses of violence: almost exclusively the violence of boys and men, which women's peacefulness then gets counterposed to. We will argue in Chapter Ten that girls' violence is displaced onto boys. This brings us to several issues which we cannot resolve here, but would like to raise for future debate. Firstly, is it not counterproductive to our moves for world peace and disarmament for us as women to deny our own violence, as though it were only located outside ourselves? Secondly, although male violence against women is a serious problem, these little girls display violent emotions, which are later outlawed as inappropriate to femininity. We will see in the next chapter how violence, hatefulness and all active emotions are outlawed for women. But we want to say something else here, by referring to two bodies of psychoanalytic work dealing with violence: Melanie Klein and Frantz Fanon.[12]

Klein's work is important because she deals more clearly than other theorists with children's hateful feelings towards their mothers. Indeed, it was this work which was transformed by later theories and the hate denied. Klein locates hate (she takes all violence to be a product of hate) in the inevitable loss of the breast, in a way which is positive and yet also slides back into the idea of instincts.[13]. By contrast, Fanon locates violence within oppression. As a psychiatrist in Algeria during the war of independence, he charted the way in which colonial psychiatric discourses understood the Algerian man as having a 'violent' (read 'pathological') personality. He locates this violence done to Algerians, although he states that the men are often driven, by oppression, to take it out on each other. It is thus that he advocates violent uprising as an opposition to the violence done to Algerians under colonialism. It is this work to which Bhabha refers (see Chapter Two), and which has been so important in supporting the idea of colonial fantasies in the discourses of oppression.

We do need some basis and understanding for our anger and an endemic hate is not enough to capture it. We are beginning to be angry, to speak it, to articulate a different discourse. 'Anger expressed and translated into action in the service of our vision and our future is a liberating and strengthening act of clarification . . . ' (Lorde, 1984, p. 127).[14]

In addition to this, while violence is permitted, sanctioned and celebrated as 'natural' in boys (see Walkerdine, 1981), it is commonly disavowed in girls, in their difference and Otherness. We would argue that such displacement and disavowal of violence relates to the issue of fantasy and fiction that we have been talking about. Of course, male violence is 'real', but we think it is no solution to regard it as an essential component of 'men'. Yet, in all this muddle, as Urwin (1985b) articulates, there is hardly space within feminism to explore what she describes as 'aggression'. What most of this work (except Fanon) misses is an understanding of power. Little four-year-old girls can make a bid for power over their mothers, which is resistance to their regulation, and can indeed tyrannise their mothers. In this analysis, power does not reside in the mother as her possession, but she can be rendered powerless by being positioned as object of her daughter's resistance.[15] Thus, blaming mothers for oppression simply serves to increase the burden of guilt felt by mothers. Judith Arcana (1981) liken mothers and children to caged animals who take out the violence of their oppression on each other. To take it further we would need to explore how mother and daughter are constituted in discourse as Other to each other and what fantasies therefore emerge.

But what we are saying about some of the working-class mothers is not that they live in an idyll of resolved violence, far from it. Rather, these mothers may more easily recognise that they live in an oppressive and unjust order. They know that you cannot have what you want. They do not believe that they are free or have access to plenty. They are poor, often live in bad housing, they work hard, the world is hard, They must teach this to their daughters and they do so often, by making their power visible. They stop, they say no, they regulate overtly. It is a liberal fantasy to believe that power is removed if regulation is made covert, if the girl believes herself (as in the quote from the Newsons in Chapter One) to be an agent of choice, of free will. This autonomy is a sham. We do not want to praise working-class resolution of violence, but to point to its place (and its opposite place in middle-class denials) in a violent and oppressive order. Is it really better to let little girls believe they can do and have what they want? What serves us better to recognise and fight our oppression and how can we do so without blaming our mothers for withholding, for their failure to allow 'autonomy'?

In our examination of 'violence', therefore, we are deliberately choosing this term (following Fanon) as opposed to 'hate'. Although other psychoanalytic work, particularly that of Melanie Klein, deals with hate, it is located within innate drives and has a problematic relation to the 'real'. We urgently need an examination of the psychic dimensions of violence within an understanding of power, oppression and exploitation. It is not possible to talk of these working- and middle-class mothers and daughters as normal or pathological outside an analysis of how people cope with the exigencies of their lives.[16] There is so much violence done to people through oppression and yet Fanon seems to be alone in psychoanalytic circles in attempting to explore its psychic effectivity.

CHAPTER EIGHT

GROWING UP THE HARD WAY

Dreaming of harmony

Mothers and daughters in perfect union – what an enticing vision! It is an idyll of sisterhood designed to break the grip of patriarchy and heal the wounds of the fraught relationship with mothers, described by so many feminists. However, despite its attractions, it is an idea which brings in the sensitive mother by the back door. We have pointed to the problems of an empiricism which locates the mother in the home and holds her responsible for meeting needs. We have suggested that this is a fantasy of enormous proportions which invests in 'woman' that which will uphold peace, harmony, democracy. Further, we are saying that it does no good either to women or children.

In the last chapter we explored the eruption in the girls of violent emotions towards their mothers. One account would have it that this violence was the result of frustration, because of the failure in sensitivity.[1] It is an account which suggests that needs *can* be met and that the goal of socialisation is the daughter who has a clear sense of herself and her autonomy because the balance has been made between the meeting of her needs and her own independence. The account is now so commonplace that it seems eminently reasonable. But there are problems in this version of events. Firstly, we are suggesting that violence does not simply result from frustration, but from the inevitability of power and regulation. Secondly, we argue that the dream of harmony ties in with the fantasy of covert regulation, which is not 'autonomy' at all, but the production of the bourgeois individual in a social order which denies power, oppression and exploitation.

In Chapter Three we examined the strong movement in the 1940s and 1950s which tried to produce the possibility of social reform through the agency of the mother. In order to facilitate reform, the pessimism of social Darwinism was countered by an environmentalism which, instead of stressing aggression and war, emphasised the possibility of social reform through love and nurturance.[2] This project of social democracy created natural mother-love as an object which was to be the bedrock of its policy. It is our aim in this section to demonstrate that although feminist work in this field has been committed to women's liberation, unwittingly much of the work operates on theoretical premises not a million miles from those produced by figures such as John Bowlby, who attempted to utilise ethology, the study of animal behaviour, to validate Freud scientifically. Bowlby moved away from the idea of instincts or drives to the notion of the evolutionary adaptedness of behavioural systems. This gave to social reformers an 'environmental' solution, which, rather than stressing inbuilt and therefore unchangeable instincts of love and hate, instead pointed to behavioural patterns of mothering which were amenable to intervention and change. As Bowlby states, the environment was understood not in terms of a complex interplay of material, economic and social conditions, not as oppression and exploitation, but as a key to social change, a manipulable solution to reform brought about through the infant's 'interaction with the principal figure in that environment, namely the mother'.

So, Bowlby and others, claiming to build upon psychoanalysis, changed it out of all recognition, by dint of an environmentalism which centred on the mother. They did this, as did many other 'object relations' theorists, by getting rid of the theory of drives in favour of an environmentalism. At first sight, such a move seems correct since the idea of instincts smacks of heredity and appears very reactionary. But this move was not as radical as it may at first appear. It became the bedrock of social-democratic reform and entailed the oppression of half the human race in the process, with the creation of the fiction of the natural mother. Such environmentalism, while it claims realism for itself, has none of the elements of a materialist analysis, and conversely, while we have stated our problems with Klein's theory of hate, nevertheless Klein and Freud, because of their adherence to drives, do not resort to a crude and simple environmentalism, but engage with the psychic production of fantasy. This makes them worthy of further consideration.

Given that object-relations approaches and developmental psychology came to be the discourses, the common sense of mothering became the bedrock of liberal training in the caring professions, it is hardly surprising that some feminist approaches came to pick up on what they saw as an environmental approach, amenable to change, rather than return to the Freud of the drives. Unfortunately that firmly roots the mother as both cause and solution to women's problems. This in effect means that, despite a certain amount of feminist rhetoric, the statements about the mothering of daughters bear remarkable similarity to those of Bowlby.

There is a strong tendency in feminist work on mothering, such as that of Nancy Chodorow (1978), Jessica Benjamin (1978), and Luise Eichenbaum and Susie Orbach (1982) of the Women's Therapy Centre, among others, to stress the reality of women's oppression, but to understand this by making statements which reduce this real to the 'real' of mothering, precisely because they utilise environmentalist theories. While theorists such as Bowlby and Winnicott offered poor conditions and poverty as explanations of why some women became incapacitated for mothering, these feminists tend to offer women's oppression, domestic labour and sex-role stereotyping as explanatory. But the argument remains virtually the same: women have been badly mothered.

The effect of renouncing drive theories is that it reduces emphasis on certain basic psychoanalytic concepts. This means in effect that when a woman presents in therapy problems in her relationship with her mother this can be interpreted in ways consonant with straight approaches, namely, that the woman's mother really was inadequate. Thus the solutions presented, of presence, bonding, attachment and shared parenting, share many similarities with the liberal approaches they claim to criticise.

For example, Nancy Chodorow argues in favour of the object-relations approach of analysts such as Balint (1954), Fairbairn (1952) and Guntrip (1961, 1969, 1971) for the following reasons. She claims that they avoid the instinctual determinism of Freud, Klein and the ego psychologists, the direct environmental determinism of the 'cultural school' of Erich Fromm, Karen Horney and Thompson in favour of a view that 'social relational experience from earliest infancy is determining for psychological growth and personal formation' (Chodorow, 1978, p. 47). If we compare this statement with that quoted from Bowlby earlier (Chapter Three, p. 51), it will be seen that they are actually remarkably similar.[3] Eichenbaum and Orbach (1982) also accuse Freud of 'patriarchal bias' when describing female sexuality. They want to propose an account which deals with 'the meaning in a girl's life of the experience of her mother's body as a positive force' (p. 107). They suggest that girls are treated differently from boys and that the 'psychic sphere reflects' that women are second-class citizens in patriarchal culture. Although it may seem pedantic, it is important to dwell on their use of the term 'reflects'. Whether the psychic sphere reflects the social or what kind of relationship there is between them is something we will need to pursue. They argue against instinctual and drive approaches precisely because of their position that the psychic is a mere 'reflection of the social'. They too, like Chodorow, opt for theorists like Guntrip because 'What comes across clearly in Guntrip's description of his work and clients is the importance of nurturance in the therapy relationship. This concept is the cornerstone of our feminist psychotherapy' (p. 113).

Here we have the classic argument. Women's problems result from inadequate mothering, in which failure in nurturance does not allow the woman to separate from her mother. Because she has not been nurtured enough, she is continually in a state of wanting and cannot separate. Women's ego development in this account is shaped less by male sexuality than by a concept of a social order which renders women bad mothers. Because daughters are valued less than sons, women fail to nurture their daughters properly and hence the daughters cannot separate and remain connected, fail to be autonomous. The rather circular explanation is that because of this order women do not get their needs met and so do not mother properly.

Of course some feminist writers celebrate this 'connectedness'. It is quite common to pose women's connectedness as important and antithetical to male rationality and individuality. Thus the pre-Oedipal mother–daughter relation is seen to be a time of women's connectedness which is outside patriarchy. Feminists as diverse as Adrienne Rich (1977) and the French psychoanalyst Luce Irigaray (1985) take variants of this position. In other words, what these accounts celebrate, in their various ways, is a very positive vision of sisterhood. Here, only positive emotions, positive possibilities, are stressed. There is a vision of possibility in which hurt, pain, violence and hatred are removed from the scene. However, we have called into question some of the denials present in this view.

Let us approach it in a rather different way. Much hinges on the concept of the 'real'. In these accounts the 'real' is taken to equate with actual presence. But if we consider the idea of harmony to be a fantasy, we might begin to ask other questions about the 'real' and what actually happens. Imagine the newborn infant – small, vulnerable, demanding. Warmth, comfort and food are available from the mother's or others' bodies. But the supply is not limitless. There are times when the other presence is absent. How does the infant survive these times? Freud suggested very early on (1900) that this was by means of 'hallucination of the breast', by fantasising that which had provided satisfaction. What is central to this account is the idea that absolute satisfaction, harmony and love are an impossible fantasy. However, instead of suggesting what *can* be achieved by limited and regulated *actual* satisfaction, he stresses the psychic consequences of loss and absence. These are the production of unconscious fantasies which have what he described as 'psychic reality'. In other words, what Freud stresses is both the inevitability of loss and the complexity of unconscious processes through which 'reality' is lived. There is no easy relation between what actually happens and the child's psychic health, precisely because the mother/other's absence is filled by the infant with fantasy. It is that fantasy which is the stuff of neuroses and psychoses, not in any simple sense the fact of the absence itself. Times of absence are inevitable and should not be confused with the idea of problems caused by mothers leaving their children.

So the crux of the impasse for feminism appears to rest on a fantasy – a fantasy of presence and harmony. Freud, on the other hand, stresses inevitability and therefore the necessity of dealing with loss. It has often been felt that Freud's phallocentrism can be countered on two fronts – one is the feminist stress on relations with the mother and the significance of the breast, the other is the importance of environment over drives. But drives need not be equated with instincts[4]. Admittedly there are many problems with such an account, but what it does allow is the recovery of those aspects suppressed in the modern account of femininity. What was outlawed was action, passion, violence and conflict, in favour of passivity, receptivity and nurturance. The drives are active, demanding. It is through fantasy that the unconscious wish-fulfilment is achieved, and it is this, not reality, which, for psychoanalysis, is paramount in understanding traumas. 'Psychic reality' then is the creation of the analysand – the wishes and fantasies, which can be experienced as very real indeed. But they cannot be 'read off' as effects of an actual event precisely because it is the gap, the absence, that is filled with fantasy (not reality).

Melanie Klein went further than this. She posited that the infant not only had positive wishes of fulfilment, but was racked by hate as well as love, and would fantasise destruction of the absent breast. These hateful fantasies are projected onto the fantasised Bad Mother. The infant thus reacts to the qualities (bad mother) it has created inside its own fantasy, and counterposes them to a split-off Good Mother. Klein sees this violent hatred as basic to the fantasies of the Bad Mother. Here then we have the basis of quite a different view from the one which presents the bad mother as 'really' bad and the good mother as a possible solution. Janet Sayers (1984) pointed this out in relation to feminism arguing that:

> 'the phantasy of the positively fused mother and infant daughter is an illusory basis on which to found the unity and solidarity of women. This can only be forged on the basis of recognising the real factors (both material and psychic) that at the same time unite and divide women as a sex – a recognition that will be obstructed as long as there is a defence against acknowledging the contradictions which inhere in relations between women. Klein does not specify all these contradictions. Nor does she consider the social and ideological forces that operate to obscure that recognition. But she does draw attention to one factor – namely splitting – that is used as a defence against recognising contradictions in social relations. And she also draws attention to the contradictions that inhere in women's relations with each other as mothers and daughters.' (p. 240)

Just as some writers have remarked on the 'neglect of hatefulness'[5] in recent developmental psychological accounts of mother–infant interaction, so the feminist accounts neglect and ignore aggressive and difficult emotions and the issue of power differences between mother and daughter, that is, the mother's regulative function. If the mother is to regulate, she must of necessity exercise power over her daughter. However, regulation goes underground in the idea that the mother can indeed meet and be sensitive to the needs of her daughter. Power in this analysis must remain invisible because the daughter must believe that she is autonomous, in control, not regulated. This creates a fantasy scenario lived out because the mother must appear to meet her daughter's needs and the daughter must maintain a fantasy of omnipotent power to control the mother. If then the daughter expresses powerlessness and aggression towards her mother it is because power has become visible. This, as we have seen, is interpreted as pathology, with the view that harmony is both possible and realisable. In our view this denies power and the inevitability of regulation and the loss and powerlessness that the daughter has to come to terms with.

Such an account is more in keeping with the complexities of power, conflict and violence as we have outlined them in this sample of mothers and daughters. The idea of 'containment' and the setting of boundaries, which we have pointed to in the regulative practices of some working-class mothers, seems to us in keeping with factors stressed in a Kleinian account and are quite different from a view of rationalisation and nurturance.

Oedipal and pre-Oedipal relations

For classical psychoanalysis, it is fantasy which provides the key to the workings of the unconscious, hence the importance of what is termed the 'transference', in which the analysand transfers her fantasies onto the figure of the analyst. This provides a good way of examining the analysand's 'psychic reality', for example, the fantasies of good and bad mother and how these have produced conscious and unconscious patterns of coping. This is carried out using the technique of free association, so that apparently meaningless or random connections can be explored. The other approach is the analysis of dreams. Both of these provide routes from the surface association or images in the dream to latent meanings held beneath, by chains of associations.

This idea of unconscious meanings, held beneath others in a chain leading to primary wishes, is a cornerstone of psychoanalysis. It is important for an analysis of meanings, such as those produced by the girls and women, because it suggests that for every manifest meaning there are a chain of latent meanings linked to fantasies, fears, wishes, anxieties, phobias etc. We can add to this the idea that fantasies and wishes also circulate at the social level through the production of meanings in scientific accounts (such as those about mothering in developmental psychology). Jacqueline Rose, for example, talks of the 'key fantasies operating at the heart of institutions' which are 'linked into the most fundamental images of sexual difference' (1986 p. 4). We could add also differences of class and race. The 'images' are constructions which operate together at the social, cultural and psychic levels and are the terms through which our lives are understood. We have tried to specify how certain fantasies circulate and how we get caught up in them. We will explore this further with respect to the meanings generated by the mothers and daughters about growing up.

A cornerstone of Freud's theory is the Oedipus complex, based on the Greek myth of Oedipus. This is particularly important because it is said to define sexual difference, whereby the child's omnipotent fantasies of controlling the mother are broken by the threat of castration for the boy and the recognition of castration for the girl. Some feminists objected to Freud's theory of female castration, accusing him of phallocentrism. To some extent, this promoted the feminist emphasis on the breast rather than the penis and the pre-Oedipal relations with the mother rather than the later triangle. It is not the Kleinian Breast, but one in which the father, patriarchy, is banished – totally banished from the primal scene. The 'new couple' of mother and daughter do not have their pre-Oedipal harmony broken. There is no Oedipus, only the girl, gradually satisfied, leaving her mother in order to fend for her own independence in the world outside. It is clear in writings such as that of Jessica Benjamin (1978) that the father is to be removed totally: 'It is this image of revolt springing from mutual recognition and nurturant activity which may guide us in our struggle against instrumental rationality toward a society without the father.' The violence of the father's removal is obvious in this account. The feminine idyll refuses to be broken by patriarchy. Here then the father is made to hold everything evil which threatens the state of harmony. There seems to be a great deal of splitting going on.

Women's anger at men and at patriarchal culture is an important aspect of feminist work, recovering again our anger and the violence of our emotions to speak of conflict, oppression. But this method of denial seems to block the emergence of those very necessary emotions by banishing them into the father, and then by banishing the father himself. The account presents the *disappearance* of patriarchy; the *disappearance* of the father. This belies the aggression of this account, and the violence of the fantasy it represents. For the father does not merely disappear, he is very forcibly *ejected*. He becomes shipwrecked: Robinson Crusoe, the economic man, marooned at last in perpetuity on the desert island. It is a good myth, a powerful fantasy. But will it be sufficient armour in the battle of and over our oppression?

We need some good myths, stories to counter the ones that we are given to understand ourselves by. There are two major debates where pre-Oedipal mother–daughter relations consistently surface as an issue. The first is around child abuse and the problem of the entry of the father as an abuser. This cannot simply, of course, be reduced to a fantasy, which is the danger in those psychoanalytic approaches which stress psychic reality over environmentalism. Yet we do need a way of understanding the materiality of abuse without situating it back within the only accounts which claim to deal with what actually happens, that is, those which centre on monitoring the mother. The second issue concerns the idea of women's desire and women's silence. It has been quite often said, differently by different feminists (*pace* Adrienne Rich and Luce Irigaray) that women are silenced within patriarchy. And yet it is to relations with the mother that feminists so often turn to examine the possibility of an-Other language.

These issues of materiality, speaking, silence and fantasy are central to our account. What do structuralism, and post-structuralism offer to these ideas? Jacques Lacan, the infamous French psychoanalyst, argues that woman existed 'only as a symptom and myth of the male fantasy'.[6] Woman in his vision is silent, silenced, imaginary. Although at first sight this analysis seems extremely reactionary, it has its important points. The first is that it tells us a lot about male fantasies, fantasies of power and domination. These fantasies, which Lacan calls the 'Law' and the 'Symbolic Order', are the discourses and practices through which we are regulated and become subjected. They are powerful, have material effectivity, but are founded upon a chimera. The masculine desire which Lacan uncovers is one of wanting to be the object of the mother's desire. The boy child wants to be that object, but is for ever wanting. It is out of this desire that man constructs a fantasy of an Other who would want him, over whom he could have omnipotent control – an infantalised, powerless Other.

'What does the woman (the little girl) want?' asked Freud and Lacan.[7] But Lacan realised that he was trapped inside his own question. Indeed, he was trapped inside his desire to 'know' woman, to master, to make us want him. He accepted that this phallic fantasy was a fraud, but one which he could never give up. We need to take apart the fantasies, to reveal the desperation on which this mastery, this desire to know sits. Thus, knowledges of us, claim feminists who use his work, are constructed entirely out of those fantasies which we are trapped inside, for when we take apart the regimes of truth, the fictional accounts and the media images, it is masculine fantasy which is there revealed.

Is there then an *Us*, women who can stand outside that fantasy? It is precisely this problem that Bhabha and Fanon pick up by claiming as we have seen that the colonised are trapped with the discourses and therefore the fantasies of the coloniser. Have we nothing then to say inside patriarchy? Is there a possibility of building an-Other language outside patriarchy, from the positive sense of our mothers' bodies?

While we think this debate is crucial, we want to point somewhere else. As working-class women we were silenced. We had the dreams that oppression created for us. But that is not all there is to say. We do not think the other dream – of what cannot be spoken – comes out of the joys of community and other romantic myths of the connectedness of working-class life. No, it comes from what was silenced, screaming to be spoken, under oppression. There *are* other stories, other accounts, there is resistance and fighting that all the covert regulation in the world cannot completely keep down. There are the discourses of opposition, the fantasies of another possibility – of feminism and socialism, of rising up against oppression. Yes, we can speak, but it is dangerous speech for which we will be punished, pathologised, silenced every time we struggle to formulate it.

Those feminists who stick closely to Freud and his follower Lacan, for example, Juliet Mitchell, Mitchell and Rose (1983), Jacqueline Rose (1983), Janet Sayers, argue strongly about the fictional and ideological nature of sexual difference – the fictions built up around the materiality of biology.[8] Although the emphasis on pre-Oedipal relations attempts to stress a positive future for women, the dyad has to be broken. If women are held responsible for the regulation of the world of the home, the private, how will their daughters fare when they approach the public world outside, where regulation is of a very different order?

Although our data does not touch on Oedipal aspects of

sexual difference, we can state that sexual difference comes to play a larger part for these girls as they grow older and that those with sensitive mothers are not in any simple sense at all better prepared, more autonomous or more independent at school, for any such moves are thwarted and challenged as threatening sexual difference the whole time.

How then do we deal with the relation between psychical and material reality? We have stressed the importance throughout the book of the discourses and practices regulating women's sexuality and the ways that these both became understood as matters of fact and implicated in policies and practices designed to produce normal citizens. These had effects on women's lives in terms of their production as mothers which can rightly be deemed material. Yet that does not mean that they are not at the same time fictitious, and have built into them powerful and enormous fantasies operating on a social level, like the fantasy of the sensitive mother. Women are held responsible for the maintenance of reason over emotion, for harmony against discord. We are made to bear the brunt of these fantasies. No wonder we experience both desire to live them out and guilt at their failure. This makes a nonsense of the classic split between fantasy and reality. We have argued that the sensitive mother is a fantasy, but it is the object of a science which claims it is real.[9]

There is no singular 'family', no normal mother, but families constituted in their difference from, and opposition to, each other. Thus different mothers and daughters struggle to make sense of who and where they are. These struggles have different psychic effects. Neither are these mothers and daughters by themselves. They are with others and in social networks which extend outside them. It is a fantasy that the mother and daughter can exist outside the confines of the social world. That world must always take the mother's attention away from her daughter. It is only in fantasy that the mother is so besotted with her baby that the reality principle never enters. We do not believe that the idea of the never joined and therefore never separated mother and daughter is the best way to understand the complexity of meanings and circumstances generated between the mothers and daughters in our sample. It is certainly the case that the mothers and daughters have to deal with power and powerlessness and with adulation, aggression, fear of loss and wanting to control the mother, but they do so in different ways, circumstances and with different consequences.

A frequently observed phenomenon in our data is that of girls resisting the notion of growing up. This resistance was articulated in various ways: for instance, by a refusal to perform practical tasks for themselves or for their mothers; by maintaining a 'helpless' position, saying things like 'I *can't* . . .' do my buttons up, reach the cupboard, etc. Some girls want to be carried or held all the time, they don't want to walk. This hostility to the idea of growing up often involved jealousy of a sibling, sometimes a younger one. In general, though, we can say that some girls expressed desires to stay 'little babies'.

In studies of siblings, this issue is often dealt with in terms of 'imitation'. Dunn (1984), in her study of brothers and sisters, notes how, in the early stages of a new arrival in the family, it is more usual for the older child to imitate a newborn sibling. This gradually works around so that, by the time the baby is eight months to a year old, it is much more common for the younger child to imitate the older one. The framework Dunn uses is essentially a 'modelling' one. She argues that the copying of an older child may be important to the intellectual development of the younger, as the older child may direct the younger's play towards a more rapid development of skills (through more mature play, for example). Copying may also have important effects on the younger child's behaviour, especially where they imitate the actions of an older sibling which have attracted adult attention.

Our evidence suggests that it is not only older siblings, faced with a newborn brother or sister, who display this kind of 'imitation'. In this study, there are some girls who at the time of recording are themselves the youngest, yet display very 'babyish' or infantile behaviour. An account which reduces this to 'modelling' and 'imitation' loses the crucial dimensions of power and emotion; of understanding the investment the child has in remaining a helpless baby. For there is, indeed, much to be gained in this position. Girls who avoid growing up and doing things for themselves, who are waited on by their mothers, can wield much power. Such work also neglects the possibility of the girl not wanting to separate from her mother, not because her needs are not being met, but because the forfeiting of such a powerful position is too frightening. Let us look at the sorts of strategies some girls use to regulate their mothers and remain helpless.

Amanda is playing a word puzzle with her mother. It is obvious by Amanda's fidgeting that she wants to go to the toilet, but despite her mother's coaxing, she steadfastly refuses to go.

> M: Darling, if you're going to walk about like that, we must go upstairs. Now come on, Amanda.
> C: No . . . Noooo!
> M: It'll be much better. Then you can enjoy it because you're just . . . I know you . . . come on.
> C: Nooo.
> M: Come on.
> C: No, no, no, no, no.
> M: Otherwise . . .
> C: No, no, no, no. Ah, err . . . no!
> M: Come on, you've got to go upstairs. You're just being silly now.
> C: Nooo!

The power which Amanda wields in her resistance is enormous. By steadfastly refusing her mother's reasonable coaxing, she is eventually positioned as a baby, for it is at this point that her mother carries her upstairs, undresses and sits her on the toilet, brings books in to her, and, when the child has finished, wipes her bottom. In a complex way, Amanda's powerful resistance to going to the toilet could be construed as a resistance to self-sufficiency, taking responsibility for her own body.

'Helplessness' as a strategy for regulating the mother, for getting her to 'service' the child, is not confined to middle-class girls. Kerry's mother is designated 'sensitive' and she spends most of the afternoon playing with and amusing her daughter. Even though Kerry has her mother's attention almost all the time, she behaves quite helplessly on occasion, often getting her mother to perform tasks that she herself could quite easily do. For instance, Kerry is sitting at the dining-table eating lunch, while her mother sits with her, drinking a cup of tea or coffee. The television is on and they discuss the puppet show that is on and how the hand puppets work. Casually, Kerry asks her mother to feed her.

> M: No, he puts his hand inside . . . puts his hand inside . . . and then he makes the puppet move . . . and then he talks . . . and it looks as though . . .
> C: Feed me. (C gives M the fork.)
> M: . . . the puppets [are] talking.

With only the slightest halt or falter in the conversation, Kerry asks to be fed and the mother complies, feeding Kerry as if she were a baby. But Kerry is no baby. She becomes powerful enough to tell her mother what food and how much to put on the fork:

> C: Put one more on.
> M: No, you can't put too much in your mouth.
> C: Yes, did you put that other . . .
> M: All right.
> C: . . . did you put some egg on?
> M: All right . . . nice?

Cathy Urwin (1984) outlines how young children can take positions which regulate the mother on whom they are dependent. This provides for them a fiction of power and control, masking their own vulnerable dependency. In Urwin's analysis, the mother becomes 'a focus for supporting the infant's illusionary control and omnipotence, to which separation is one amongst many possible threats' (p. 314). Regulating the mother who regulates you is very powerful. Thus, being helpless or attempting to remain a baby can be both the site of enormous power and refusal of the terror and pain of losing the mother. Simultaneously, of course, their daughters' growing up may be very painful for the mothers.

When we are talking about a 'struggle', it is not only the girls' struggle to grow up which is significant. There is the struggle between mother and daughter, and, in addition, there is the struggle of the woman herself. For the daughter is not the only one with fantasies of satisfaction. Although much feminist work has concentrated on the 'myth of the maternal instinct',[10] there is also, for many women, a considerable amount of desire involved. 'Wanting' a child and how that is both understood and regulated is important for us to consider. Not only can a child be desired, and itself become viewed as an object that can potentially 'satisfy' a woman, but clearly there is considerable pleasure in a relationship with a child. Many women look for the satisfaction of met needs in their children (having failed to find it with men) and attempt to be a 'perfect mother'. Babies can make women feel wanted and needed. Their dependency can be very appealing precisely because it offers love which will not go away, threatened only by one thing – the child growing up and not needing the mother so much. If the modern concept of sensitive mothering sets so much store by the mother as guardian of the future social order, mothering is certainly given considerable importance. It is quite possible, then, that many women in this position, who long for satisfaction, pleasure, being needed, having an important job to do, will find it very hard to let their daughters become 'big girls'. Urwin (1985a) gives this as a reason for many women having another child, which then produces difficult problems around jealousy. Mothering indeed *is* set up as a rewarding job for women whose only alternative may be hard and menial labour, with long hours, poor conditions and low wages. In terms of job satisfaction, mothering appears to offer many rewards (Oakley, 1984). Urwin points to the pleasure women she interviewed expressed in 'seeing or anticipating the next stage' (p. 191). Here, developmental psychology gives a positive socialisation role, stressing both its normative qualities and its possibility. It is hard to face the pain of giving up that idea of socialisation when it is presented with such enticing positivity. Mothering is clearly both painful and intensely pleasurable.

Big girls or babies, sensible or silly

With these issues in mind, what does it mean to be a child from the point of view of the adult women, the mothers in the study? That is, the mothers in their interaction with their daughters give to them covert and overt meanings and rules through which they are to understand what it means to be a child and what and how a child should be. These are different for the working- and middle-class girls in the study. Indeed, it is fair to say that they are more or less the converse of each other. Basically, the middle-class mothers tend to sanction physical dependency and yet push their daughters hard to be intellectually independent. Conversely, the working-class mothers tend to expect their daughters to be physically self-reliant and are much more willing to tolerate that their daughters are 'little' and therefore 'do not know' about intellectual matters. This is perhaps most starkly expressed in Amanda's case, in which the mother tolerates and sanctions the girl's failure to be able to wipe her bottom after going to the toilet, allows her to be a baby in this respect and yet the same girl has a reading age way above her chronological age, and is pushed by her mother to achieve more. There is a stark contrast between kinds of 'childishness' which are permitted and expected and what counts as adult behaviour.

What are the consequences for the two sets of girls of these demands and assumptions? If we think back to the previous chapter, we will see that the middle-class mothers' mode of regulation related to the intellectualisation of conflict, so that sensitive mothering was achieved by mothers' avoidance of direct confrontation and power and by resorting to intellectualisation and injunctions about their feelings. Thus, the push to intellectualise on the part of these mothers can be understood as something very central to what it means to be in control of your own life as well as to become middle class, to enter the professions. Not only does the world have to be mastered, so do the emotions.

Conversely, the self-reliance demanded by some of the working-class mothers relates to the problems of work and time and to the necessity of the girls getting on by themselves, being physically independent, to allow the mothers space and time to do their domestic work. Their mode of regulation therefore demands and sanctions this kind of independence, just as growing up for these women for the most part means undertaking kinds of physical labour, paid and unpaid. They are women who did not succeed at school, who left with no qualifications and therefore it is not surprising that there is too a sanctioning of their daughters' fears about intellectual work. We will explore this aspect of their 'not knowing' in the next chapter.

How then is the world outside the home, the adult world of being a woman that the girls must grow up to enter, represented by the mother? Is it presented to the daughters as knowable or frightening? What does it mean for each mother to watch her daughter growing up to be a woman like her? How does the mother see herself? While in this data we have no interviews with mothers which explore these issues, what we do have is what they tell their daughters about the world outside and we can extrapolate from that some aspects of their own anxieties. For example, we get instances where working-class mothers get their daughters to rehearse what they would do if they got lost outside the home, to recite their address and so on.

Dawn and her mother are watching the television. There are horses in the TV programme which remind them of a day when the family saw horses in the park. They discuss the events of that day:

C: Big Joe got lost.
M: Did they?
C: Yeah.
M: What did they do?
C: The police take he home.
M: That's why we tell you to stay near me. That's why we tell you to stay near me, don't I?
C: Yeah.
M: Otherwise you'd get lost.

Here, as in the following example, the intervention of the police is noteworthy. Margaret's mother was helping her write her name when the episode became a lesson in survival skills. The mother pushes Margaret to rehearse what she must do if she is in the frightening situation of being lost.

M: What do you say to a policeman? If you're lost.
C: If you're lost.
(———)
M: You tell him your name.
C:Yeah.
M: And what do you tell him?
C: Do your name.
M: No, you don't do your name.
(C laughs.)
M: What do you say to him? Policeman? Mr Policeman, I'm lost.
C: Yeah.
M: And he'll say to you, 'Where do you live?'
C: I says . . .
M: What do you say?
C: What did he say?
M: No! No. (M and C laugh.) Be serious, Margaret. When you . . . when he asks you, 'Margaret, where do you live?'
C: I said I live down by the grass.
M: Down by the grass! You know the address?
C: Yeah.
M: And what do you say to him . . .

C: Um? I've, I said . . .
M: What number house?
C: Um . . . number six.
M: No, you don't live at number six.(———) You say, 'My name is Margaret Johnson.'
C: Yeah.
M: I'm age four.
C: Yeah.
M: And I live at 11a . . .
C: Queen's Park Flats.

The pair continue to practise the address for a while.

M: . . . this is when you're lost. When you get lost.
C: Where?
M: Well, you never know, 'cos you're going down to the beach in the summer, aren't you?

Although this episode is, at times, fun for the child, and she and her mother laugh together when Margaret plays about, her mother nevertheless treats this as a very serious exercise, and one which must be 'got right'. Both Dawn's and Margaret's mothers stress self-reliance, getting the girls to recognise danger (the danger of being alone and away from home) and making sure they know how to get out of this danger. In so doing, Margaret's mother presents the world outside the home as unsafe, a place where you might get lost and have to know, above all else how to reach home again. But they never say what the danger actually is. The object of the lesson is survival, without letting the child *know* the nasty things that can happen to her – from this knowledge she must be saved.

Does the mother herself then regard that world as frightening? She certainly gives that impression and one can envisage the sense of anxiety of the housewife who may be trapped, depressed, at home, but for whom the outside world is infinitely more terrifying. You do not have to master the world but you must know how to get home again. Yet, interestingly, Tizard and Hughes are cautious about the value of such conversations as learning contexts and instead focus on the unease and confusion this particular example provoked in the child.

> Not only has [Margaret] forgotten her flat number, but she now seemed worried by the idea of being lost, and by the possible appearance of a policeman. She found it difficult to grasp the idea that she needed to be told what to say *if* she got lost, and *if* she met a policeman. This confusion seemed to be made worse by her mother's use of 'when', rather than 'if', and it was never finally resolved. (p. 71)

In our view this analysis misses the point. It misses the mother's anxiety and the seriousness of the lesson she has to teach her daughter about growing up. This cannot be reduced to sensitivity but is bound up with the position of the adult women themselves. It may well be that the mother communicates her anxiety to her daughter, but this is an anxiety about her life which cannot simply be wished away by an injunction to be sensitive. After all, these women are for the most part on low-paid part-time work, they have heavy domestic responsibilities and they live on little money in bad housing conditions. The world is a frightening place, and one in which they have to learn to cope. The lessons of coping that they must teach their daughters are not pleasant and it is little wonder that some of them may want to shield their daughters from these facts of life. They communicate fear but rarely tell them what is frightening. They teach them how to cope and survive. But what is the latent content of these manifest meanings? That there are good and bad men in the world outside the safety of home and the mother? That the mother does not want her daughter to grow up and leave her?

Conversely, the middle-class, sensitive mothers can be understood as dealing with their anxiety by intellectualising it. They present to their daughters a world which can be known and mastered, a world which is safe. Their mothers are indeed well-qualified women and yet they are at the bottom of the professional labour market. Those who work do so part time and are exploited as teachers and so forth. All their intellectual endeavours have not allowed them to master the world nor saved them from the contradiction of this independence and the serving of children. Thus, they might present a picture of safety to their daughters, that teachers are like mothers, school like home. But they do not give them the tools with which to cope with the fear and anxiety of oppression. They are expending all their energy in teaching them to intellectualise, as though that were a magic charm that could ward off the struggles they will inevitably have to face in adult life. When the working-class girls leave home, they may become like their mothers or become distant from them by barriers of class. Whereas the middle-class girls may strive either to be like their mothers or to be successful professionals as these women are unable to be. For both groups, then, separation is complex, difficult and different.

Where mothers are chronically constrained by their material circumstances, this has effects on the girls. Seeing their mothers always working, always rushing, never having enough money and so on may make the girls want to remain babies, not want to grow up to be like them, but to be protected from the world of growing up. Gill's mother presents graphically the drudgery which awaits her daughter:

> M: You'll have to do this [darning] when you're bigger.

And Dawn's mother:

> C: Mummy, I doing ironing today.
> M: Yes, when will you be big enough to do all mine?

The pair of 'big girl'/'baby'[11] is often used as a regulative device in the working-class homes, especially in those homes in which the mother appears under a lot of stress to get housework finished at a particular time, and with girls who are especially fractious. The working-class girls more frequently expressed the desire to remain babies than the middle-class girls. This point needs some clarification, as it is also true that the middle-class girls were often likely to display dependence and helplessness, and moreover, to insist that they couldn't achieve some task (usually practical) by themselves. But while the working-class girls more often expressed their wish to be helpless babies, this wish was consistently, although not always successfully, resisted by the working-class mothers. It is these situations that the pair 'big girl'/'baby' is most frequently evoked, though not always in these exact terms.

> M: Nicky, you're not helpless, you're three years old, you can quite, all that go up the stairs and put 'em in yourself.
> C: I can't!
> M: You're not a baby.
> C: I am, I am.
> M: If you wanna act like a baby, Mummy'll treat you like a baby.

To be big, a big girl, is closely linked with growing up, and, characteristically, maturity relates to physicality and self-reliance, not to intellectuality. Being a baby – helpless, wanting to be carried – is not a position which these working-class girls are so easily allowed to occupy.

> M: I'm not touching it, I told you . . . you've got two good legs yourself, go and put it up yourself.

Sometimes, as with Kerry, who is demanding, tired, tearful and helpless for much of the afternoon, mothers attempt to resist the child's dependence by mockingly calling her 'baby'. For example, Kerry wants her mother to give her a piggy-back, but her mother refuses. She cries and climbs onto her mother as she sits down.

> M: Oh, poor little baby, get down.
> C: You won't, you won't carry me.
> M: I've been carrying you for ages.

There is more weariness in her mother's comment 'I've been carrying you for ages' than even she would probably care to admit. This use of 'baby' does relate to regulation, even though, as a strategy, in this case it does not work. Issues about being a helpless baby then also become the site for conflict and resistance.

Jenny wants her mother to carry her downstairs; her mother resists, using the same mocking tactic as Kerry's mother:

> M: Oh, are you a little baby?
> C: No!
> M: Well, come on then.
> C: Will you carry me down?
> M: I only carry babies down. (———) Can't you walk down then?
> C: No.
> M: Baby!

The middle-class girls can occupy a position of physical helplessness because *intellectual* self-reliance is stressed by the mothers. Often the same helpless behaviour that is marked in the working-class transcripts by struggle and resistance is dealt with by the middle-class mothers in quite a different way, one which is not seen as punitive in the same way as a working-class mother refusing to help her daughter get dressed is seen.

For example, Jenny's and Kerry's mothers resist their daughters' demands by teasingly calling them 'baby', a pejorative term. While this strategy is unsuccessful in that it does not curb the girls' demands, the mothers nevertheless do not give in. For the middle-class mothers, however, there is not the same investment in resisting the child's desire to be a baby.

> M: What do you want, darling?
> C: Some of Ribena in the little bottle, some Ribena in the little bottle. (She is given a baby's bottle.)
> M: There you are, baby.

These working-class mothers stress physical independence from the mother. Big girls are girls who can keep out of Mum's way when she is busy, they can play by themselves, go to the toilet by themselves, wash their own hands. They can 'look after themselves' in the home, and learn how to survive in the dangerous world outside. There are also strong elements of nurturance, for big girls look after not only themselves, but others too. This comes up most often in relation to helping Mum and in the care of younger siblings.

Growing up for both sets of girls is about leaving behind a fantasy. The fantasy of the isolated mother and child is exacerbated by the practices we have outlined, particularly the middle-class ones, which stress that mothers can always be there. The fantasy that must be given up therefore is the one that says that you can have the mother all to yourself. We have seen that psychoanalysts such as Winnicott deal with this by the idea of the 'good-enough' mother, the one who is there enough and can therefore deal with the child's frustration. But we have argued that this has simply served to further entrap women. No, the fantasy is presented as real and the pain of the realisation that you cannot have this is difficult. Growing up and away from the home has to be coped with – the terrible, creeping realisation that you will not always be the baby, who can demand so much attention. Fears of replacement emerge too.

Anna is playing fantasy games, parts of which take place in a doll's house. There is a sticker on the house which Anna wants to peel off. Her mother, who has been watching Anna play, says:

> M: Leave it on, 'cos another little girl might have it one day.

Anna's reaction to this comment is very interesting. Despite her mother's reproval, she begins to pull the sticker off. Her mother tells her it's silly to do that and repeats ''cos there might be another little girl that wants it'. *Am I not the only little girl in the world? Am I not* your *only little girl? Won't I always be a little girl?* These are our own interpretations of the possible fears and fantasies lurking beneath Anna's reaction.

How very frightening to have, inevitably, to share with others the one on whom you so depend. Anna certainly resists the idea of her replacement:

> C: No one else won't want it.

Jealousy and growing up

All the girls express fears of growing up, in some form, at some time during the afternoon. Jealousy of older and younger siblings also is a common phenomenon, and is linked to fears about getting older and having to leave the mother. However, jealousy of this kind was generally expressed more frequently and more forcefully by the middle-class girls. Their fears appear very wound up with their chronological position in the family; whether they are the youngest and therefore the baby, or whether there is a younger child, sometimes a new baby, which has displaced them from this privileged position. For all the girls, however, meanings of size terms like 'big', 'little' and 'baby' become signifiers for growing up. So we have many examples where girls' fears of growing up are linked with their physical size.

Teresa wants to try on a coat that is much too small for her. Despite her mother pointing this out, Teresa persists in trying it on.

> M: Too small for you, Teresa.
> C: Can you get it down and see?
> M: No, look, it's too small, you don't like it anyway.
> (M gets the coat down anyway.)
> M: Look at the arms. (Laughs.) It's for a baby. You're a little baby in that.

Nicky wants to wear a particular jumper to nursery school tomorrow, but her mother will not let her:

> M: You're not, it's too small for you. It's Jane's [little sister].
> C: It is not! (Moans.)

This episode quickly turns into an argument. Nicky is clearly jealous of her little sister and insists that the jumper is hers, but eventually concedes to let Jane *borrow* it.

A fairly common occurrence was girls trying to sleep in baby cots or pushchairs, places that were far too small for them to sleep in. Often their mothers tried to resist this but the girls who used these strategies were fairly adamant. Sarah sits in the baby's buggy:

> M: That's a very silly place to lie.
> C: Why?
> M: I mean it's too small.
> (C climbs in the buggy anyway.)

With a small minority of girls, there emerged evidence that they harboured feelings of hatred towards babies; not always their own baby siblings, but other babies that came up in conversation. Their jealousy was also often expressed in *size* terms; either wishing that the baby remain small, or in the case of Julie, actually expressing a death wish towards the child. We would suggest that the slippage from wishing a child to remain small to wishing it *away*, wishing it *dead*, is minimal.

Naomi and her mother are chatting about a family friend who is expecting twins:

> M: We'll have the babies born before Christmas.
> C: No they won't.
> M: They will.
> C: No, no, no, they come out and they be about that size. (Holds out arms.)
> M: Will they?
> C: No, I want to see them small.
> M: You want to see them small? Well, they may. They may be born when they're small. Don't know. Don't want them to be *too* small.
> C: Yeah.
> M: If they're too small, they'll have to stay in hospital to be looked after.

Fear of growing up and having to leave home can be expressed implicitly. In the following extract, Katy and her mother are looking through the kitchen window, watching the birds come to eat the bread they have put out for them.

> M: Look, there's a big bird. (———)
> C: Oh, I like, I like weeny birds and not big birds. (———) Where's baby ones?
> M: Ooh, I don't know.
> C: Oh!
> M: They're probably growing big now.
> C: Oh, can they stay with us?
> M: Dunno, they'll grow big. (———)
> C: Like mummy birds?
> M: Mmm, some of those are mummy birds.
> C: Oh, some is not no mummy birds.

Siblings, fathers and others get in the way of this pleasant dream of remaining the mother's only baby. Intense anxiety is often expressed in the form of jealousy: of wanting to take the place of a baby sibling who demands so much of the mother's time. For some girls, intertwined with giving up this fantasy is the suggestion by the mother that growing up means losing her but that the girl can one day take the mother's place and have a baby of her own. Patsy has a conversation with her mother about babies, during which her resistance to the notion of growing up emerges strongly. In this scene Patsy gets quite angry and in an attempt to cajole her out of this, as well as resist her desire to be the baby, her mother says:

> M: One day you'll have a baby to push yourself then, won't you? When you're big.

We are faced with the importance of emotion and anxiety in what it means to grow up. These meanings are therefore charged with emotion and emotion may indeed be the charge which leads to the creation of new meanings. Elena Lieven (1982) points to such an idea in a study in which Eve first used quite complex time adverbials. Her baby sister was being given a bottle. Eve wanted to take her sister's place and have the bottle herself, to be in the position of the baby. It was in this electric setting that she first used a new grammatical construction. The emotion had pushed her to verbalise. We can speculate that for some children, such a situation might go underground, they might not be able to express the strength of their feeling. Not only did Eve learn a new construction, but she uttered something which allowed articulation of her anxiety.

What is important here is the way in which a traumatic event, fed by jealousy, provokes a move into a different kind of coping with that anxiety: verbalisation. Freud suggested (1920) that an infant could deal with the presence and absence of the mother by vocalising to accompany the pushing and pulling of a cotton reel – '*Fort-Da*', 'here', 'gone' – so the mother's absence could be in some senses controlled. This is one reason why Lacan (1977) used structural linguistics to link language to the forms and meanings of chains of associations. What is important is the way that manifest meanings of the girls and women are linked both to struggles to grow up, as Lieven's example suggests, and back to basic fears, hurts, pains of dealing with dissatisfaction, loss and absence.

Cathy Urwin (1984) suggests that such new utterances also serve to give the child an imaginary fantasy of control over the mother. It is 'imaginary' in the sense that the young child is of course extremely dependent upon its mother, but as in the cotton-reel game, the dependency can be masked by a fantasy game of control. The girls in our study did this kind of thing often, getting their mothers to play at being babies, or telling them off.

Penny is fiddling with the radio and trying to turn it on. Her mother tells her to leave it off.

> C: Now *I'm* a mummy!
> M: Yes, all right.
> C: But I want it on.

Not only are these the taking up of positions, regulative

devices, they are at the same time ways of dealing with anxiety – the anxiety of their dependency. In this sense, regulative power is always related to its counterpoint, powerlessness. The ambivalence and struggles of these little girls and their mothers can be seen in this light.

In this way certain important changes are possible to existing accounts of language and cognitive development, as Urwin points out. These are crucial in relation to the critique of 'sensitive mother' accounts. We noted in Chapter Four that the mother was held responsible by some accounts for interpreting her child's gestures and vocalisations, thus creating meaning 'intersubjectively', through her own sensitivity. These accounts speak of a child trying to express what it needs and a sensitive mother interpreting. We criticised this view of meaning, just as we were critical of an account of cognitive development which saw the child as acting upon its environment, a process of adaptation and cognitive mastery in which the mother became part of the environment.[12] In the account we are proposing, cognitive and linguistic processes are at the same time deeply affective: they relate to strong and deep emotions. Not only this, but the mother does not 'make' meanings for her daughter. Meaning inheres in the discourses, historically defined, which regulate mothering, in the regulative practices, in cultural forms and practices, in which the mothers and daughters find themselves and try to make some sense of their situation. But, the meanings are both social, regulative, ideological and also layered in chains of associations into unconscious fears and ways of dealing with the inevitability of loss – they are the link to fantasy, to psychic reality.

Classical psychoanalysis is utilised in clinical settings, not with the material we are dealing with here. This means that, while it has crucial insights, it could not possibly provide an account of socialisation. Some feminists, for example Jacqueline Rose (1983), have argued that it is quite misplaced to see psychoanalysis as an account of how people are fitted into place. Psychoanalysis deals with trauma, with the failure of consciousness to deal with the everyday. Freud dealt in dreams, slips of the tongue, apparently nonsensical associations. In this sense, what is on the surface, conscious, is not all there is to say. Far from it, the surface shows part of a struggle to deal with the pain and inevitability of growing up. This means that psychoanalysis cannot be an account of effective and 'proper' mothering, as it is a clinical practice which deals with the effect of conscious and unconscious strategies which make us ill. Jacqueline Rose (1983) stresses that therefore psychoanalysis testifies that the socialisation of girls and women does not work, because it is dealing with the failure of socialisation, the resistance of the psyche:

> What distinguishes psychoanalysis from sociological accounts of gender (hence for me the fundamental impasse of Nancy Chodorow's work) is that whereas for the latter, the internalisation of norms is assumed roughly to work, the basic premise and indeed starting-point of psychoanalysis is that it does not. The unconscious constantly reveals the 'failure' of identity. Because there is no continuity of psychic life, so there is no stability of sexual identity, no position for women (or men) which is ever simply achieved. Nor does psychoanalysis see such 'failure' as a special case, inability or an individual deviancy from the norm. 'Failure' is not a moment to be regretted in a process of adaptation, or development into normality, which ideally takes its course [. . .]. Instead 'failure' is something endlessly repeated and relived moment by moment throughout our individual histories [. . .] viewed in this way, psychoanalysis is no longer best understood as an account of how women are fitted into place [. . .]. Instead psychoanalysis becomes one of the few places in our culture where it is recognised as more than a fact of individual pathology that most women do not painlessly slip into their roles as women.

Most accounts of little girls growing up *are* accounts of socialisation. They assume that the processes work and that the girls are stereotyped into roles. This is partly because of a kind of assumed empiricism. You read the *surface* (the manifest content) of the observations of these little girls and their families, their homes and their schools, and you see with much empirical clarity 'socialisation going on'. Empirical psychology and sociology then use socialisation approaches to posit cause and effect. As we have seen, psychology is fond of using statistics to tell the truth, to find the norm, to look for the cause. Psychoanalysis makes such an empiricist, surface reading impossible. Socialisation, if it is ever achieved at all, is a struggle. It is that struggle that we have tried to begin to chart in this chapter.

We need, however, to add to Rose's account. She implies that socialisation does not work, but the inevitability of the failure of identity can be overstressed or too simplistically stated. That 'failure' is lived as difference and difference as pathology. Women are consistently positioned as lacking, as abnormal, and this has great and painful effect in their insertion into practices which regulate them, as we shall see in Chapter Ten. The gender and class divisions cannot easily be crossed. This is why we need an account which understands what Bhabha describes as the stereotype within discursive practices. We will see that when girls go to school, these fantasies are put into practice, since in the classroom there is usually something found to be wrong with them. We will examine these issues more closely in the next two chapters, exploring how the mother is held responsible for preparation for her daughter's schooling and its success, and what happens to these girls when they are at school.

CHAPTER NINE

HAVING THE KNOWLEDGE

The mother is often held responsible for the educational success of her children. By producing the correct early environment, she is to allow them to 'separate' from her. This separation then paves the way for independence and autonomy which is taken to lead to educational success. We have stressed that separation, leaving home, involves entering a world of difference, division, Otherness, which cannot easily be crossed, and that theories of separation hold the mother responsible while failing to deal with these issues. The fact that leaving home is difficult, painful and different for the different groups of girls is something we wish to explore here. Their mothers are set up as guarantors of a certainty which, in practice, it is impossible for them to produce.

The 1950s and the post-war democracy

The 'sensitive mother' as a strategy of regulation became, in the 1950s, a way of producing as natural the truth of a liberal social democracy. In Britain, the post-war Labour Party opted for a strategy of 'equal opportunities' through education, rather than a policy of equality.[1] While the organisation of the welfare state is certainly not to be lightly criticised in the era of its dismantling by Thatcherism, nevertheless there is a way in which Britain's liberalism produced a humane state as a latter-day form of charity. If the USA adopted a strategy of 'making it', Britain provided access to the bourgeoisie for those with the 'aptitude' and 'intelligence'.

The introduction of a meritocracy meant that the eradication of class divisions was now to be accomplished by allowing certain 'bright' working-class children into grammar schools. Evolutionary biology had been used to talk of both heredity and adaptation to environment. Clearly, there was much impetus to stress what could apparently be changed – the environment – over what could not. As we have argued in Chapter Two, ideas about instincts were out of favour, replaced by ethology. We have shown how this line of study led directly to maternal behaviour as the thing to be changed.

More and more it became the private domain, the home and essentially the mother which was to ensure the upward mobility of working-class children. The onus was on the working class to demonstrate that they could put right the 'lack' in themselves which was blocking their route, through education to upward mobility, to a place in the bourgeoisie.

Denise Riley (1983a) looks at how nursery provision was argued for throughout the war years on the basis of 'relieving the tired mother' and upholding the ideologically powerful conception of the 'free mother'. It is not surprising that the opposition 'freedom'/'oppression' was used, for the effects of the recent world war on political ideology were inevitably great. British mothers and children had to be free from the tyranny of an oppressive state.[2] The hope of the future, they must be able to experience that freedom of spirit which is, the nation was told, the right of every individual. For mothers, this liberation could be facilitated by easing the financial and emotional drudgery of childbirth and child care. Thus emerged campaigns for contraception, better obstetric practices, and nurseries for working-class women.

In the post-war years the retention of nurseries was argued for but the rationale for this had shifted considerably. Previous rhetoric about tired mothers became arguments about the inadequacies of mothers to 'mother'. Nursery provision was to become a site for badly needed re-education for such incompetence. 'Help' and 'training' went hand in hand:

> We cannot afford not to have the nursery school: it seems to be the only agency capable of cutting the slum mind off at its root and building the whole child while there is yet time. ('Our Towns', report from Hygiene Committee of Women's Group on Public Welfare, Quoted in Riley, 1983a)

This sort of sentiment came from conservative and social-democratic philosophies alike. Fabian humanists took a strong line in nurseries as schools for mothers, stressing nutrition, cleanliness and physical education, such was the strength of the rejection of the notion of heredity by liberal, humanist and social-democratic thought in explaining working-class failure. Heredity arguments fed right into the implicit fear of a working-class uprising by supporting ideas about the inevitability of conflict. Social-democratic thought was more concerned to work on the premise that revolution was not inevitable, that something *could* be done. What could be done was to educate the masses.

Working within an environmentalist framework, the Labour Party of the post-war years set out to attack deprivation. Fabian and Labour ideologies were actively struggling to build a truly meritocratic society, to 'help' those whose home and community life disabled them from entering fully into the meritocratic process. Education became the principal route through which the state could claim that it was 'fair'. The post-war meritocratic sociology demonstrated that the advantage of middle-class pupils over working-class pupils in gaining grammar-school places remained intact.[3] J.W.B. Douglas's 'Home and School' study placed the mother as central guarantor, as pedagogue, of the success (getting to grammar school) of working-class children. His account also documented that children who succeeded tended to have mothers who were better educated than average:

> In ambitious working-class households it is not unusual to find that the mother comes from a middle-class family and supplies the drive and incentive for her children to do well at school. (1964, p. 42)

In this influential study, Douglas positions mothers as the main key to the transition to primary school as well as later success in selection examinations. The mother is central to fostering educable and educationally successful children.

> We know that for many young children it is the early contacts with their mothers that are likely to have the greatest influence on learning, and at later stages too, it is often the mother who is more concerned than the father with school problems, and has the closest contact with the teachers. (p. 43)

Throughout Douglas's work he upholds a notion of 'the family' as underpinning educational success. Attitudes towards education and child-rearing practices are what make middle-class children succeed:

> His (*the child's*) own attitude to his work will be moulded by theirs (*the parents'*), and if they are ambitious for his success, he will have the further advantage of home tuition in reading and probably other subjects. (p. 43, our emphasis)

Failure in working-class families can only be attributed to a lack of these attitudes and practices. Parents (read mothers) who know or come to realise the value of education will consistently encourage their children's progress at school, as well as become pedagogues at home.

From Douglas's work subcultural theories emerged in the 1950s: this large body of work focused on working-class 'subcultures' (by their very name viewed as essentially sub-standard).[4] Thus the notion of 'culture' arose from work on the family and community. The physical environment was simply not enough to explain continuing working-class failure.[5] After all, something was being done about this. Research within this area came to incorporate analyses of the 'values' and 'norms' of different social classes, and in the USA of different ethnic and social groups.[6] Working-class culture was found wanting (as was black culture in the United States): it was deprived.

Norman L. Friedman (1976) traces the development of the idea of cultural deprivation and notes that the ideas which were to make up the popularly grasped notion of the 'culturally deprived child' were first stated in 1955 at an American Psychological Association conference (three years before Harlow's presidential address on 'love') with particular reference to New York children. Failing children within the low-income sections of the city were said to have low self-conceptions, experienced feelings of guilt, shame, distrust and most important 'emotional deprivation'. The solution to these problems was packaged in programmes of 'cultural enrichment' for these children. By the 1960s a further twist was introduced in the form of the importance of pre-school years (critically three to four years). Douglas, too, attaches much importance to these pre-school years, concluding that middle-class children receive greater attention and stimulus from their parents, and attributing 'many of the major differences in performance to environmental influences arising in the pre-school years' (1964, p. 42).

These conclusions then are echoed in the 1950s and early 1960s, although by this time, the 'environment' had become the 'culture'. In the American discourse on cultural deprivation, those same early years were increasingly viewed as the time when enrichment could be most effective. The aim was to work out ways in which to get working-class pre-school children to develop in the same way as middle-class children, or those who were culturally privileged. The theme by the 1960s within the deprivation accounts was within a developmental framework. Not so much emphasis on reading, or indeed any other 'subject' as such, but rather on experience, learning and discovery – the true basis for development within a Piagetian model. However, the idea of reading has returned and is now firmly secured with PACT schemes[7] in many primary schools in Britain.[8]

There has been a vast literature on the concept of deprivation.[9] The work of Tizard and Hughes falls within this framework. Yet, by stressing 'equal but different', or the 'wealth of working-class culture', it is impossible, as we have argued, to engage with oppression.

Throughout all work on education, there is an underlying 'them' and 'us' theme, underpinned at least partially by a fear of working-class uprising. It is this fear which gave rise to the IQ debates, the environment arguments, debates on good mothering practices. All these things focus on different sites at which it might be possible to allay the fears: mothers, the family, the community. The transition from home to school is basically about or based on the notion that 'they' will be entering into 'our' world – obviously a difficult stage for the children to progress through. This concern is only limited to the difficulty which working-class children experience. Or is it? Does anyone talk about how difficult middle-class children find the move from home to school?

Thus we have a profoundly unfair and unjust social order which treats inequality and oppression as an effect of 'intelligence' (if you had it you could become middle class, 'succeed') and naturalises inequality as a just system. On top of this, it lands mothers with the guilt of failing to produce a proper environment (the 80 per cent of the 80/20 heredity/environment couple)[10] for development which would lead to educational success. Class then becomes naturalised, as though we all could potentially be middle class with the right brains and the right mothers. In addition to this, women teachers are burdened with guilt. They simultaneously blame parents for children's failure (see Chapter Ten) and blame themselves, since the other fiction is that 'correct development' could be ensured through adequate knowledge and monitoring of each child. Hence pedagogy props up the meritocratic fantasy – this 'could' be possible, if we could only get development right.

How then, if you were working class in the 1950s or subsequent periods, were you to understand what was happening? We were both working-class girls who went to grammar schools. How were we to deal with parents who in the face of our success protested their stupidity, who naturalised and legitimated their own pain and the brutality of their lives? How were we to cope with our class and culture being read consistently back to us as bad and stupid. How were we to avoid seeing ourselves as 'special', and others, our parents, brothers and sisters, as ignorant and stupid? How were we to deal with the terrible price to be paid for entry into the bourgeoisie – the loss of home, for a life on the margins, never belonging anywhere, except as professional carers, 'helping' somebody else's children?

It is not only this. We felt constantly that this was supposed to be our 'right' (free meals, uniforms). But these things were handed out to us as though it were charity, and we were made always to be grateful for those offerings, to be grateful for being chosen to leave our class, in this disgusting and oppressive (but oh so helpful) system. And of course we wanted out. As we said in Chapter Two, this constructed our dreams, we believed the stories. We wanted to marry the prince, wear fine clothes and live in a big house. We almost bought the dream, almost but not quite. Always, underneath, there was the silenced pain screaming to be spoken, with no discourse for its enunciation except pathology.

Equal opportunities and gender

The failure of working-class children to become upwardly mobile led to the stress on the mother at home. Inequality, oppression or exploitation do not feature in these accounts of how failure is produced, but an unsupportive, unstable home life is seen as the cause. Something, in other words, is taken to have gone wrong before the child ever gets to school. It is early socialisation which was and is held responsible. Later, when attention turned to gender and women's entry into non-traditional careers in the 1970s, the selfsame arguments were used. That is, girls and women were failing to enter traditionally masculine professions and the cause for this failure was also to be found in the home.[11]

The impact of the women's movement in the 1970s meant that a similar meritocratic discourse of equal opportunities was brought in to quell the talk of women's oppression. Where in the 1950s mothers were held responsible for the mobility of working-class boys, so in the 1970s mothers began to be held responsible for the early socialisation of their daughters. A similar meritocracy held off the threat of feminism by incorporating a liberal vision that women could gain access to the power and status of men, be like men in fact, if they were afforded entry through education. Much educational work has sought to prop up the system in this way and has had recourse to socialisation arguments to do so.

So, here too, as we have seen in Chapter Eight, feminist work condoned a version of a socialisation account, based on mother–daughter bonding, which held the mother responsible for the later educational and occupational possibilities of her daughter by stressing that environmentalist empiricism of cause and effect. It was still common to assert or to imply that working-class mothers were again the worst, most stereotyped, with the most rigid roles, thereby confirming this, conveniently, as the reason it was harder for working-class girls to gain mobility and entry into non-traditional class and gendered occupations.

In addition to the above arguments, there was another source of emphasis on the mother during the 1970s. This period saw the burgeoning of work on language development, which began to place language and literacy also at the hands of the mother. Educational success became linguistic development – and this was produced by the mother. In the words of the Bullock Report, mothers were advised, 'when you give your child a bath, bathe him in language'.[12]

What we want to explore here is the idea that the working-class mother is seen as lacking. Frequently, working-class parents are held up by primary schools as 'getting it wrong'.

They do not 'understand children's needs' and are either blamed for not helping their children or for doing it in the wrong way. They teach them sums instead of letting them explore concepts, they buy the wrong books and toys. The whole discourse of parental involvement assumes that teachers must teach parents (almost always mothers) how to prepare and help their children in the right ways. The target is, almost always, black and white working-class parents. There is no sense of listening to and learning from the parents – for they are already defined as wrong and reactionary.[13]

But the working-class mother who 'lacks' also knows a lot, as we have seen. She, like Margaret's mother, implies that the world is frightening and how to get home. She prepares her for the world as she sees it, but this is a frightening lesson and not a cosy reassurance. Often, then, the working-class girls acquire at school knowledge which their mothers do not have. They read books, sing songs, do work that is unfamiliar to these women. The middle-class mothers 'know'. They often have the books at home and therefore present to their daughters a sense of safety and similarity of home and school. Most of the middle-class mothers seemed much more familiar with the discourse on learning of the nursery school, knowing the methods used to teach the alphabet, for example. This was sharply contrasted to working-class women, who seemed puzzled by, and even resistant to, the 'new ways of learning'.

Sally's mother attempts to get Sally to do a 'real' lesson where she actually 'teaches' her the 'correct' art of writing, exactly what she is not supposed to do. She writes SALLY at the top of a page and asks Sally to copy the letters.

> M: You try and copy that.
> C: No!
> M: Underneath, you do it underneath.
> C: I want to do see . . . (Mumbles.)

Sally's mother knows how the nursery school approaches writing – they get the children to trace over the letters, rather than copy them. But she does not want the child to do it like that and so she pushes her to do it *her* way.

> M: Not over the top of it. Not like you do at school, you do it by yourself, underneath. You try and copy it.
> C: Can't. (Sally makes a scribble.)

The entire episode is punctuated by the child's resistance to her mother's way of teaching. She often says she 'can't do it', thereby resisting her mother's attempts to introduce a different practice. There exists then a strong tension between school practice and what the mother considers to be real pedagogic practice. Eventually and begrudgingly, Sally complies with the lesson, but then only to reject her mother's help.

> M: Put a little bump.
> C: *I'm* doing it.

We could understand this as the child's struggle to be independent from the mother, to strive for intellectual independence through 'confident challenge'. But her rejection must also be bound up with what she perceives as her mother's lack of knowledge. Sally must gain control of the lesson, because as far as she's concerned her mother has made it clear that she does not know what is right.

The working-class women are therefore rendered powerless and this gives their daughters considerable power, as in the case of Nicky, who has to teach her mother the songs she learned at nursery school.

> C: I will tell you mine.
> M: You help me. You gotta help me.
> C: Come on then.
> M: 'Cos I never learned that one at school.

This might be a powerful lesson for Nicky. She, like many working-class girls, is picked out as 'clever' and 'knowing' at the age of ten and it gives her considerable status, which will be quite important to her. But to see it only in this way suppresses another aspect: that is, the pain of the gap, the widening chasm of difference between the girl and her mother, a difference which the mother seems powerless to rectify. The mother 'lacks', she does not have the knowledge and this must be very painful to many little girls. Her knowledge is stupid, wrong, pathological and it is therefore no knowledge at all. We suggest that the problems of 'separation', of going to school, leaving home and growing up, are, in the literature, totally conflated with insensitivity. This is not a hopeless mother, but a powerless one. It suggests power, difference and the pain of splitting as opposed to the safe and cosy transition much beloved in the developmental literature.

However, we should not give the impression that everything in the middle-class garden is lovely. The 'sensitive mother' account also belies the fact that middle-class girls may not make the cosy transition to autonomy spelled out in the literature.[14] Many ten-year-old middle-class girls are terribly anxious. What in all that security could have produced such anxiety? Sensible girls are rational: they have been pushed to achieve and to hide and gloss over that pain and anxiety of growing up, of transforming their terrifying emotions.

The early years of childhood and the difficulty of the transitional period between home and school have been highlighted as one of the main areas of concern for educationalists. Failure is accounted for by the inadequacy of mothers to meet 'needs' and by the subcultural and culturally deprived experience of the working-class child. But just how valid is it to talk about transition to school in these terms? The 'gap' which the mother is central in bridging is a cultural one. The chasm between middle- and working-class children is about *experience*. Middle-class children, so the story goes, have culturally enriched childhoods; they experience at home the joy of learning, of development. Their thirst for knowledge and discovery is quenched and yet at the same time heightened by the sensitive mother who allows and helps them to experience and crave for mastery.

> She is a very ordinary little girl . . . the things within her scope are not the things of the more intelligent children . . . she's got a nice home, don't get me wrong, but it's a very ordinary home . . . her idea of going out is to go shopping and to go out for tea. She doesn't get taken to anything stimulating . . . She's that kind of good, conscientious girl, but not brilliant.

This is said about Maureen, a working-class girl, by her class teacher when she is ten. Her father is a foreman in a factory, her mother a cleaner and they live in a terraced house with a back yard. But what is important for her teacher, in the psychoeducational discourse she uses, is bourgeois culture. The teacher unproblematically equates brilliance with 'getting taken to anything stimulating', not shopping, teas out, or nice homes. Immediately any happiness the child might feel in such outings is denigrated, and the parents' attempt to provide a 'nice home' is presented as nothing, for nothing, it seems, short of bourgeois culture is capable of lifting her out of being good and conscientious into brilliance. In teachers' comments the bourgeois culture of museums, galleries, music and so on is often equated with brightness.

Many working- and middle-class girls expressed intense fears of school, relating it strongly to growing up and leaving the home. In the following extract, Jacky has gone along with her mother to take her older sister back to school after lunch. When they return, Jacky plays with her doll. Quite out of the blue she voices her fears about going to school in a fantasy episode.

> C: She's sick, Mummy.
> M: Pardon?
> C: She's sick.
> M: Sick? What's the matter then?
> C: She can't go to school.
> M: Mmm?
> C: 'Cos she's sick – again.
> M: Oh, poor old thing.
> C: She not big enough.

M: Isn't she? I thought you said she wasn't well.
C: No, she not well.
M: Oh dear.

It is interesting that Jacky's original rationale for why the doll cannot go to school is that she's ill, and then changes to that she is not 'big enough'. Of course, illness and small size are powerful ways of remaining dependent and therefore not facing the difficulties of having to grow up.

Penny is playing a fantasy game with her mother. She pretends she is a mother also, with children. Penny asks her mother what she's been doing.

M: Taken my little girl to school.
C: Who?
M: Penny.
C: Yes, what . . .
M: She likes it at school now.
C: Does she?

Penny's mother uses this conversation to bring up the issue of school. By her comment 'she likes it at school *now*', we get the impression that Penny may well have experienced some difficulty in making the transition to nursery school. However, the sense of resolution of this initial problem is not so clear-cut.

M: How's your little girl getting on?
C: Um, all right.
M: Does she go to school now?
C: Um, yes, the same school.
M: That's nice, does she like it?
C: Yes, she just, she just started on um, Wednesday. It's not Wednesday today.
M: Ooh, that's nice.
(———)
C: She doesn't go to playgroup.
M: No.
C: So she thought she would, um, go school every day.
M: Oh, I see.

C: Well, um, she doesn't want to go, grow bigger, so she can't.
M: She doesn't want to grow bigger? No.
C: She 'cos, she want to stay at the same school.

This example shows clearly how the issue of school, of leaving the home, is undeniably a site of struggle for the child. The transition is difficult – that cannot be overstated. But for Penny, a middle-class girl, as well as for Jacky, a working-class girl, the root of that fear seems to lie in making the transition from a baby who can lay almost complete claim to her mother for five or six hours a day, who can enjoy the intimacy and ownership of her mother as a *dependent* child, to an independent big girl, one who must leave the home, and with that leaving, she will lose much power through dependency. She must grow up, grow *big*.

Susan and her mother are talking about something else altogether when Susan pipes up:

C: I, I, you got, I'm not gonna school.
M: Aren't you? Oh, all right.
C: I can't go to school.
M: Why?
C: 'Cos I don't like schools.

Still a few others seem quite happy about the whole idea. Gill seems to welcome the idea of her mother going out to work, even when the mother tells her that she can only do this after Gill goes to primary school:

C: Mummy when . . . when will you go to work?
M: When you go to school.
C: I already go to school.
M: You only go in the mornings.
C: Mum, no, you mean when I go to big schools?
M: Yeah. When you go to the big school with Mary. If I can get a job. Why? Do you want me to go to work?
C: Yeah.
(———)

M: I wouldn't be here to cook your dinner if I went to work.
C: Doesn't matter.

No longer can we afford to view the 'difficult transition' in the same light, to see it as predominantly a working-class problem, born out of deprivation and a lacking, inadequate mother. These constructs belie the immense complexity of working-class children's failure and at the same time explain it away, make it not 'ours' but 'their' problem. By pathologising working-class culture, working-class mothers, a particular, historically produced 'norm' can remain intact. The working-class girls of this study, even at four (and certainly by ten) are *failing* compared to the middle-class girls. But they are not deprived, their mothers are not inadequate or pathological (though we have shown how they are patholo*gised*).

School is a frightening place, and not only for little girls. As we have shown, there is for working-class mothers a 'gap' between the home and the nursery school in terms of knowledge, a gap much less marked for the middle-class mothers who 'know' the world of school. The gap has been filled, or so they tell us, by a culturally enriched experience facilitated by a sensitive, nurturant mother. Middle-class girls then should have no problems, should they? Middle-class children may not be 'failing' educationally, but their success in no way means that they do not find the transition just as difficult. They too are just as afraid of leaving home, of growing up.

Our evidence suggests that the transition for middle-class girls may be only partly bridged by the mother's knowledge of the school pedagogy as well as (not unproblematically) her own experience of education. Often, in stark contrast to an easy familiarity with educational discourses, we witness the working-class parents' fear of school: of how it was an unhappy time in their own childhood, punctuated by failure.[15]

In Chapter Eight we criticised the view that mother–daughter bonding created the possibility of an independent girl who gradually separated from her mother to full autonomous status. We argued that girls do not leave their mothers to nothing, that patriarchal culture is not so easily banished. When a girl leaves the safety of her mother's arms, where does she go? Many have argued that school is a place where phallocentric knowledge (what Lacan and others call the 'Logos') is produced. Going to school then is not simply a place where autonomous girls can skip happily towards independent and fully fledged entry into social democracy. The 'big school' is a place where new meanings are created, new associations linking to old meanings in tortuous and complex ways. The meanings through which schools understand and identify pupils draws heavily on precisely the same naturalistic discourses which define mother and child. These discourses are heavily gendered. Here, then, the girls are to meet the full force of sexual difference as they are classified, not as good or poor pupils, but as good and poor, working- and middle-class white *girls*. There is no easy autonomy, no simple crossing over the gender divide thanks to the sensitive mother holding the safety net over the chasm below.

CHAPTER TEN

SCHOOL GIRLS

The girls at ten

When they were four, all the girls in this study were paired so that there was at least one working-class and one middle-class girl in the same nursery school. By the age of ten only one of the original pairs, Julie and Patsy, remained in the same junior school. Five of the middle-class girls attended preparatory schools in the Girls' Public Day School Trust. The sample, apart from this, had become much more split along class lines. Basically, while the areas from which the sample had been drawn when the girls were four contained a mixture of working- and middle-class families, private owner-occupied and rented housing and public housing, by the time they were ten class differences in location had increased dramatically. The working-class families still lived in the same kind of housing, even if they had moved location, like for example the family which had left London for a council house on a new town estate. The middle-class families, by comparison, had been far more mobile. Apart from those whose increase in living standards had allowed them to pay for their daughters' education, one had moved to live in Switzerland and others had moved to better and more expensive accommodation. This is not surprising. Professional career patterns mean that parents in professions enter a long career ladder and even women returning to professional work, although treated badly, would be likely to earn far more than their working-class counterparts. In other words, the gap between the standards and lifestyles of the two groups had widened.

More dramatic and depressing was the huge gap in educational attainment between the two groups of girls. The attainment of all the working-class girls (and other boys and girls in the same year at their school) was very poor compared with that of the middle-class girls and their classmates. We have described how the responsibility for the academic attainment of working-class children has been laid at the door of their mothers. We have also argued that sensitivity has been posited as the basis of greater equality through the medium of greater equality of opportunity. Yet, from looking at the girls when they are ten, it is distressingly evident that 'sensitivity' is no such guarantee.

Some of the attainment figures for the different schools highlight the performance gap and demonstrate the complexity of the link between the psychic and the social.[1] Some of the working-class girls were doing well compared with their classmates, they were highly regarded by their teacher and thought well of themselves. They believed themselves to be clever and good at their work. They also had high expectations. Yet, if we compare their performance with that of the middle-class girls, often with lower self-esteem, it is like comparing chalk and cheese. It will be many times harder for such girls to attain professional careers than their middle-class counterparts. They are likely to experience pain and frustration at best, because of the struggle they will have to face in relation to their ambitions. Methodologically, this is important. It is quite common for large surveys of attainment to ignore data such as the position of the child in class and the teacher's estimate in favour of national comparisons. But this completely skews the picture, which emerges as far more complex and disturbing when it is recognised that many working-class girls are doing well in comparison with their classmates and appallingly badly when compared with middle-class pupils.

The highest attainment was to be found in the public schools and in those state schools in upper-middle-class areas which were effectively regarded as state preparatory schools, feeding the nearby public schools.

Rank order of school means[2]

(p) = private

Test scores	*Middle class*	*Working class*
124.48	Emily (p)	
119.08	Samantha (p)	
117.34	Helen	
116.25	Naomi	
115.91	Charlotte (p)	
112.44	Gill	
112.24	Penny	
112.15	Liz	
111.50	Amanda (p)	
108.36		Jacky
108.12		Jenny
106.65		Maureen
106.65		Teresa
104.70		Nicky
104.11		Susan & Katy
102.08	Diana	
101.97	Angela	
101.37		Anna
98.85	Julie	Patsy
96.64		Kerry
94.87		Dawn
92.15		Sally

Nicky and Dawn are two working-class girls who at four were said to have fairly insensitive mothers. Their respective relationships with their mothers were judged (by Tizard and Hughes) to be fraught with wrangles and disputes. Bowlby would probably have found their mothers egocentric, the Newsons might have accused them of not being concerned enough about fostering autonomy and 'good' feelings in their daughters. We could expect to find these two girls at ten failing dismally at school. This is not the case. Both girls are doing well within their classes and schools. Their teachers evaluated them highly, as did the girls themselves. But there is a large sting in the tail of this 'happy ending' from an unhappy start. For while the girls are positioned as 'good' in their own schools, and their performance is better than that of their classmates, their scores, when viewed in relation to the scores of the rest of the sample schools, present quite a different picture. For while Nicky is ranked by her teacher as among the top in maths, and described as an 'ideal pupil', her score actually places her as only average when compared on a wider scale. Dawn's position is much more worrying. She came among the top three in her class in the test, completely fulfilling the teacher's expectations of her; she regarded Dawn as one of her top children, and evaluated her all-round performance extremely positively. However, Dawn's position in relation to the rest of the sample bears no real comparison. She is, all of her class are, performing appallingly when compared in this way. So badly that the top score for her class was the lowest in the sample at 103, lower than the *bottom* scores of two of the private schools.

The situation of girls like Dawn cannot be encompassed within a cosy 'equal but different' explanation. She is not equal at all and her difference, effectively her class position, is not going to be changed by a rhetoric which attempts to value 'working-class culture' as if exploitation and oppression simply did not exist. The discourse of Equal Opportunities is here held out to be a chimera. Only massive changes in the British education system would make it possible for her to do anything other than fail and become one more figure in the ridiculous self-fulfilling prophecy of the attainment of working-class pupils.

Conversely, how are girls like Patsy and Katy produced as 'having no ability', when they, of all the working-class girls, had, according to the developmental literature, the brightest futures, a head start, because of their sensitive mothers? Given this insight, how can we now judge their performance so simply?

Selection practices formulated during the post-war period were aimed at siphoning off the bright working-class children. This was the upward road to social mobility, but it was a road open only to boys, and one which led away from home. It had to lead away from home because it was the poor environment of that home that held them back in the first place, kept them sinking in the 'pool of wasted talent'. Through a rhetoric of 'equality of opportunity' many promises were made. Selection as the way of catching this talent came to be frowned upon by the philosophy of progressivism. But selection at eleven was not forfeited by many education authorities, who kept their tripartite systems intact, paying only lip service to the new god. From the data on these ten-year-old girls, it is painfully clear that, if selection at eleven is based on the sorts of tests we gave to them (and it is), very few working-class girls could even *enter* the competition against the middle-class girls: they are complete non-starters. In some of the working-class schools, the children had rarely, if ever, taken such a test; they were confused by both the procedure and content of the tests. These children, not surprisingly, did worst in relation to the rest of the schools. Contrast this with the public schools, where the girls were familiar with testing as a classroom practice, and even laughed at the easiness of it.

What we wish to explore now is what it means to be a 'school girl' by examining the definitions of these girls and their classmates by their class teachers. We examined how teachers in all the schools categorised the academic performance of girls and boys. Although not asked to make gender differentiations, the teachers' judgements were highly gender-differentiated in all schools.

In the middle-class schools the teachers consistently used terms such as 'natural ability' to describe the top pupils, but these terms were rarely used to describe girls. Even girls who were doing very well indeed, both in terms of the test score and the teacher's rating, were rarely described in such terms. Sometimes words like 'flair' would be used, but it was far more common for the teachers to describe even high-ranking girls as 'hard-working'. This was used in such a way as to render it as an opposition to 'ability' and 'flair'. In other words, it had pejorative connotations, as for example in the following quotation, where a classmate of Diana's is said to be a 'very, very hard worker. Not a particularly bright girl . . . her hard work gets her to her standards.' Take the teacher's comments about Diana herself: 'Technically she's very good, and creatively she has the ideas . . . she's not outstanding, no . . . but always does her best.' This phenomenon, of 'downgrading' the 'quality' of girls' good performance because it is viewed as not being produced in the right way, is extremely common.[3] It is common within child-centred discourses and early mathematics education to contrast the 'old ways' of hard work and following rules with the new concepts of development, activity and discovery.[4] This view has serious implications. It suggests that any child who is seen to be working *must* be lacking in 'ability' or 'flair' – the qualities which must apparently produce good attainment without effort or work.[5]

Its effect is fairly devastating for the girls in our study. We have already seen that many of the middle-class mothers pushed their daughters to intellectualise to a very high degree, but here we are presented with girls who, for the most part, are succeeding in the education system, and yet there is taken to be something wrong with their work. It will come as little surprise then that the majority of the middle-class girls themselves are very anxious that their performance is not good enough, an anxiety that most of the teachers seem not to see. How then can it be the case that girls who were brought up to be independent, rational thinkers, the independence and autonomy supposed to be produced by sensitive mothering, are now categorised as 'hard-working', a term which implies a failure in almost all the girls to display the very characteristics their upbringing was supposed to produce?

Angela, a middle-class girl, scores the top mark in her class. When asked, she has a clear idea of why she ranks her classmates as she does, putting emphasis on the amount of work they do, and thus how many 'right' answers they get, making the connection between effort and attainment clear. Angela's teacher, however, draws a distinction between hard workers and those with flair, when talking of Angela herself:

'If she comes across something new it needs to be explained to her whereas some of these will just be able to read what they're to do and do it . . .' Angela does quite well, then, but she is certainly not 'brilliant': 'She's very hard-working, very quiet.' Angela is positioned classically as a 'good girl' and 'ideal pupil', but she does not have that elusive gift, 'brilliance' – she must rely on hard work. What has happened here? When Angela was four years old we saw how 'sensitive' her mother was. She is an articulate child, and at nursery school was one of the few children who found it easy to chat away to the teachers. Why then at ten, even though she is outstanding in her class (surely coming top is an indication of achievement), is she designated a quiet, shy girl who only comes top through sheer hard work?

While almost all teachers in working-class schools also described high-achieving girls as hard-working, most of them viewed it as a positive phenomenon. In other words, for most of these teachers it did not have the pejorative connotations it had for the middle-class teachers. Hard work was highly valued. And it is noteworthy that the high-achieving working-class girls did not display the anxiety about the inadequacy of their performance present for the majority of the middle-class girls. This may have been partly because the standard of attainment was overall much lower in the working-class schools, and the girls who were doing well were more likely to be picked out as 'good'. It may also be because their position as 'helpers' is constantly reaffirmed, by the teachers and other children. Working-class girls whose performance is poor, and even those who are 'average', often refer to 'helping' as an attribute of those girls who came top of the class, and will often put themselves in the position, not of helper, but of needing help. For instance Sally, who is performing quite well, says of the girl she ranks as among the top in her class: 'Um, like if you can't do something you can always go to her because she'll help you.' While only a couple of the ten middle-class girls who were top in their classes talk about 'helping', the issue of who helps and who needs help emerges as a recurring theme with *most* of the working-class girls, who also *put themselves forward* as helpers. Talking of a classmate Dawn says: 'Sometimes she does need help, but she always asks me for it . . . Most people ask me.' Even girls who do not promote themselves as helpful are said to be so by the teacher and this is highly evaluated. For instance, Anna's teacher sits her deliberately next to a poorly achieving girl because she knows Anna will 'help and be kind' to this girl.

Another term which was used to refer to girls of both classes was 'mature'. This turned out to be quite an ambiguous term, meaning different things; some meanings are pejorative. On the positive side, mature girls have a good, a 'mature' attitude towards their work. They are well behaved, they settle down quickly and quietly to their work. They may not abound with confidence, but this, in girls, can be an asset. For example, Maura is said to be 'very mature and understanding . . . and does her best all round in her work generally . . . She is never pushy. She's not overconfident . . . That's part of her whole charm . . .' Dawn is 'very good, she's very mature and if you give her some information and say "go away and find out about it", she'll do it, even though she doesn't perhaps understand.' Penny is, 'umm, quite mature really in her attitude to her work . . . But she's mature in her attitude to life as well really. She's totally organised.'

Maturity also signifies aspects of the good girls' positions in relation to their classmates and their teachers. Being 'kind', 'considerate and helpful', they can also, whether of their own volition or because they are called upon to do so, become sub-teachers. But being a mature girl can carry other, more pejorative meanings. There is a curious double-edged element in the perceived maturity of some girls. That is, mature girls may mislead us into thinking that they have an ability which is not really there. For instance, Jenny is 'quite big for her age and because she's able to talk and hold very good conversations with adults, I think we tend to believe she is capable of more than she really is.' The slippage is greater here, the meaning of 'mature' has shifted again. Here it refers specifically to Jenny's physical maturity and her apparently adult articulateness. It does not describe her work habits or position as a good girl. But her mature demeanor only fools the teacher. Conversely, when we take the same characteristics in a boy in this class, they are read in a completely opposite way. Rather than overestimating the boy's 'real' ability, his apparent lack of maturity indicates for this teacher his hidden potential; he is really 'not achieving as much as he could'.

Generally, boys were very rarely said to be mature, rather their 'immaturity' was often pointed out. While teachers of the working-class girls term their good girls as mature and link this with hard work, boys, on the other hand, both high and low achievers, are referred to as *late* maturers, *late* developers. By the juxtaposing of 'maturity' and 'development', the implication is that boys' intellectual development is what is being commented on, but a more worrying aspect of girls' sexuality underlies their maturity. This suggests that mature girls have already developed intellectually, while boys are *late* in their development.

In other words, in very many cases negative terms were used to transform girls' positive attainments, independence and achievement into undesirable qualities. These qualities, as we shall explore later, can be linked directly to the terms in which women's attainment and their sexuality have been feared for a long time. The categories too which are used often imply an active sexuality in girls who show independence of thought, which is seen as an undesirable and unfeminine trait.

If we turn to the teachers' categorisations of poorly attaining girls, a different picture emerges. It will be remembered that only one middle-class girl, Julie, was doing very poorly at school. All other poorly achieving girls were working class. They tended to be characterised by teachers and other working-class girls not as *working* hard, but as *trying* hard. All the poorly attaining working-class girls were viewed as unconfident by their teachers, but while there is a tendency to see them as 'sensitive', this was often at the same time viewed as a sham. For instance Katy 'might look sensitive, but in fact it's like water off a duck's back'.

These girls may well only be *acting* sensitive, they may well be truly 'hard' underneath it all – images of working-class women: 'hard as nails', 'tough'. Conversely the evidence from their interviews makes it clear that they feel a lot of pain. This is mostly expressed in the way all but one of them report victimisation, and talk of (mostly) boys who hit, kick, punch, pinch and bully them. While other girls report bullying, what is striking about these girls is that all their categories are directed towards *themselves*. They all appear confused about why children are good or poor in their work, concentrating only on what those children are like to them and whether they will help them.

All the girls who did badly were vague and confused about their reasons or rationale for why they and others achieved the position they did. They all conveyed a sense of not really knowing or understanding why children are either doing well or failing – 'it's just that they are'. Some of the girls, most notably Patsy, were so bound up with their position as victim that they simply could not engage with the exercise and could not actually distinguish between who was good or poor at all. Others did better. Katy, Kerry and Jacky were aware of their own and others' position in the class, but had no understanding of why or how.

Not all the girls viewed themselves in the same terms as their teachers: in fact the working-class girls had a much clearer impression of themselves, while some of the middle-class girls considerably underestimated their performance, placing themselves in low groups and saying they were 'not good enough', 'Awful! Um, I don't know, I just am . . . Yeah, I just get nervous.' This is a girl who achieved the highest score in her class, and in the whole sample! They tended to undervalue themselves and be very anxious about their performance. All the private schools lay great emphasis on testing, as the girls were being prepared for highly competitive entrance examinations to public schools.

> You have to keep it in their minds with the . . . tests . . . and just move on rapidly to new learning so that the tests are really to get them into the habit of learning quickly. (teacher)

Good performance was always praised, but it was not picked out as especially noteworthy in the middle-class schools, while the working-class girls were given much status and praise for their good performance (even though it is average or even poor compared to the rest of the sample). The middle-class girls were *expected* to achieve a very high standard, thus they were never sure that they were 'good enough'. After all, nearly everyone in their class achieved similar levels of attainment, and this was not remarked on as outstanding.

For all of the girls at ten, growing up is difficult. For the working-class girls who were coping we are presented with the sham of their equal opportunities. It is perhaps salutary that almost all of them expressed the desire to join the helping professions when they grow up, mentioning 'helping people' as a rationale. Perhaps then some small percentage of them will be able to have the equal opportunities to join the professions inhabited by the mothers of the middle-class girls. Are these girls being educated in effect simply to be sensitive mother substitutes? Do we dare to call that equality?

Most of the middle-class girls are put in a double bind. That is, they are good but not good enough because they are quite simply and starkly, not boys. They are put on a ladder of struggle on which they can never succeed until and unless we succeed in confronting sexual difference and women's oppression.

Gender and sexual difference

The kinds of classifications the teachers make of girls are not mere rhetoric. As we have explored elsewhere these 'truths' are as likely to lead to practice as any which shape the domestic and mothering practices of the home.[6] We have seen earlier that the feminist account of mother–daughter bonding is to lead to autonomous and independent girls who can separate from their mothers. We also noted that other feminists stressed the breaking of the dyad by the father – that separation is never simply to leave the mother. Lacan, using linguistics, refers not to the actual father, but to the 'paternal metaphor'. Here he makes reference to structural anthropology, to the 'law of exogamy', the exchange of women by men.[7] The classification of girls and boys, differentiated as they are, places certain capacities 'in' boys: they possess the 'phallus', that is they are talked of as possessing some capacity, some potency, as yet invisible, but known to be there. The bourgeois male is also endowed with 'reason' and it was woman's job to be guardian and container of the irrationality, which left him free to hold 'reason'.

We cannot detail here the channelling of irrationality onto women. But it is central to an understanding of the fictions and fantasies inscribed in difference.[8] This is part of a series of splittings in which the Other comes to hold certain characteristics. We have seen that women as mothers must ensure the maintenance of liberal democracy. Thus mothers become not knowers themselves but nurturers of knowers: caring and the caring professions together make possible the autonomous children who will become the free, liberal, rational thinkers.

Women's bodies were stripped of their active sexuality, of their passions, to become nurturers of knowers. Here, teacher after teacher tells us that boys 'know' and that boys' violence (their passions) are just the road to knowing. Small wonder, then, that the girls too split off from their own violence, which we witnessed forcefully such a little while ago, and displace it onto boys.

If teachers invest boys with capacities which cannot be seen and deny that they see such capacities in girls, again there is no simply empirical 'real' for us to find. We find fictions instead, fantasies, splittings. And everywhere we find sexual difference. No matter how much their mothers prepared them, this is what the girls have to face. They can manifest the same behaviour as boys until they are blue in the face but this will never 'mean' the same thing. If they are independent they may be a 'madam', if they are strong they may be 'selfish'.[9]

We are arguing that the proof of masculinity as rational, as possessing knowledge, as superior, has constantly to be reasserted and set against its equal and opposite proof of the failure and lack of femininity. To say this is not to collude with the idea that women, and all other excluded groups, really 'are' lacking, but to demonstrate the great investments in proving this to be the case. Such 'proof' is based not on an easy certainty, but on the terrors and paranoias of the powerful, who are always afraid of the loss of that which they have so forcibly conquered. It is necessary to understand then how those Others, and other narratives, become a constant threat. Disproving them alone, without showing up the fantasies for what they are, means we are fighting a losing battle.[10] But because women are so caught up in those fantasies, we need to free ourselves from the story of our subjugation in this order.

Girls do not grow up to autonomy. They grow up on one side of a sexual divide, already replete with myth and fantasy, but myth and fantasy with material consequences. They will be discriminated against because they are not men. Some will want to prove that they are like them, others will resist their place in other ways. The struggle they face is not easy and it raises many contradictions for the women with whom they come into contact. For example, their women teachers see in their female pupils many of the difficulties they faced themselves. This can be quite painful. Freud suggested that identification with someone was a difficult and fraught process. On the surface women may deny that they are like their mothers because deep inside they fear they are all too like them. Many women teachers in this study were extremely contradictory about the girls in their charge. Sometimes they would admit to girls being like them, but it was always ambivalent and full of pain:

> She's basically a big softie (like me), y'know, in some ways she's not like me, she's not as outgoing as I can be, but she's going to have to be careful she doesn't get walked on.
>
> I hate[d] having to be spoken to in class, I absolutely hated having to be the centre of attention . . . She used to be like that. I found myself very easy to relate to her and if ever she was pulled out by the headmaster, she used to sort of, she used to panic – 'I don't want to go, I don't want to go' – I can imagine myself being like that.

At other times, teachers would go out of their way to deny that girls were having any problems. So we would be confronted with girls who, in our interviews, talked of their anxieties but whose women teachers denied they felt any.

By stark contrast the teachers found anxiety in boys all the time. Not only this, but they 'contained' it – they took it upon themselves to alleviate it.

> He's the one that went into a sulk . . . and he can't be told anything, you can't even tell him to change places. But I'm pleased with the way he gets on. He's quite bright.

We have seen that a similar splitting and denial occurs with violence in boys and girls.

There is no simple sense in this data in which boys really 'have' something (brains, flair) which girls are lacking. Yet socialisation approaches operate as though this were precisely the case. Girls fail at school because they are 'stereotyped', they can't break out of rigid roles, they haven't had the right play experience at home. This assumes that boys really are 'the Law', really do possess that which history, culture, science has accorded them and that girls are surely lacking and must be more like boys to succeed. But what of boys' masculinity? The power of patriarchy is not 'real' in that sense, but a fantasy, a fiction operating as fact with real oppressive effects. How much would be needed to keep this fragile illusion in play in consciousness?

We have argued against a simple notion of 'meeting needs' as the antidote to the 'patriarchal family', 'the society without the father'. Sociologists like Michèle Barrett and Mary McIntosh (1982) play right into this idea by supporting this view and talking about *the* family. Black women have been rightly vociferous in pointing out the normative assumptions in that concept.[11] There is no single family. We have examined differences in modes of regulation across social class in these families. These make it clear that while the regulation of mothering might affect both working- and middle-class white women, it operates differently. Here, we have pointed towards different meanings of what it means to grow up in different practices. Pain, loss, anxiety and satisfaction may appear universals but the meanings in which they are inscribed differ from family to family with different and *specific* histories. We have attempted to show why the specificity of those meanings is important for understanding the unconscious as well as conscious social processes.

If teachers deny anxiety in girls, they fail to give the girls support. At the same time teachers feel that they have to shoulder the burden of responsibility for the failures and violence of the boys. Thus, anxious and violent girls become pathologised in practices which help produce the splitting of sexual divison. At ten, the girls are struggling. They struggle towards a fragmented and divided adulthood and a harsh world outside. It is not uncommon within feminism to see as 'beyond the pale' girls (usually working class) who do not easily opt for 'non-traditional' choices. The voluntarism of such a view denies the struggles in which the girls have to engage. It is not easy to face racism, to leave one's class or to cross the gender divide. Rather than a feminist moralism that blames girls, teachers and mothers for failing to live up to some rarefied notion of a feminist consciousness, isn't it about time that we engaged in the complexities of that struggle, which is a struggle, though differently lived, for all of us, all the time?

Facing the future

'This is an old fiction of reliability,' says Denise Riley of mothers in her poem which we quoted at the beginning of the book. We have attempted to outline many fictions in this volume – fictions which we are caught and enslaved in. If we are constructed in the gaze of those Others who invest us with their hopes and fears, how do we move outside an intense sense of hollowness, that 'we' are nothing? We do not believe that redefining motherhood for feminism is an answer. We have to understand the scale and complexities of the fantasies in which we are subscribed: the huge edifices of the Enlightenment, of colonisation, of capitalism, of patriarchy. All these build upon the regulation of Others to be held in check, to ensure the possibility of government.

We have tried to begin to turn the tables on these fantasies, to produce a counter-discourse, a counter-memory. For that which claims to describe us cannot tell the whole story. We need to look to what has been silenced and how that silence too has been read. Let us give one final example. An unemployed woman, a mother of three children, seeks work in a university to teach women's studies. The male professor presents her as an 'invasion by feminism'. Let us examine for a moment the terror inscribed in his fantasy. There is no women's studies at this point. She is unemployed. He has tenure. Yet, he can constitute feminism as an 'invasion' – so precariously does he view the power of his reign. What kind of delusion is it that talks of invasions, of armies, of hordes – of masses? Only one in a precarious omnipotence, only one with the power to oppress. Sometimes the oppressor can seem very benevolent and offer us a vision in which the chains that bind us are almost invisible. In liberal democracy we could almost be free – almost, were it not for the massive and hidden regulation. We have a dream, not of bolting any more for the door of the bourgeoisie, asking to be let in, but a dream of a freedom, a dangerous dream. We want to offer our dream to counterpose the fantasy of freedom, the benevolent gaze which tries to make us imagine that we are the originator of our actions, in control of our destiny, the dream of bourgeois, liberal democracy.

It may, however, seem hollow to make such a plea in the late 1980s when the Right has all but eroded the last vestiges of liberal humanism. But there are some things we feel we need to say about re-visions for the future. The situation which we have documented in terms of what happened to the girls at ten is horrific. No amount of equal opportunities could make the chances of the working-class girls in a meritocracy anything more than minimal. We exist in an education system in which 75 per cent of the pupils fail in terms of access to professional careers. What hope for upward mobility? Yet, it is precisely this that has been seized on by the Right, with its rhetoric of testing, benchmarks and standards. It seeks to sweep away the sponsored mobility that we have grown up with. We need to remember that we – VW and HL – did well out of liberal democracy: it provided our path to privilege, to home ownership, to high salaries, but at the expense of others left behind. It is necessary now to defend rights to higher education, to full grants.

The Tories would like to make Britain more like North America, where no one gets grants. No one knows what it is like, except the wealthy, to believe at least that you have a right to free higher education. We need to think very carefully, for in the USA it is no longer easy even to talk about class, since anything other than middle class is considered a pathological category (black, poor) – those who haven't, by dint of their own efforts, escaped. It is a dream which has some mileage for working-class people with their understanding of hard, grinding work and hatred of handouts and charity. We want to remake and rework the discourse of class, to enunciate it before it is so late that, as in the US, it can no longer be spoken, making socialism almost impossible any longer to remember as a vision.

One one level it seems ironic that we should want to bring back issues of class now. And yet now is precisely the time that we feel it is necessary to bring them back. For years we have been told that issues of class operate *against* those of gender, as though we could indeed 'divide' our 'loyalties'. To grow up a working-class girl but to become a middle-class woman through education and profession does not mean that nothing remains of the working-class girl. It is only the Left and the women's movement which splits and fragments our history this way, as though we did not live our class, our gender and our race simultaneously.

What we have to say is not easy for us. White women have been made to look at the contradictions of power and oppression in our position, that we are part of the oppression of our black sisters. We want to examine class too in these terms. The project we have in mind is *not* a denial of feminism, nor a return to class. However, it is, for us, a chance to articulate something and to engage in a politics for us which is about the present moment, a political engagement for feminism with the politics of the government of a social democracy and the struggle for freedom. It took black women a long time to beat down the door of white feminism, to demand a hearing, not plead to be let in. We want to move forward to a politics for the 1980s and we think that, at this very moment, one which denies class denies it at its peril.

But it is not any old discourse of class, for we are certainly not arguing for a return to an old-style class politics. Rather we want a politics which can engage with differences, with our different constitution in shifting plays of power and powerlessness, of class, of race, of gender. We must tackle these and work together, but no longer out of a spurious sense of unity which evades and eludes the differences between us, painful and fraught as they are. We can no longer countenance a liberal democracy that rests on the oppression of women. We agree with Laclau (1987) that the working class is not a unified or unitary body (if it ever was – see Chapter Two) and that it cannot be the only agent of political transformation. He argues that the Left has wanted to invest too much in the working class, relying on concepts of the universal subject, science and truth which are no longer tenable. We would add to that the massive fantasies, hopes and fears invested in the working class that we have discussed in the previous chapters. Laclau goes on to argue that the category of working class does not have the same reality as it did in Marx's time:

> We can see why: to be a worker in the nineteenth century meant to spend many hours in the factory, to live in certain areas, to have certain patterns of consumption, to participate only in rigidly defined ways in the political and cultural life of the country. But the strict correlation among all these forms of social participation becomes looser and looser as the increase in productivity means less and less hours are spent in the factory, as the expansion of the welfare state means that the social identity of the worker is going to be decreasingly determined by his/her location in the means of production. The participation of the worker in a variety of social relations means that many more areas of his/her participation in social life, *not strictly depending on his/her location in the relations of production*, can be the sites of new and radical social struggle. (p.23)

We think that it must be a long time since Laclau participated in white working-class life, otherwise he simply could not conceive of uttering the words in the above paragraph. We spent some time in the Introduction describing the daily lives of our families, lives that have not changed substantially in the 1980s. We see too in the transcripts the hours spent working, the conditions, the rigidity, which he seems to think we left behind in the nineteenth century. The spurious argument about changing patterns leads Laclau to argue for policies based on a 'radical democracy' of rights and equality, the very bourgeois democracy we have spent so much time discussing in this book. His problems with class seem to lead him to act as though exploitation and oppression also belonged in the nineteenth century. While we agree that class is an ambiguous term, we think that it is a necessary one.

Similar arguments have been made about the concept of

'black'. Of course black people are a diverse and not a homogenous grouping. But it is the importance of racism which gives 'black' its meaning, not cultural homogeneity. 'Black' then is a political category, defined by a politics that opposes racism, through which it is constituted as object. In our view, 'class' must function in a related way. 'Working class' as a designation is the object of exploitation, and is Other to the bourgeoisie. It is a political term which deserves to be kept in the armour of our fight against oppression. We might even go as far as saying that it is social democracy, the democracy of rights and responsibilities, which has redefined the working class and made it into a new object inside a set of discourses and practices designed to promote upward mobility. Yet this is read back onto them, when they long for a bourgeois lifestyle, as an indication that they are now reactionary, that class has no value and that it is an out-of-date concept. If it is so easy to rob the working class of their history then no wonder that they feel dumped and that there is no place for white working-class people in the 'new politics'.

But what hope is there of defending anything in the present political climate? In terms of education it is necessary to remember that it was the Labour Party which opted, in the first place for a meritocracy – for a tripartite system, for comprehensive schools, for the Great Debate, for standards and the needs of industry. We, the authors of this book, have done well out of that, but millions have not, and the millions have voted with their feet, wanting to believe that the Tories' way might give them more than the empty promises of progressivism, of relevant, meaningful education which left them right where they were – at the bottom.

It is easy in this climate for the Left to move to the right to combat Thatcher.[12] But not only is that a further betrayal, it will not work. Only an aggressive defence of socialism, of a move for education for equality, is worth fighting for, not some spurious aim of national competition. But what would an education for equality look like? And how could it be part of a strategy for socialism? It cannot even be considered outside other strategies for socialism, struggles to counter oppression. But they cannot be strategies which simply seek to let a few more into the elite. Mass strategies do not defend privileges. Some of us will have to suffer and to understand that we need to look at what we are so fearfully hanging on to.

Let us return to the place from which we began this book. Social democracy was to be achieved by certain strategies of regulation. Children were to be taught how to be democratic citizens. The place where this was to begin was the democratic kitchen, where mothers would achieve a socialisation of their children which would ensure the correct path to an education for equal opportunities. We maintain that there is no easy socialisation that mothers can be accused of failing to do, or through which feminism can ensure the future generations. We have argued against an easy empiricism for a more complex blending of fact and fiction, of materiality and fantasy. Just like these little girls and their mothers, all women resist where they can, when they can, how they can. It is vital now, more than ever, that we begin to recognise and explore the differences between us so that we might then struggle as women together.

APPENDIX I

GIRLS' NAMES

Middle Class	*Working Class*
Naomi	Susan
Emily	Katy
Angela	Caroline
Gill	Nicky
Deborah	Patsy
Julie	Jenny
Sarah	Margaret
Diana	Kerry
Charlotte	Teresa
Penny	Maura
Liz	Sally
Victoria	Maureen
Samantha	Jacky
Amanda	Anna
Helen	Dawn

NOTES

Introduction

1. John Osborne, *Look Back in Anger*, 1959
2. Carolyn Steedman particularly notes how these men eulogise and romanticise their working-class mothers. C. Steedman, *Landscape for a Good Woman*, 1986.
3. Jeremy Seabrook, *Working Class Childhood*, 1982; R. Hoggart, *The Uses of Literacy*, 1959.
4. J.W.B. Douglas, *The Home and The School*, 1964.
5. There is a huge literature. One recent British example would be Beverley Bryan, Stella Dadzie and Suzanne Scafe, *Heart of The Race*, 1985.
6. See for example S. Yeo, 1989.
7. For example in V. Walkerdine, 'Dreams from an Ordinary Childhood' in Liz Heron (ed.), *Truth, Dare or Promise*, 1985.
8. They were both Registrar General's social class IV. We explain this system of classification in Chapter Two.
9. It may be argued that this is a considerable caricature of that work and that movement. We do not wish to denigrate the important work in structuralism and post-structuralism, the huge importance of the New Left, or the rise of new issues and new constituencies, but we are arguing that the relationship between the labour movement, working-class people and these constituencies and concerns has never been fully explored. This exploration is long overdue, both in theory and in practice. In relation to the latter, Banks and Tomkins, quoted in Bianchini, 1987, argue that the Greater London Council never took the London white working class seriously: 'For this crucial group' (the 'white', 'respectable' working class) 'little was done' (Bianchini, p. 114).
10. See for example Goldthorpe and Lockwood, 1968; Hill, 1976; Gorz, 1982.
11. Developments in theories of ideology moved from the idea that ideology was simply a distortion, to a system of representations

in which the working class were taken to live, not in a real relation to the conditions of their exploitation, but an imaginary one. See, for example, Althusser, 1975; Hirst, 1976. We do not wish to denigrate this strand of work, which had enormous importance, but it still tended to see the working class as both the problem and the solution.

12. See for example H. Beynon, *Working for Ford*, 1973; R. Cavendish, 1982; S. Westwood, *All Day, Every Day*, 1984. Of course, since George Orwell and before, the upper classes have stepped into the worlds of poverty, only to step out again swiftly to document what they saw for the voyeuristic fantasies of the bourgeoisie and upper classes.

Chapter One: It's Only Natural

1. B. Tizard and M. Hughes, 1984. See Introduction.
2. As we pointed out in the Introduction, there is a whole tradition of work which does this. However, from the 1970s the mother was targeted specifically by psycholinguists and developmental psychologists who battled over whether or not the mother was capable of providing an adequate preparatory environment, or indeed was better at the job than any nursery or school.
3. See for example arguments in Lynne Segal (ed), 1983, *What Is To Be Done About The Family?*
4. We are not going to argue, following Elizabeth Badinter, 1981, *The Myth of Motherhood: An Historical View of the Maternal Instinct*, that the idea of the maternal instinct is a myth. Rather we want to examine how the idea that children have needs to be met by natural mothering came to have a currency in, and be the bedrock of, arguments for bourgeois democracy.
5. For example, N. Friday, *My Mother, Myself*, 1979; J. Arcana, *Our Mothers' Daughters*, 1981; L. Eichenbaum and S. Orbach, *Outside In, Inside Out*, 1982.
6. See for example the arguments surrounding deprivation in M. Rutter, *Maternal Deprivation Reassessed*, 1972.
7. W. Labov, *The Logic of Non-Standard English*, 1978.
8. See for example K. Millett, *Sexual Politics*, 1969.
9. One-to-one correspondence is a concept which comes from the work of the developmentalist Jean Piaget, whose work has

become deeply embedded in modern approaches to early education and child development.

10. See T. Adorno, 1982, and later work such as R. D. Laing, *The Politics of The Family and Other Essays*, 1971.
11. See particularly H. Marcuse, *An Essay on Liberation*, 1969; *One-Dimensional Man: Studies in the Ideology of Advanced Industrial Society*, 1964.
12. See L. Segal in Segal (ed), 1983, for a review.
13. This is documented by, for example, B. Campbell, in 'Feminist Sexual Politics', *Feminist Review 5*, 1980.
14. For a critique of the idea of the System, see J. Henriques et al., *Changing The Subject*, 1984.
15. To the workers in Paris in 1968, the students' demands that they join their struggle must have seemed like 'much wants more' (see Introduction). Students, the sons and daughters of the middle and upper classes, already had so much privilege. It might have seemed more appropriate to the workers if the students had supported increased entry for the sons and daughters of the workers to the kind of privilege that it now seemed the bourgeoisie was not content with.
16. W. Reich, *The Mass Psychology of Fascism*, 1975; *Children of the Future: on the Prevention of Sexual Pathology*, 1983.
17. This is documented in W. Hollway, 1989.
18. J. Donzelot, *The Policing of Families*, 1980.
19. D. Riley in L. Segal (ed), 1983.
20. E. Badinter, 1981.
21. Ursula Le Guin, *The Left Hand of Darkness*, 1973; Marge Piercy, *Woman on the Edge of Time*, 1979.

Chapter Two: Taming Nature

1. See for example Centre for Contemporary Cultural Studies, *Unpopular Education*, 1981.
2. But see J. Henriques et al., 1984, section 2.
3. For example A. Phillips, *Divided Loyalties*, 1987.
4. See for example A. H. Halsey, *Originis and Destinations*, 1980.
5. For example P. Cline-Cohen, *A Calculating People: The Spread of Numeracy in Early America*, 1982; I. Hacking, *How Shall We do the History of Statistics, Ideology and Consciousness*, I. & C., 1981;

E. Hobsbawm, *The Age of Revolution, 1848-1875*, 1975; M. Foucault, *Discipline and Punish*, 1979.

7. His work has been and continues to be very important in struggles of oppressed peoples. See for example F. Fanon, *The Wretched of the Earth*, 1967; *Black Skin, White Mask*, 1969.
8. See P. Q. Hirst and P. Woolley, *Social Relations and Human Attributes*, 1983; B. Eastlea, *Science and Sexual Oppression*, 1981; S. Bovenshen, 1978.
9. See for example M. Foucault, *The History of Sexuality, Vol 1*, 1981. This argument is that everything outside reason has become the object and target of medical discourses and practices, which then created it as illness and sought a cure. Jacqueline Rose, 1983, demonstrates how this was intimately tied to the pathologisation of certain groups of women in the nineteenth century. These were bourgeois women who wanted to be educated and proletarian women who were on the streets and not in their homes.
10. See C. Hall and L. Davidov, *Family Fortunes: Men and Women of the English Middle Class 1750-1850*, 1987, for a discussion of what happened to bourgeois women.
11. V. Walkerdine (1986b), 'Video Replay', in V. Burgin, J. Donald and C. Kaplan (eds), *Formations of Fantasy*, 1986.
12. See L. Stanley and S. Wise, *Doing Feminist Research*, 1983.
13. Elsewhere it is suggested that the idea of proof and retelling creates a fantasy of timeless omnipotence – mastery over the laws of nature, which covers over the fears of the Others (the masses) who are the object of the calculation. See H. Bhabha, *The Other Question: the Stereotype in Colonial Discourse*, 1983; V. Walkerdine, 'Science and the Female Mind: the Burden of Proof', 1985b; V. Walkerdine, *The Mastery of Reason*, 1988.
14. There is ample evidence of this in a study carried out by V. Walkerdine where the working-class family realised that if the daughter did not speak it would be thought she had nothing to say. At the same time her parents tried to get her to say the 'right' things, like 'the rain in Spain falls mainly on the plain' (V. Walkerdine, op cit).
15. This has been emphasised in recent debates, for example, the History Workshop series on Psychoanalysis and History, as well as in the work of L. Passerini, 1987.
16. We can point to similarities in all these women's work as well as

differences between them. Despite the massive differences in the sort of work they do, and how they got into that work in the first place, their working experiences and conditions bear some similarity by virtue of its part-time nature. Constrained from taking up full-time work by domestic responsibilities, they are all subject to discriminatory practices leading to low pay and lack of security.

17. There is a general acknowledgement within recent sociological literature on class that we can no longer assume a simple relationship between the bourgeoisie as owners of capital and the proletariat as workforce. Increasing professionalisation and development of complex management structures have produced what J. H. Goldthorpe and A. H. Halsey, 1980, have called a 'service class'. Consisting of professionals who possess 'valued skills made available in educational institutions' B. Bernstein, 1977, p. 126) this group is known as the 'new middle class'. For further details on the debate see Abercrombie and Urry, 1983; J. Westergaard, 1984.

Chapter Three: Caged Animals

1. See M. Safouan, *Men and Women: A Psychoanalytic Point of View*, 1984, for a further discussion.
2. See related articles by L. Bland, 1981 and 1982.
3. U. Brofenbrenner, *The Ecology of Human Development: Experiments by Nature and Design*, 1979.
4. Most notably M. Rutter, *Maternal Deprivation Reassessed*, 1972; W. Sluckin, M. Herbert and A. Sluckin, *Maternal Bonding*, 1983; Tizard, *On Mothering*, 1986.
5. L. S. Crnic et al., 'Animal Models of Human Behaviour: Their Application to the Study of Attachment', in R. Emde and R. Harmon (eds), 1982.
6. Cf. D. Riley in L. Segal (ed), 1983.
7. See C. Urwin, 1984, for further details.
8. For example G. Wells, 'Language, Literacy and Educational Success' in *Learning Through Interaction*, 1982.

Chapter Four: Women's Work is *Always* Done

1. It was very common to use experimental and ethological evidence about animal behaviour to support the 'natural mother-love' theme. For example, Bowlby, 1971, made reference to the work of the zoologists Konrad Lorenz and Nikolaas Tinbergen.
2. One easy analysis of the above two examples would indeed be to 'find' pre-mathematics in their work and then give these mothers the normative accolade for confirming theories of natural development.
3. A. Foreman, 1977; J. Gardiner, 1975. For a comprehensive review see E. Kaluzynska, 1981.
4. A. Pollert, 1981; R. Cavendish, 1982; J. Wajcman, 1983.
5. K. Marx, *Capital*, Volumes I (1976a) and III (1976b).
6. Of course, there are those who would disagree that women's oppression is caused by their economic dependence on men, and therefore a consequence of capitalism. Much feminist work uses theories of patriarchy to account for the subordination and oppression of women. See H. Hartman, 1979, V. Beechey, 1979, A. Kuhn and A. M. Wolpe (eds), 1978, D. Adlam, 1979, for a discussion of the debate.
7. K. Marx, *Capital*, Volume I (1976a).
8. See A. Phillips, 1987, for a review.
9. This position is taken by C. Harman, 1984.
10. For example H. Gavron, 1966; A. Oakley, 1974a.
11. M. G. Boulton, 1983.
12. H. Gavron, 1966; H. Z. Lopata, 1971; A. Oakley, 1974a.
13. Those who have waved the 'wages for housework' banner (M. R. Della Costa and S. James, 1972) argue that all labour power under capitalism is a commodity, thus, women who expend this in their role as housewives are also workers and therefore produce value and surplus. Others (Seccombe, 1982) agree that value is produced, but argue that because she does not put the produce of her work on the open market, the housewife cannot produce *surplus* value.
14. V. Beechey, 1979.
15. R. Cavendish, 1982; A. Pollert, 1981.
16. V. Beechey, 1983.
17. M. Porter, 1983.

18. A. Oakley, 1974b.
19. For example, A. Oakley, ibid.
20. M. G. Boulton, 1983, notes that while both working- and middle-class women felt the pressure of conflicting demands of housework and child care, middle-class women were more likely to 'put the children first' as a solution to the conflict.
21. B. Bernstein, 1977, uses this term to describe practices which are predominantly working class, which are contrasted with what he calls the more 'personal' orientation of many middle-class families.
22. This is the term used by the psychologists quoted in the last chapter.
23. See Note 1.
24. M. Klein, 1975a and b; Piaget: see H. Gruber and J. J. Voneche, 1977, for a concise review of his work.
25. This is explored in some detail in relation to educational practices in V. Walkerdine, 1984.
26. ibid; C. Urwin, 1985a.

Chapter Five: A Question of Meaning

1. By B. Tizard and M. Hughes, 1984, p. 123.
2. This is a term used by Piaget to describe a universal embodiment of the individual.
3. It would be wrong to infer that a publisher's editorial assistant is a well-paid job. It is of course too easy to discount the woman's low wages as 'pin-money', supplementing those of her highly-paid husband. However, it is likely that the family is 'comfortable' in a way which is most unlikely for a working-class family in which the man is a window cleaner.
4. This issue is discussed at greater length in V. Walkerdine, *The Mastery of Reason*, 1988.
5. This is a hypothesis advanced by psychologists, such as M. Bierwisch, 1970, in the 1970s which suggests a universal sequence of the acquisition of meanings, which is ultimately derived from 'perceptual universals' (cf. H. Clark, 1973).
6. In the tree-branching structure, terms with 'less' features are said to be acquired before those with 'more' (see E. Clark, 1973).

7. That is, it has fewer semantic features.
8. V. Walkerdine, 1988.

Chapter Six: Democracy in the Kitchen?

1. We will explore the idea of the failure of socialisation in Chapter Eight.
2. See for example P. Adams et al., 1972.
3. See sources quoted in N. Rose, 1979, especially Ch. 7.
4. Teresa's mother is one of those working-class women who do indeed excel in doing all the 'right' things. She spends the entire afternoon with Teresa, doing no housework at all. She reads, engages in fantasy play and seizes every opportunity to impart some sort of knowledge to her. Yet, unlike Samantha, who at four has a high IQ score of 123, Teresa only gets a score of 104. This throws into confusion the idea that doing this sort of thing with and for your child will automatically ensure her educational success. It also makes a nonsense of the predictive power of such tests, for Teresa is performing well above the average for her school when she is ten years old.
5. V. Walkerdine, 1988.
6. For more detail see V. Walkerdine, 1988; R. Walden and V. Walkerdine, 1985; Girls and Mathematics Unit, 1989.
7. D. Bar-Tai, 1978; C. Dweck and M. Repucci, 1973; J. Parsons, 1983.
8. B. Bernstein, 1977.
9. B. Bernstein, 1977, uses the concepts of 'classification' and 'framing' to describe this, suggesting that many middle-class families have 'weak boundary maintenance'.
10. Remember the quotation cited near the beginning of Chapter Four which told mothers not to make 'mathematical play' into a 'lesson'. See also R. D. Hess and V. Shipman, 1965, where working-class mothers are said to prepare their children for teachers as authority figures. For a discussion, see V. Walkerdine in C. Steedman, C. Urwin and V. Walkerdine (eds) 1985.

Chapter Seven: The Suburban Terrorist

1. C. Lasch, 1977, *Haven in a Heartless World*, criticises this view of the family. See also M. Barrett and M. McIntosh's discussion of it in *The Anti-Social Family*, 1982.
2. J. Benjamin, 1978, uses this term. See discussion in Chapter Eight.
3. As F. Fanon, 1967, was able to do in relation to male violence in colonial Algeria.
4. J. Newson and E. Newson, 1976.
5. This argument is developed in V. Walkerdine, 1981. See also J. Brophy and C. Smart, 1982, who argue that women's power in custody cases is similarly fractured and fraught because it is accorded them only by virtue of an oppressive discourse of mothering. It is here based on post-structuralist approaches to power as in M. Foucault, 1979. See also J. Henriques et al., 1984.
6. See for example Chapter Five.
7. See A. S. Neill, *The Free Child*, 1953; P. Adams et al., 1972.
8. See B. Bradley, no date.
9. A view propounded strongly in relation to aggression, childhood and war during the period of the Second World War. See D. Riley, *War in the Nursery*, 1983.
10. V. Walkerdine, 1981. Here two four-year-old boys develop a rhythmic chant in opposition to their nursery teacher. In the article it is discussed in terms of violence, power and resistance.
11. Cf V. Walkerdine in C. Steedman, C. Urwin and V. Walkerdine (eds), 1985. We also want to take issue here with the return to a universalising morality in the analysis of E. Laclau, 1987. Laclau makes arguments about the changing composition of the working class that are important and highly pertinent, but he ends the argument by arguing for exactly the kind of universalising morality we are objecting to. See Chapter Ten.
12. M. Klein, 1975a and b; F. Fanon, 1967 and 1969.
13. See also J. Sayers, in *Feminist Review*, summer 1986, for a further discussion.
14. There is, of course, another discourse about violence; a libertarian one which understands violence done *by* the family *to* the individual – especially the repressive nature of the authoritarian family. Here, violence is to be allowed to be

displayed – a 'freeing' the subject – but the authoritarian family (and especially the pathological mother in R. D. Laing's analysis) is said to produce schizophrenia. See also D. Riley, 1983, for a critique.

15. See Note 5.
16. See for example L. Breslow Rubin, *Worlds of Pain*, 1976; R. Coles and J. Hallowell Coles, *Women of Crisis*, 1978.

Chapter Eight: Growing up the Hard Way

1. This is sometimes referred to as the frustration/aggression hypothesis. See for example J. L. Dollard et al., 1939.
2. The evolutionary arguments, which we have barely touched on in this book, are highly significant because they naturalise bourgeois democracy as the most civilised and most highly evolved form. It is the higher primates, and particularly *Homo sapiens*, which are taken to have evolved to a state requiring certain needs to be met. In Chapter Three we saw how psychologists in the 1950s used ethological arguments to strengthen the idea of behavioural systems produced out of evolutionary adaptation rather than drives or instincts. This meant that this state was amenable to intervention and behavioural regulation to ensure the possibility of civilised life. These scientific arguments were crucial to their incorporation into practices of regulation in the bourgeois order.
3. J. Sayers, 1986, sets out cogently the problems with Chodorow's account and we will not reiterate them here. Rather, here we are seeking to demonstrate the similarity of these accounts with the approaches which they are critiquing.
4. J. Mitchell and J. Rose (eds), 1983, p. 34.
5. For example B. Bradley, no date.
6. J. Lacan, 1977. See also J. Mitchell and J. Rose (eds), 1983.
7. S. Freud, 1931; J. Lacan, in J. Mitchell and J. Rose (eds), 1983.
8. J. Mitchell, 1975; J. Mitchell and J. Rose (eds), 1983; J. Rose, 1983; J. Sayers, 1986.
9. In V. Walkerdine, 1986b.
10. E. Badinter, 1981.
11. We are using the idea of the word pair here as a contrastive opposition, like the more/less pair examined in Chapter Five.

Our point here, as there, is to demonstrate how meanings are not 'universals' but produced in the regulation of practices.

12. This account of development towards rationality uses an evolutionary framework to suggest that just as a species evolves (phylogenesis) so a species-being (a child) evolves (ontogenesis) in the same manner through adaptation to the environment. Thus mastery over nature is presented as evolutionarily inevitable and natural and not a huge and dangerous fantasy.

Chapter Nine: Having the Knowledge

1. Centre for Contemporary Cultural Studies Education Group, 1981.
2. Unlike German mothers, who were financially penalised if they did not go in for large families, but who did not have welfare services to support them.
3. A. H. Halsey et al., 1980; J. W. B. Douglas, 1964.
4. See for example A. K. Cohen, 1955 and 1966; B. Sugarman, 1970, in M. Craft (ed).
5. A. H. Halsey et al. 1980.
6. For example H. H. Hyman, 1967, in R. Bendix and S. M. Lipset (eds).
7. Parents and Children Together. This has been used as a way of getting working-class parents involved, but also of trying to make sure that they do it in the right way. If they are involved, standards of literacy are supposed to rise and this will aid the educational success of working-class children.
8. By 1964, the concept of cultural deprivation was firmly established in the United States through the work of psychologists and educational researchers. In 1963 the American government instituted and allocated millions of dollars to a number of schemes to 'fight back' against such deprivation; the 'War on Poverty' was launched with operation Headstart and project Upward Bound and, in 1964, the Job Corps. Deprivation in the USA, and to a lesser extent in Britain with the Educational Priority Areas, became a spur to legislation. This was testimony to the wide appeal of the concept.
9. See for example S. Kessel and A. W. Siegel, *The Child and Other Cultural Inventions*, 1983.

10. This was a very common fraction used to explain intelligence, which was felt to be two components added together, heredity and environment.
11. Many accounts place considerable emphasis on early socialisation and sex-role stereotyping. See for example J. Chetwynd and D. Hartnett, 1978; R. Deem, 1980.
12. A. A. Bullock, 1974; G. Wells, 1982.
13. See for example M. Craft (ed), 1980; T. Becher, 1981; P. Clift, 1981.
14. Most therapeutic accounts using this model opt for 'separation' as a kind of end-point, leading to later maturation, independence and adulthood. See how L. Eichenbaum and S. Orbach (1982) develop a feminist version of this argument.
15. In a previous analysis of data on six-year-old girls at home and at school, many working-class parents stressed their daughters' happiness at school. 'As long as she's happy' was often said even when the girls were failing badly at school, as though being happy was the most that could be hoped for.

Chapter Ten: School Girls

1. We administered a NFER Standardised Mathematics Test. See Chapter Two for more detail.
2. Two of the middle-class girls were not available to be included in the follow-up study. There were also four occasions when, due to lack of time, the classes could not be given a standardised test. Thus, although they were tested, the results could not be included in this table.
3. R. Walden and V. Walkerdine, 1985.
4. G. Corran and V. Walkerdine, 1981.
5. 'Work' is an aspect of the old pedagogic discourse of chalk and talk, bringing with it the fear of authoritarianism. Girls' performance is therefore seen to be caused in the 'wrong way' and presents a threat or danger. See Walkerdine, 1988 and 1985b, for a fuller discussion.
6. V. Walkerdine, 1988; R. Walden and V. Walkerdine, 1985; The Girls and Mathematics Unit, *Counting Girls Out*, 1989.
7. E. Cowie, 1978; G. Rubin, 1975.
8. G. Corran and V. Walkerdine, 1981; V. Walkerdine, 1985a and b.

9. We think that it would be possible to develop an argument linking the suppression of violent emotions in women, their capacity for anger and to rise up against the oppressor, and active sexuality. Certainly, in producing the natural mother, passionate, active sexuality was to be replaced by passive nurturance: a femininity only directed towards the 'new couple', mother and child. This is not, however, at all the same as arguing that women are naturally passive.
10. For whenever we try to enter their game of proof, the ground shifts and new arguments and evidence appear. That is why we think it is crucial to refuse to play and to expose the fraudulence upon which the proof is based. See V. Walkerdine, 1985b.
11. For example B. Bryan, S. Dadzie and S. Scafe, 1985.
12. G. Benson and S. Lansley do exactly that in their article on education and the working class in the *New Statesman*, 1987, building upon Tory rhetoric and completely failing to come up with any vision, after having rightly criticised the failure of liberal democracy.

BIBLIOGRAPHY

Abercrombie, N., and Urry, J., *Capital Labour and the Middle Classes*, Allen and Unwin, London, (1983).

Adams, P. et al, *Children's Rights*, Panther, London, (1972).

Adlam, Diana, The Case Against Capitalist Patriarchy, *M/F 3*, pp83–102, (1979).

Adorno, T. et al, *The Authoritarian Personality*, Norton, New York, (1982).

Ainsworth, M.D.S., Patterns of Attachment Behaviour Shown by the Infant in Interaction with his Mother, *Merrill-Palmer Quarterly*, 10, pp51–8, (1964).

Ainsworth, M.D.S. et al, Individual Differences in the Development of some Attachment Behaviours, *Merrill-Palmer Quarterly*, 18, pp123–43, (1972).

Althusser, L., Lenin and Philosophy and Other Essays, *Monthly Review Press*, New York, (1975).

Anzaldua, G., *This bridge called my back*, Persephone Press, Watertown, Massachusetts, (1981).

Arcana, J., *Our Mother's Daughters*, Women's Press, London, (1981).

Aries, P., *Centuries of Childhood*, Penguin, Harmondsworth, (1960).

Badinter, E., *The Myth of The Motherhood: An Historical View of the Maternal Instinct*, Souvenir Press, London, (1981).

Balint, A., *Primary Love and the Psychoanalytic Technique*, Hogarth Press, London, (1952).

Banks, T. and Tomkins, A., in *New Socialist*, February, (1986).

Barrett, M., and MacIntosh, M., *The Anti-Social Family*, Verso, London, (1982).

Bar-Tai, D., Attributional Analysis of Achievement-Related Behaviour, *Review of Educational Research, 48*, (1978).

Becher, T., *Policies for Educational Accountability*, Heinemann, London, (1981).

Beck, J., *World's Apart: Readings for a Sociology of Education*, Collier MacMillan, London, (1976).

Beechey, Veronica, On Patriarchy, *Feminist Review*, 3, pp66–82, (1979).

Beechy, Veronica, What's so Special About Women's Employment? *Feminist Review*, 15, pp23–46, (1983).

Bendix R., and Lipset, S.M., (eds) Class, Status and Power, Routledge and Kegan Paul, London, (1967).

Benjamin, J., Authority and the Family Revisted, *New German Critique*, no 13, pp52–3, (1978).

Benson, G., and Lansley, S., Education – Failing the Masses, *New Statesman*, Vol. 114, No. 2946, September, (1987).

Bernstein, B., *Class, Codes and Control*, Vol. 3, Routledge and Kegan Paul, London, (1977).

Beveridge, M., (ed), *Children Thinking Through Language*, Edward Arnold, London, (1982).

Bevis, P., Spacial-Visualisation and the Cerebro-gonadal Access, Unpubl. PhD., South Bank Polytechnic.

Beynon, H., *Working For Ford*, Allen Lane, London, (1973).

Bhabha, H., The Other Question: The Stereotype in Colonial Discourse, *Screen*, Vol. 24, no. 6, pp18–36, (1983).

Bianchini, F., GLC R.I.P. Cultural Policies in London, 1981–1986, *New Formations, 1*, pp103–117, (1987).

Bierwisch, M., Semantics, in Lyons, J., (ed), (1970).

Bland, L., The Domain of the Sexual: A Response, *Screen Education*, Summer 1981, No. 39, pp56–68.

Bland, L., Guardians of the Race or Vampires on the Nation's Health, in E. Whitelegg et al (eds). (1982).

Blehar, M.C., Lieberman, A.F., and Ainsworth, M.D.S., Early face-to-face Interaction and its Relation to Later Mother-Infant Attachment, *Child Development*, 48, pp182–94, (1977).

Boulton, M.G., *On Being a Mother: A Study of Women with Pre-School Children*, Tavistock, London, (1983).

Bovenshen, S., The Contemporary Witch, the Historical Witch and The Witch Myth, New German Critique, No. 15, pp83–119, (1978).

Bowlby, J., *Attachment And Loss, Vol. 1*, Penguin, Harmondsworth, (1971).

Bradley, B., The Neglect of Hatefulness in Psychological Studies of Early Infancy, Mimeo, Cambridge, Cambridge University Press.

Breslow Rubin, L., *Worlds of Pain*, Basic Books, New York, (1976)

Breugel, Irene, Women as a Reserve Army of Labour, *Feminist Review*, 3, pp12–23, (1979).

Brofenbrenner, U., *The Ecology of Human Development: Experiments by Nature and Design*, Harvard University Press, Cambridge, Mass, (1979).

Brophy, J., and Smart, C., From Disregard to Disrepute: The Position of Women in Family Law, *Feminist Review*, 9, (1982).

Bryan, B., Dadzie, S., and Scafe S., *The Heart of The Race*, Virago, London, (1985).

Bullock, A.A., *A Language For Life*, (Committee of Enquiry), HMSO, London, (1974).

Burgin, V., Donald, J., and Kaplan, C., (eds), *Formations of Fantasy*, Routledge and Kegan Paul, London, (1986).

Campbell, B., Feminist Sexual Politics, *Feminist Review*, 5, pp1–18, (1980).

Cavendish, R., *On The Line*, Routledge and Kegan Paul, London, (1982).

Centre for Contemporary Cultural Studies Education Group, *Unpopular Education*, Hutchinson, London, (1981).

Centre for Contemporary Cultural Studies Women's Group, *Women Take Issue*, Hutchinson, London (1978).

Chetwynd, J., and Hartnett, D., *The Sex-Role System*, Routledge and Kegan Paul, London, (1978).

Chodorow, N., *The Reproduction of Mothering*, University of California Press, Berkeley, (1978).

Clark, E., What's in a Word? On the child's acquisition of semantics in his first language, *in*, T.E. Moore (ed), (1973).

Clark H., Space, Time, Semantics and The Child, *in* T.E. Moore (ed), (1973).

Clift, P., Parental Involvement in Primary Schools, *Primary Education Review, 10*, (1981).

Cline-Cohen, P., *A Calculating People: The Spread of Numeracy in Early America*, University of Chicago Press, Chicago, (1982).

Cohen, A.K., *Delinquent Boys*, The Free Press, Glencoe, (1955).

Cohen, A.K., *Deviance and Control*, The Free Press, Glencoe, (1966).

Coles, R., and Hallowell Coles, J., *Women of Crisis*, Dell Publishing Co., New York, (1978).

Corran, G., and Walkerdine, V., The Practice of Reason: Volume I, Reading the Signs of Mathematics, Mimeo, University of London, Institute of Education, (1981).

Corrigan, P.R.D., and Sayer, D., *The Great Arch: English State Formation as Cultural Revolution*, Blackwells, Oxford, (1985).

Cowie, E., Woman As sign, *M/F. 1*, (1978).

Craft, M. (ed), Family, Class and Education, Longmans, Harlow, (1970)

Craft, M. (ed), *Linking Home and School*, Harper and Row, London, (1980).

Crnic, L.S. et al, Animal Models of Human Behaviour: Their Application to the Study of Attachment, *in* Emde, R., and Harmon, R., (eds), (1982).

Curran, J., (ed), *The Future of the Left*, Polity Press, Cambridge, (1984).

Deem, R., (ed), *Schooling for Women's Work*, Routledge and Kegan Paul, London, (1980).

Della Costa, M.R., and James, S., *The Power of Women and The Subversion of the Community*, Falling Wall Press, Bristol, (1972).

Dollard, J.L., Doob, N.E., Miller, D.H., Mowrer, D.H. and Sears, R.R., *Frustration and Aggression*, Yale University Press, New Haven, (1939).

Donzelot, J., *The Policing of Families*, Hutchinson, London, (1980).

Douglas, J.W.B., *The Home and The School*, McGibbon and Kee, Glasgow, (1964).

Dunn, J., *Sisters and Brothers*, Fontana, London, (1984).

Dweck, C. and Repucci, M., Learned Helplessness and Reinforcement Responsibility in Children, *Journal of Personality and Social Psychology*, 25, pp109–116, (1973).

Eastlea, B., *Science and Sexual Oppression*, Weidenfeld and Nicholson, London, (1981).

Eichenbaum, L., and Orbach, S., *Outside In. Inside Out*, Penguin Harmondsworth, (1982).

Emde, R., and Harmon, R., (eds), *The Development of Attachment and Affilliative Systems*, Plenum, London, (1982).

Evans, S., *Personal politics. The Roots of Women's Liberation in the Civil Rights Movement and the New Left*, Vintage, New York, (1979).

Fairbairn, W.R.D., *Psychoanalytic Studies of the Personality*, London (1952).

Fanon, F., *The Wretched of The Earth*, Penguin, Harmondsworth, (1967).

Fanon, F., *Black Skin. White mask*, Penguin, Harmondsworth, (1969).

Foreman, A., *Feminity as Alienation – Women and the Family in Marxism and Psychoanalysis*, Pluto Press, London, (1977).

Foss, B., (ed), *The Determinants of Infant Behaviour*, Methuen, London, (1961).

Foucault, M., *Madness and Civilisation*, Tavistock, London, (1967).

Foucault, M., *Discipline and Punish*, Penguin, Harmondsworth, (1979).

Foucault, M., *The History of Sexuality. Vol. 1*, Penguin, Harmondsworth, (1981).

Fraser, R., *In Search of a Past*, Verso, London, (1984).

Freud, S., *The Interpretation of Dreams. Standard Edition, Vols. 4–5*, Hogarth Press, London, (1900).

Freud, S., Beyond the Pleasure Principle, *Standard Edition, Vol. XIV*, Hogarth Press, London, (1920).

Freud, S., Female Sexuality, *Standard Edition, Vol. 21*, Hogarth Press, London, (1931).

Freud, S., *Standard Edition. Vol. 23*, Hogarth Press, London, (1937–39).

Friday, N., *My Mother/Myself*, Fontana, London, (1979).

Friedman, N. L., *in* J. Beck (ed)., (1976).

Gardiner, J., Women's Domestic Labour, *New left Review*, no 89, (1975).

Garnsey, E., Women's Work and Theories of Class and Stratification, *in* Giddens, A., and Held, D., (eds)., (1982).

Gavron, H., *The Captive Wife: Conflicts of Housebound Mothers*, Routledge and Kegan Paul, London, (1966).

Giddens, A., and Held, D., (eds), *Classes, Power and Conflict*, Macmillan, London, (1982).

Gilligan C., *In a Different Voice: Psychological Theory and Women's Development*, Harvard University Press, Cambridge, Mass, (1982).

Girls and Mathematics Unit, The, *Girls and Mathematics: Some Lessons for the Classroom*, Economic and Social Research Council, London, (1987).

Girls and Mathematics Unit, The, *Counting Girls Out*, Virago, London, (1989).

Glastonbury, M., The Best Kept Secret: How Working Class Women Live and What They Know, *Women's Studies International Quarterly*, 2, pp171–81, (1979).

Goldthorpe, J.H., *Social Mobility and Class Structure in Modern Britain*, Clarendon Press, Oxford, (1980).

Goldthorpe, J.H., and Lockwood, D., *The Affluent Worker: Industrial Attitudes and Behaviour*, Cambridge University Press, Cambridge, (1968).

Gorz, A., *Farewell to the Working Class: An Essay on Post-Industrial Socialism*, Pluto, London, (1982).

Grender, I., and Mannion, C., (eds), *The Open Home*, 3, 4, 5 Publishing Ltd., Henley.

Gruber H. and Voneche, J.J., *The Essential Piaget*, Routledge and Kegan Paul, London, (1971).

Guntrip, H., *Personality Structure and Human Interaction*, Hogarth Press, London, (1961).

Guntrip, H., *Schizoid Phenomena, Object Relations and the Self*, International Universities Press, New York, (1969).

Guntrip, H., *Psychoanalytic Theory, Therapy and the Self*, Hogarth Press, London, (1971).

Hacking, I., How Shall We do the History of Statistics?, *Ideology and Consciousness*, No 8, pp15–26, (1981).

Hall, C., Private Persons and Public Someones: Class, Gender and Politics in England, 1780–1850, *in* Steedman, C., Urwin, C., and Walkerdine V., (eds), (1985).

Hall, C., and Davidov, L., *Family Fortunes: Men and Women of the English Middle Class 1750–1850*, Hutchinson, London, (1987).

Halsey, A.H. (et al), *Origins and Destinations: Family, Class Education in Modern Britain*, Clarendon Press, Oxford, (1980).

Hareven, T.R., *Family Time and Industrial Time*, Cambridge University Press, Cambridge, (1982).

Harlow, H., The Nature of Love, *in* American Psychologist, Vol. 13, (1958).

Harlow, H., The Development of Affectional Patterns in Infant Monkeys, *in* Foss, B., (ed), (1961).

Harman, C., Women's Liberation and Revolutionary Socialism, *International Socialism*, 23, pp3–41, (1984).

Hartman, H., The Unhappy Marriage of Marxism and Feminism: Towards a More Progressive Union, *Capital and Class*, 8, pp1–33, (1979).

Henriques, J., et al, *Changing The Subject: Psychology, Social Regulation and Subjectivity*, Methuen, London, (1984).

Heron L. (ed)., *Truth, Dare or Promise*, Virago, London, (1985).

Hess R.D. and Shipman V., Early Experience and the Socialisation of Cognitive Modes in Children, *Child Development*, Vol. 36, No.3, pp869–886, (1965).

Hill, S., *The Dockers*, Heinemann, London, (1976).

Hirst, P.Q., Althusser and the Theory of Ideology, *Economy and Society*, Vol. 5, no. 4, pp385–412, (1976).

Hirst, P.Q., and Wolley, P., *Social Relations and Human Attributes*, Tavistock, London, (1983).

Hobsbawm, E., *The Age of Revolution, 1848–1875*, Weidenfeld and Nicholson, London, (1975).

Hoggart, R., *The Uses of Literacy*, Penguin, Harmondsworth, (1959).

Hollway, W., (forthcoming), *History of Industrial Psychology: a Reader*

Hooks, B., *Ain't I a Woman?* Pluto, London, (1982).

Hyman, H.H., The Value Systems of Different Classes, *in*, R. Bendix and S.M. Lipset (eds), (1967).

Irigaray, L., *Speculum of The Other Woman*, Cornell University Press, Ithaca, New York, (1985).

Jones, K., and Williamson, K., The Birth of The Schoolroom, *in Ideology and Consciousness*, No. 6, pp59–110, (1979).

Kaluzynska, E., Wiping The Floor with Theory: a Survey of Writings on Housework, *Feminist Review*, 6, pp27–54, (1981).

Kessel, S. and Siegel A.W. (eds), *The Child and Other Cultural Inventions*, Praeger, New York, (1983).

Klein, M., *Envy and Gratitude and Other Works, 1946–1963*, Hogarth Press, London, (1975a).

Klein, M., *Love, Guilt and Reparation and Other Works, 1921–1945*, Hogarth Press, London, (1975b).

Kuhn, A., and Wolpe, A.M., (eds), *Feminism and Materialism*, Routledge and Kegan Paul, London, (1978).

Labov, W., The Logic of Non-standard English, in *The Study of Non-Standard English*, National Council of Teachers of English, Urbana, Illinois, (1978).

Lacan, J., *Ecrits: A Selection*, Tavistock, London, (1977).

Laclau, E. and Mouffe, C. *Hegemony and Socialist Strategy: Towards a Radical Democratic Politics*, Verso, London, (1985).

Laclau, E., Class War and After, *Marxism Today*, April, pp30–33, (1987).

Laing, R.D. *The Politics of the Family and Other Essays*, Tavistock, London, (1971).

Lasch, C., *Haven in a Heartless World: The Family Besieged*, Basic Books, New York, (1977).

Lewis, J., The Debate on Sex and Class, *New Left Review*, 149, pp108–120, (1985).

Lieven, E., Context, Process and Progress in Young Children's Speech, *in* Beveridge, M., (ed), (1982).

Lopata, H.Z. *Occupation Housewife*, Oxford University Press, London, (1971).

Lorde, A., *Sister Outsider*, Crossing Press, Trumansburg, New York, (1984).

Lyons, J., (ed), *New Horizons in Linguistics*, Penguin, Harmondsworth, (1970).

Marcuse, H., *One-Dimensional Man: Studies in the Ideology of Advanced Industrial Society*, Routledge and Kegan Paul, London, (1964).

Marcuse, H., *An Essay on Liberation*, (1969).

Marx, K., *Capital, Vol. I*, Penguin, Harmondsworth, (1976a).

Marx, K., *Capital, Vol. III*, Penguin, Harmondsworth, (1976b).

Marx, K., T.B. Bottomore and M. Rubel (eds), *Karl Marx: Writings in Sociology and Social Philosophy*, Penguin, Harmondsworth, (1967).

McRobbie, A., Working class Girls and the Culture of femininity, *in*, Centre for Contemporary Cultural Studies Women's group, *Women Take Issue* (1978).

Millett, K., *Sexual Politics*, Doubleday, New York, (1969).

Mitchell, J., *Psychoanalysis and Feminism*, Penguin, Harmondsworth, (1975).

Mitchell, J., and Rose, J., *Jacques Lacan and the Ecole Freudienne: Feminine Sexuality*, Macmillan, London, (1983).

Moore, T.E., (ed), *Cognitive Development and Acquisition of Language*, Academic Press, New York, (1973).

Neill, A.S., *The Free Child*, Jenkins, London (1953).

Newson, J., and Newson, E., *Seven Years Old in the Home Environment*, Allen and Unwin, London, (1976).

Oakley, A., *The Sociology of Housework*, Penguin, Harmondsworth, (1974a).

Oakley, A., *Housewife*, Penguin, Harmondsworth, (1974b).

Oakley, A., *Taking It Like A Woman*, Cape, London, (1984).

Osborne, J., *Look Back In Anger*, Longman, Harlow, (1959).

Parsons, J., Attributions, Learned Helplessness and Sex Differences in Achievement, *Journal of Educational Equity and Leadership*, No. 3., (1983).

Passerini, L., *Fascism in Popular Memory: the Cultural Experience of the Turin Working Class*, Cambridge University Press, Cambridge, (1987).

Phillips, A., *Divided Loyalties*, Virago, London, (1987).

Piercy, Marge, *Woman on the Edge of Time*, The Women's Press, London, (1973).

Pollert, A., *Girls, Wives, Factory Lives*, Macmillan, London, (1981).

Porter, C., Let's Fall In Love, from the musical, *Wake Up and Dream*, (1929).

Porter, M., *Home, Work and Class Consciousness*, Manchester University Press, Manchester, (1983).

Reich, W., *The Mass Psychology of Fascism*, Penguin, Harmondsworth, (1975).

Reich, W., *Children of the Future: on the Prevention of Sexual Pathology*, Farrar, Straus, Giroux, New York, (1983).

Reiter, R., (ed), *Towards an Anthropology of Women*, Monthly Review Press, New York, (1975).

Rich, A., *Of Woman Born*, Bantam, New York, (1977).

Riley, D., *War In The Nursery*, Virago, London, (1983a).

Riley, D., The Serious Burden of Love, *in* Segal, L., (ed), *What Is to be Done About the Family?* (1983b).

Rose, J., Femininity and its Discontents, *Feminist Review*, 14, pp5–21, (1983).

Rose, J., *Sexuality in the Field of Vision*, Verso, London, (1986).

Rose, N., The Psychological Complex: Mental Measurement and Social Administration, *Ideology and Consciousness*, No. 5, pp5–68, (1979).

Rose, N., *The Psychological Complex: Psychology, Politics and Society in England 1869–1939*, Routledge and Kegan Paul, London, (1985).

Rousseau, J.J., *Emile*, Basic Books, New York, (1979).

Rubin, G., The traffic in Women; notes on the "Political Economy" of Sex, *in* Reiter, R. (ed), (1975).

Rutter, M., *Maternal Deprivation Reassessed*, Penguin, Harmondsworth, (1972).

Safouan, M., Men and Women; a Psychoanalytic Point of View, *M/F. 9*, pp61–70, (1984).

Said, E., *Orientalism*, Routledge and Kegan Paul, London, (1979).

Sanders, D., and Reed, J., *Kitchen Sink or Swim? Women in the Eighties: The Choices*, Penguin, Harmondsworth, (1982).

Sayers, J., *Biological Politics*, Methuen, London, (1982).

Sayers, J., Feminism and Mothering; a Kleinian Perspective, *Women's Studies International Forum*, 7, 4, pp237–241, (1984).

Sayers, J., *Sexual Contradictions*, Methuen, London, (1986).

Schaffer, R., *Mothering*, Open Books, London, (1977).

Schaffer, H.R., and Emerson, P.E., The Development of Social Attachments in Infancy, *in Monographs for the Society for Research in Child Development*, 29, (94), (1964).

Schools Council, *Early Mathematical Experiences*, Addison Wesley, London, (1977).

Seabrook, J., *Working Class Childhood*, Gollancz, London, (1982).

Seccombe, W., *The Housewife and Her Labour Under Capitalism*, I.M.G. Publications, London, (1978).

Segal, L., (ed), *What is to be Done About the Family?* Penguin Harmondsworth, (1983).

Sluckin, W., Herbert, M., and Sluckin, A., *Maternal Bonding*, Basil Blackwell, Oxford, (1983).

Stanley, L., and Wise, S., *Breaking Out: Feminist Consciousness and Feminist Research*, Routledge, London, (1983).

Stanworth, M., Women and Class Analysis: a Reply to John Goldthorpe, *Sociology*, 18, March, (1984).

Steedman, C., "The Mother Made Conscious": The Historical Development of a Primary School Pedagogy, History Workshop Journal, Vol. 20, pp151–163.

Steedman, C., *Landscape for a Good Woman*, Virago, London, (1986).

Steedman, C., Urwin, C., and Walkerdine, V., (eds), *Language, Gender and Childhood*, Routledge and Kegan Paul, London, (1985).

Sugarman, B., Social Class, Values and Behaviour in Schools, *in* M. Craft (ed), (1970).

Tansley, A.G., *The New Psychology and its Relation to Life*, Allen and Unwin, London, (1920).

Thorne, B., and Yalom, M., (eds), *Rethinking the Family*, Longman, Harlow, (1982).

Tizard, B., On Mothering, *Thomas Coram Working Papers. No. 1*, (1986).

Tizard, B., and Hughes, M., *Young Children Learning*, Fontana, London, (1984).

Urwin, C., Power Relations and Emergence of Language, *in*, Henriques J. et al. (1984).

Urwin, C., Constructing Motherhood: the Persuasion of Normal Development, *in*, Steedman, C., Urwin, C. and Walkerdine V. (eds), (1985a).

Urwin, C., Review of D. Riley, *War in The Nursery*, in *Feminist Review*, 19, pp95–100, (1985b).

Wajcman, J., *Women in Control*, Open University Press, Milton Keynes, (1983).

Walden, R., and Walkerdine, V., Girls and Mathematics: from Primary to Secondary Schooling, *Bedford Way Papers. 24*, Heinemann, London, (1985).

Walkerdine, V., Sex, Power and Pedagogy, *Screen Education*, 38, pp1–24, (1981).

Walkerdine, V., Developmental Psychology and the Child-Centred Pedagogy: the Insertion of Piaget into Early Education, *in* Henriques, J., et al. (1984).

Walkerdine, V., On The Regulation of Speaking and Silence, *in* Steedman, C., Urwin, C. and Walkerdine V. (eds), (1985a).

Walkerdine, V., Science and the Female Mind: The Burden of Proof, *Psych Critique*, Vol. 1, No. 1, (1985b).

Walkerdine, V., Progressive Pedagogy and Political Struggle, *Screen*, (1986a).

Walkerdine, V., Video Replay: Families, Films and Fantasy, *in* Burgin, V., Donald, J., and Kaplan, C., (eds), (1986b).

Walkerdine, V., *The Mastery of Reason*, Methuen, London, (1988).

Walkerdine, V., and Watson, D., (forthcoming), *Young Girls and Popular Culture*.

Wells, G., Language, Literacy and Educational Success, *in* Learning Through Interaction, Cambridge University Press, Cambridge, (1982).

West, J., (ed), *Work, Women and the Labour Market*, Routledge and Kegan Paul, London, (1982).

Westergaard, J., The Once and Future Class, *in* Curran, J., (ed). (1984).

Westwood, S., *All Day, Every Day: Factory and Family in the Making of Women's Lives*, Pluto, London, (1984).

Whitelegg, E., et al., *The Changing experience of Women*, Martin Robertson/Open University, Oxford, (1982).

Widdowson, F., *Going up into the Next Class: Women in Elementary Teacher-Training*, WRRC/Hutchinson, London, (1983).

Williams, E., and Shuard, H., *Primary Mathematics Today*, Longman, London, (1976).

Willis, P., *Learning To Labour*, Saxon House, Farnborough, (1977).

Winnicott, D.W., *Mother and Child*, Basic Books, New York, (1957).

Wright, P., *On Living in an Old Country*, Verso, London, (1985).

Yeo, S., (in press).

INDEX